CW01661893

Dedication

This book is dedicated to all my family members for their devotion and never ending support. Especially my mother Petronella Tuni and Father Lesio Svikiro for their endless prayers, kindness and unselfishness.

Copyright © 2019 by Andy Israel Svikiro. All rights reserved.

This edition published by Creapac publishers.
Dirschauerstr 46
10245 Berlin

No part of this book may be used or reproduced in any manner whatsoever without written permission, except for brief quotations embodied in critical articles and reviews.

Andy Israel Svikiro asserted his right to be identified as the Author of this Work in accordance with the Copyright, Designs and Patents Act 1988

ISBN 9 78 3 9820 999 0 3

CREAPAC

www.andyisvikiro.com

Part I

Quotes and Sayings From The Author:

You cannot declare to know a man until you have experienced his presence in tranquility.

A knowledgeable man suffers the most among scholars.

Scattered seeds weakens the bond.

Leaders with no vision are like antelopes taking a drink in a crocodile infested river.

A woman of class knows where her beauty lies.

I came in blind

Tales of a young African in Germany

by Andy I. Svikiro

Chapter One

Shortly after she landed at Tegel airport, Berlin, on the 22nd of March 2013, her stomach cramped. She felt weak and nauseated. For a moment she was in darkness. "Good lord is this what happens when you change continents," she uttered to herself as she gazed around at other passengers to watch their reactions.

She took a long breath of fresh air and still could not believe that she had made it all by herself. As she strolled away from the gigantic Lufthansa plane, across the tarmac to a waiting bus, she was in awe. Her head was weightless as fear and excitement gripped her emotions.
She-cat walked out of the arrivals luggage collecting zone, and when she exited a large crowd was gathered, flooding the area with laughs and praises for their loved ones. She choked a bit expecting to be greeted by a sign with her name scribbled on it. Her face soon became pale as she looked around in vain, forcing a smile pretending like she knew what she was doing.

She adjusted herself and followed other fellow passengers whilst frantically searching for her host. She walked casually with her bags on tow, hoping someone would tap her on the shoulder or call out her name. She stood by a fashion window looking at the reflection trying to catch out Mr. Schneider.

Finally she took out her phone and connected to the free airport wifi with a big fake permanent grin on her face. "I've just landed my sisters, right now I am chilling with Angie Merkel, about to go and explore the Brandenburg Tor. Maybe I'll scribble my name on the Berlin wall if I get a chance. But right now I am gonna gulp one of these tasty German beers. It is what it is ladies, peace out," topped with a selfie, Chipo wrote on her Instagram wall as she stood posing between two heavy suitcases, lost and in despair.

She had been stuck at the airport for four hours. Her instincts kicked in and her stomach smelt of deceit. She wondered if she might have been swindled and left to fend for herself. Her fourteen-hour journey which took her from Zimbabwe via South Africa filled with a lot of promises and full of hope was heading for a derailment. Her dreams and determination of studying and becoming an IT specialist were fast becoming a curse.

She was in a foreign land, abandoned and shattered. Her mind raced wildly, with no firm conclusion. She had flashbacks, of the sacrifices her parents had made, vivid memories of happy smiling faces of her family and friends who had accompanied her to the airport and wished her well. She thought hard and deep, as she gazed up to the cold freezing sky and for once in her life, she actually felt helpless. She had no idea where to start. Everything was moving so aggressively fast and strange.
But she couldn't cry as only the gentle puff of air made her snuffle. She sat on a wooden metal bench with her head down, trying to gather some strength and figure out what had ensued. Buses and taxis whizzed by. The airport was busy with people flocking silently like robots. There were individual travelers and groups of tourists.

Heavily armed policemen walked around aimlessly. Deep in her thoughts, it was starting to register she had been neglected, deserted, and hung out to dry.

Her agent who had been so promising and prompt had abandoned her.
She had been waiting for a good five hours, she was very much concerned. She couldn't eat as all appetite had disappeared. As she gazed at every male that passed by, she had become like a newly born puppy curious, panic-stricken, not knowing who she belonged to. The passport size photo of a well dressed Mr. Schneider was soaking in sweat as she desperately scanned every face that went by. She tried to convince herself, "I am at the wrong place, maybe even the wrong airport," she whispered silently.

Her head was getting crazy she was starting to think she was in the wrong country. But again, his phone was constantly busy as if her number had been blocked. She exhaled, "soon it would be dark, this is not the time for cry babies," she talked to herself. In a crazy world like this, she could be easily taken advantage of.
The language alone was incomprehensible yet she needed to think fast and act appropriately.

Chapter Two

From nowhere a foreign voice shook her, "Guten Tag, ist alles in Ordnung?" (Good day, is everything ok?) She slowly raised her head and was greeted by a smiling neatly dressed old man, holding a pipe. His small eyes glowing through his spectacles.
Chipo observed him in hesitation."Sorry, I don't speak German," she replied politely.
His smile became even wider, "uh English, English I knew it. Very sorry you have to pardon me for being impolite," as he tipped his hat and folded his walking stick.
"I thought you might be French, Salut! –"Hi!" Bonjour – "Good day"
Ça va? – "How's it going?"
And he chuckled, Chipo was amused, she had almost forgotten she could smile.
"My name is Gunther or König Gunther," as he extended his hand, "I just arrived from Cameroon," he went on, "a great country, lovely people, the food, oh my God amazing.
Do you mind if I sit down and chat with you, I have a lot to tell," puffing his pipe?
"Sure please do sit." She made space for him, pushing herself closer to the edge of the bench. He sat himself down and lit his pipe again.
"I should have stayed in Gambia, this country is too cold, too depressing. Everything is too bureaucratic, full of greedy heartless people, with no feelings.
I love the beer though," he giggled.

"German beer is the best beer in the world. Look at the Belgians they have more than a thousand tasteless beers," he cracks up. "I don't know why they can't learn from their neighbors just across the border, the Germans, of course, quality is important, not quantity.
Focus, work hard to develop something, not eat Döner."

He was laughing by himself, Chipo remained silent and observant.
"I can buy my beer from anywhere, anytime, the easiest and cheapest thing to get, now we are all alcoholics, we should be ashamed of ourselves, but you have to agree with me without beer the world would be a very lonely place.
When I drink I can dance, I can talk to a woman, I can laugh, even ask for a cigarette from a stranger. So alcohol improves my manhood too, blotto!" He blurted and giggled. "The problems are, we are still living with the same old rules, rules that were created by the dead and forgotten. Rules that were meant for the Germans, maybe they did work but now it's a different era, you need to move with the time, you don't see a horse-drawn cart competing with a train or a bus, it's impossible.
I am German and I know that and believe me only a German person can understand another German."
Chipo felt like the nurse sitting on a bench in the forest Gump movie listening to Forest Gump.
"I wish I could take up to the sky and cruise again, fly like a kite," he spoke as he looked up watching a plane about to land.
"Huh, my memory is a bit vague, not so precise anymore. But I am not so old, no Germans don't get old, they just get murky and mysterious.
I was born of natural birth, purebred, no surrogate child," he howled.
"Can I tell you a secret, a very interesting one?"

"Please go ahead," Chipo encouraged him. "You know what happened to me during my birth?"
Chipo looked at him curiously, he chortles, "I was infused with African blood," he whispered, and laughed. "They said my mother had a terrible accident and needed a lot of blood transfusion urgently. The only blood type that matched was from Shuvai, a lady from Cameroon," and before he could finish, in a flash he threw himself back and sort of convulsed, Chipo screamed and was about to loosen his tie, when he scoffed, "just a mild seizure," he smiled, "It happens sometimes nothing serious though, I guess it's attributed to the mixture of blood," and he burst out laughing.

"My parents, of course, they are German," scoffs, "they moved from Bavaria, Bayern Munich, you know the football team, yeah everyone knows it," he answered himself. "They migrated here when I was young very young two years old, but I remember everything like it was yesterday.
They all died during that stupid Nazi war, I don't remember that part," as he scratched his head, "uh nothing," he shook his head. "It was terrible of course, nothing is nice about the Nazis," he whispered. "I don't know if my parents were Nazis, so don't ask me," he said furiously causing Chipo to twitch.

"Are you ok?" She asked. "Who me? I am great and as fit as a fiddle," he grinned, "perfectly fine, sometimes I think about it though and it bothers me, I guess they didn't have a choice, not because they wanted to, but like most people in that time, it was either that or get hanged. My father was clever, or should I say a coward, the guy loved life, women too, hahaha! I am sure he pretended to be one of them, to save his ass, so he could keep on drinking. He was a genius hey."

He shuddered, trembled, almost as though he was trying to shake off the memory. Chipo couldn't make head or tail of his stories. She was suffering to figure out what he meant.
She thought the old man was a bit cuckoo, missing a few screws in the head, but she didn't mind, she prompted him to continue.
"You are good company," she smirked.
"I know there is this perception that all Germans are Nazis. That's not true, Nazis represent a tiny fraction of the total population of Germany.
There are good and bad people, I agree but in this day and age, we are all fans of Michael Jackson. It doesn't mean if you are born in a Nazi family, you stay Nazis, nope you choose your own way, your own destination.
We are a democratic country there is no Mobutu Sese Seko here.
We have a very strong judicial system, but, don't get me wrong. We still have a few bad elements, it's normal. Can you imagine if we were all oranges and no apples, it would be a very dull and an uninteresting world," he yawned.

"I like apples," she interrupted him.
"Believe me, no one likes them, they massacred all of them."
"The apples?" She asks sarcastically.
"No," he burped, "sorry too much garlic," he whispered, "I am ashamed."
"You are ashamed of garlic?" She questioned him,
"No I am ashamed to say I am German," Gunter replies. Chipo burst out laughing, "No, you are old school, old man not everyone sees it that way, it's you who thinks like that because psychologically its in your head, it's embedded in your Medulla oblongata. The world has moved on, World war two ended in 1944 or was it 45?

The new generation has long forgotten about it, I am not willing to suffer for the sins of my fathers, no way. Do you think I give a shit about that, there was slavery, but I wasn't around during that period, what matters to me right now, is me, myself and my life. All this psychological bullshit is nonsense. What you can do, I can do better and always stay positive that is my Motto."
"It's easier said than done, and you are too young to understand," he continued, "Nazis still exist," he argued.
"They are like some kind of a time machine, always adjusting and developing, a terminator thing. I love that film, Arnold Schwarzenegger big muscular guy, I WILL BE BACK," and he laughed, hilariously, coughing at the same time.
"Oh man and he comes back and kills everyone tiktaktak," as he mimics a machine gun.

Chipo was taken aback by his sudden quickness and reflex.
"Do you own a gun?" She asked, but he ignored her and carried on with his maze of interpretations.
"When I remove my glasses and stare at someone and look straight into their souls, with my sharp angry pointed eyes, they back off, because they can see and feel death."

He groans as he rolls his eyes, chuckling.
"They realize I am damn serious, they can't mess with me, I am the godfather." He sighs. "That was good hey, admit it, come on." He prods her and continues, "I should have been an actor yah, in a western movie, Clint Eastwood, missed opportunities, regrets of a coward," he murmurs to himself.
"You are very good and you should have been an actor," she aided him.He jumps up, making her nervous. "Are you traveling? Are you going somewhere?"

Chipo stammers, "uh um I, well I just arrived about six hours ago."
"Whoa that's an awful long time," he gasped. "What are you still doing here? I can fly from here to London and back, twice in six hours. Isn't that a long time to observe our mini built airport. It's a shame for a big city like Berlin to have such a small airport. But I should say, it's very efficient, in and out in a split second, no long queues.

"Uhh!" He exclaimed. "Now I got it," he stood you up, "he didn't come to pick you up huh? Oh man what an idiot. Is he so stupid? How can he not turn up? Is he just late or he is non existent? Your boyfriend right?"
"No, not my boyfriend," she corrected him. He let's out a loud laugh.
"What sort of a man does that? My crazy father would have spanked me for making a girl wait. Women are precious, you should always safeguard them, protect them and they'll bear you healthy offsprings, my papa used to tell me. He doesn't deserve you, you need to let him go, cut him loose, he is no good. Who makes such a pretty young lady like you wait for so long. He is a dirty cow, if he was my son I would beat him up, and hang him by his dirty balls. Spill his blood," he snapped, as he slit his throat with his thumb.
"There is no way he can be German, oh man," shaking his head and he leaned towards her, "James Brown died yah, king of soul, like a sex machine uh uh," as he tried to dance.

Chipo was disturbed by his character, but she thought these were just acts of an old man. "No way he cannot be," he asserted.
"He is not German right?" Biting his lips. "He is not yah," he asked her again, curiously. Before she could

answer he blurts out, "I knew it, he is not, he can't be, I don't think he is German," shaking his head.
"Don't tell me that lie. We Germans are always on time, come rain come thunder. Wir sind immer pünktlich," *(we are always on time)* he says boldly, in a proud way. "That's one thing I admire about the Germans, always on time," nodding his head, "Uhh like the song from Ashanti," and he started singing. "Babe I am always on time, I am always there."
Chipo was entertained she laughed out loud,
"you know that song, oh my god, you are something else Mr. Gunther."
"Yah, yeah you know it too, you know it, nice woman, very nice lady, good voice. Always on time babe, babe, babe, babe," he continued singing.
Chipo was so impressed and amazed by him.
She was laughing uncontrollably. Although she could not figure out everything he was saying, it made her loosen up, relax and be aware that some people were open for a conversation.
This old man was from another world, "a marvelous creature," her father would have said.
She wandered if he was the miracle she had been waiting for.

He jumped from one story to the next and back again to the original story. She would grin, laugh and giggle just to appease him, although she could not follow his flow.
She was nervous of his quick sudden movements. It was hard for her to comprehend his attitude. She was just glad she had someone to talk to, he made her forget about her problems.
"Wild meat tastes really good, I have eaten a lot of animals in my life, I am shocked by vegetarians. How can you live without meat? They have no idea, it's the same as having a wife and no sex," he chuckled, as Chipo tried to conceal her laughter.

"Are you sure this person is coming to pick you up? Maybe he went to the wrong airport," as he stared at her while puffing his pipe.

"No, not really," she answered him calmly. "One it's not my boyfriend,"
"So no one is coming then," he cut her off rubbing his beard in the process.
"Well someone was supposed to come but unfortunately, he hasn't turned up until now."
"How is that then?" He was looking at her suspiciously.

She sniffed, "to cut a long story short, it's my first time in Berlin, Germany as you can see. I am here to study, I am a student and should be able to start my language course tomorrow, God willing. And after that, I would like to do IT management."
"Oh, you seem to have everything planned and worked out, young lady, you must have German blood in you," he smirked. " Planning and organization are the core of every business, very important," he emphasized. "In Germany we take our time to think, to plan and to execute."
He was looking at her very seriously.
"That's the only way you are guaranteed success, hard work pays off. The only minor obstacle though yah, is we are not flexible, when we plan to go west, we intend to go west, whether there is a storm coming or a wildfire, our plans stay intact, west not east. If you want us to go east then we have to go back to the drawing board, unlike the Americans or the British they are very versatile. Maybe not perfectionist, like The Made IN Germany slogan," and he roared out with laughter.
Chipo sighed, "my father was crazy about Germany made products, if it ain't Germany it don't work," he would boast.

"Your father is right, we are inventors not copycats." As he sniffed the air.

"Germany goods are well respected," Chipo said, "until today unbeatable. It's a pity the Chinese have flooded the market with their 2cents goods. That's one of the reasons I chose to come here, Germans are known as perfectionist. My agent who brought me here, after my parents paid so much money, 8,000 euros to be exact, does not seem to be living up to the German standards, he didn't turn up, just like that."

"Did you call him?"

"Yes I did more than 20 times but it was just mail-box."

"That's very unusual," he voiced.

"And very weird too," she interrupted him.

"Chinese products are laughable, everything they do, it's either it has been stolen, copied or smugg-led. Hard to blame them though, a billion people huh, they are breeding like snakes. Do you know how they eat chicken."

And he starts laughing shaking his head.

Chipo is caught up in his world, she starts laughing too.

"Let's call him up, You want me to do it? I can call him for you. Do you have an address? It's easy, we can pay him a visit." Out of nowhere he becomes serious again.

Chipo was super grateful, "Oh that sounds perfect, can you do that for me, that would be awesome," she said excitedly.

"Quite generous of you, thank you very much I really appreciate it," she applauded him.

"I am generous yes I know and kind too, yes yes, like the red light district girls, where is the number of this so called agent of death, give it to me before I change my mind?"

She panicked and nervously searched for the number, as he gazed at her.
"You didn't tell me your name, it's my fault though, I talk too much, my dead wife, always said the same thing."
"Oh, I am truly sorry about your wife,"
"No need to be sorry," he scoffed. "You are really sorry?"
He repeated shaking his head, "well then I am sorry too because right now I don't have to do shit for you." He screamed.

Chipo was afraid and confused, "are we talking about your wife," she stammered, "I mean she died right?"
"Huh my wife yeah hahaha," And he laughed.
"She died, she died before I was born, stupid woman, It happened a long time ago."
"She was mad you know, I didn't shed one tear for her, for 30 years I had to eat my food secretly in my car, because she didn't allow me to eat certain foods, she thought there was going to be another war coming, we spent our lives rationing out food," he cracked himself up.
"She thought I was playing along the whole time, yet after she slept I would sneak into my car and eat porkpies and cold chicken huh smart hey. She was an original blonde woman, she used to make a jug of coffee and keep it for days, she believed Kalter Kaffee macht schöner," *(cold coffee makes you more beautiful)* and he roared with laughter.
"You can call me Chipo, Chipo Doviwa, I am from Zimbabwe," she interrupted him.
"Sipoh," he twisted the pronunciation, "Do-vovivi-wa, oh forgive me I am bad with strange ancient Greek God names."
He lit up his pipe and looked for a while into her eyes shakig his head, "the Germans or should I say the Europeans, excluding the Bulgarians and

Romanians yes yes, no there are not Europeans, you agree, don't you."

She was caught off guard.
"They are going to mispronounce your name, you might as well get used to being called Sipoh. Wait a minute you are from Zimbabwe?" His face flushed and looked worried.
"Zimbabwe," he shouted again and began to laugh. "Huh, your president has got some hardcore skills and balls of an elephant. He chased away all the white people, oh my God, that is like walking into a lion's den. Look at what happened to the economy," he screamed, "But you know what? I praise that man, I am a fan of him. How can a white person go to Africa and be a racist? That is very strange and weired.
He is quite intelligent you know? Even the Queen of England, yes Queen Elizabeth laid out a red carpet for him. He was a darling of the West until he broke the first rule, I don't know what happened, but it happened so fast, overnight the economy collapsed. The whole country went bankrupt, that was unbelievable. Do you think it was Tsungirai?"

Chipo shrieked, "Oh mama mia, Gunther you have so much information, you killing me right now, where do you know about all that?"
"Maybe it was due to old age like Moses," he chuckled, "you people don't even have your own local currency yah," shaking his head, "corruption, corruption, mansion here mansion there, yacht here yacht there, I feel sorry for the younger generation."
"Can we please call this Schneider, you have the number in your hand," Chipo demanded, annoyed and showing no interest in politics. "You are not a political refugee are you?" He rattled.
"No, hell no," she yelled angrily, "too young, I love

my country, I am not running away from anything," her eyes rolling, appearing insulted, "I am all about education Kulez," *(grandfather)* she shouted. Gunther scratched his head, "I do agree though, Germany has the best educational system in the world," he bragged. "We have the best pharmaceutical companies ever, well I mean they had some advantages, underhanded tactics. You know that, don't you, experimental tests on the oppressed," he whispered looking around restlessly whilst nodding his head. "It's a crazy world out there."

Chipo looked at him in amusement.

He scrutinized the paper in his hand, "oh there is a physical address. It's not far from here, we can actually go there, I know where that is, Adenanuer Platz, very nice area, expensive too, he must be wealthy, maybe from your money," and he giggled. I am sure he has a big office, with a voluptuous blonde secretary. I can see him drinking iced cognac and smoking Cuban cigars. How much did you say you paid him?

Did you say 8,000 euros or bonds?"

Chipo just chuckled.

"I don't think you are the only one he scammed though, son of a mule," he jeered.

"I love cigars, Fidel Castro yah yah, let's see if he is available. My handy (cell phone) is quite old but it does the job" as he punches the numbers into his phone.

"Does he have a name? Oh yeah I see it, Schneider yah, Schneider."

"Herr Schneider yep and you are Schippo right, yah yah," as he confirmed her name.

"Chipo," she corrected him."

"Don't worry we will find a solution, Schipoh Swappo whatever," as the phone rang. She noticed that he trembled and shook randomly, she observed him with a cautious eye.

"Hallo Hallo," he sat up, as if preparing himself for a long conversation, "Ja, guten Tag, Gunther am Apparat. Könnte ich bitte mit Herrn Schneider sprechen?" *(Hello good day, can I speak to Mr. Schneider please, this is Gunther on the line?)*
There was a moment of silence, only fidgeting paper sounds where audible from the other side of the line. Schneider cleared his throat, "Ja, hallo, wie kann ich Ihnen weiterhelfen?" *(Yes, how can I help you?)*
"Ah, Sie sind Herr Schneider! Gut, gut. Ich bin hier mit einer sehr schönen Dame am Flughafen Tegel. Schippo, Schipoh, ja, richtig. Dodoviwa heißt sie, ich kann den Namen nicht richtig aussprechen. Sie kommt aus Simbabwe und wartet schon seit sechs Stunden auf Sie. Ich versuche nur zu helfen.
Können Sie bitte kommen und sie abholen? Aber sofort! Bald wird es dunkel und es ist auch sehr kalt, (hustet) so behandelt man andere Menschen nicht!"

(Oh you are Mr. Schneider, that's very good, I am here at Tegel airport with a very beautiful lady, her name is Schippo Dodoviwa. I cannot pronounce her name very well, she comes from Zimbabwe and she has been waiting for you for almost six hours, I am just trying to help her, can you please come and pick her up immediately, soon it will be dark and it's getting cold, you don't mistreat other people like that.)

Schneider was silent and stammered, "Ehm...Ehm, ja, danke für Ihren Anruf, sehr aufmerksam. Könnte ich bitte mit ihr sprechen?"
(Thank you for your call, I really appreciate it, can I talk to her please?)
Gunther:"Ja, sicher aber sie ist eine junge Dame und alleine hier. Ich finde das unverschämt. Bitte bleiben Sie am Telefon. Ich bleibe mit ihr hier, bis Sie da sind. Oder wir kommen zu Ihnen. Sie könn-

te Sie auch verklagen, sie hat 8.000 Euro bezahlt! So geht das nicht! Ich gebe Sie weiter an Schippo." *(Yes you can, of course, she is a nice young lady, here alone I find that rude, to make her wait so long, I will wait with her here until you come, or we will come to you, otherwise we will sue you, she paid you 8,000 euros, it does not work like that, here is Schippo for you)*

She sighed as she took the phone from him, trying very much to be calm, "Mr. Schneider, I don't understand, what's going on here?" She yelled.
"Hallo Schneider speaking here, is that Chipo, yes Chipo uh I am truly sorry, I don't know how I overlooked your date of arrival. Today I picked up almost 22 other students, from all over the world, China, India, Russia, Africa, from everywhere, it was a very busy day today. I am really sorry about that, I don't know why your name wasn't on my schedule, but it's no problem we can find a solution, who is the gentleman with you?"
"It's my father's friend, he came all the way from Munich to assist me. I am here for almost six hours if not seven. So what's the plan?
When are you coming to pick me up? Since you have already picked up the others, it's very cold and I am tired, I need to sleep," she demanded.
There was a long silence, "Mr. Schneider are you there, hello?"
"Yes, I am still here, uh your father's friend right, okay, uh I am trying to think how we can do it because right now I have a very important meeting with the Chinese ambassador.
They want me to bring in almost 2000 students from Xinjiang, it's absolutely important that I meet with him. I cannot afford to miss this meeting, it's very crucial. However what I can do is, there is a place called Mutare hostel, it only costs 10 euros a day,"

He ranted. "What do you mean? Should I find my own place to stay?" She complained, "In the letter, you sent to my parents you wrote that accommodation for 3 months and language school fees are all included in the 8,000 euros they paid you."
"Yes, yes but the thing is so many students arrived today and my secretary messed up, everything is so confusing, as a matter of fact, I just fired her, if you could bear with me, only for a few days, I would sort everything out, otherwise you will get a full refund from me. I work with the German government, everything I do has to be above board."

"Oh man," she was getting really annoyed, "so basically I am stuck and homeless. How do you expect me to find this Mutare hostel? I called you more than 20 times no one picked up the phone," she blasted him.

"The place is in Charlottenburg Wilmersdorf," he completely ignored her, "not far from where you are, I will send you the address and I will make sure they have a room for you, and I will also pay for the next 10 days."
"Ten days you expect me to be in a hostel for ten days," she yelled.
"Now I really have to go and don't forget your language course starts tomorrow, you have all the information in your email, by the way, welcome to Berlin, and good luck."
"Hold on I need um," she stuttered. But he had already hung up. She buried her face into her hands and remained like that for some time. She sneezed and coughed, wiped her nose, sighed heavily and bit her lips. All the while Gunther had no idea what to do. He coughed and looked at her from the side of his eye, his lips tightened. "Who are you, what do you want from me? You lost your mama?" Chipo

was stunned. "Er ist ein richtiges Arschloch." *(He is big asshole.)*
Still dazed she forced out a smile although she didn't understand what he had said, and gave him his phone back.
"Thank you very much, for your help, well I guess that's it, I need to get to this Mutare hostel. Looks like it's gonna be a long day," she said in a gloomy way.

"Mach dir keine Sorgen, wir werden ihn verklagen." *(Don't worry about it, we will sue him)* Gunther said furiously. "Did you have a contract with this man, surely if it states that upon your arrival you are supposed to be picked up, then you should be picked up?" He questioned her.
"If soldiers give the coordinates, then the pilot should be able to land and whisk them away, So ist das."*(That is how it is.)*

"Gunther, I am just confused, right now, I don't know what's right or wrong anymore. I don't know what to believe right now. All I wanted was to come over here and study. I know of at least five other girls that came through, with the same program using the same agent. And no one ever said anything negative about this company or this guy."
"So why don't you try to get hold of these other girls," Gunther asked curiously.
"This morning when I arrived I did send them messages on WhatsApp since I don't have a German number but no one has replied yet," she pouted.
"Ooh, friends indeed," exclaims Gunther.
"Reminds me of my buddies in the army. In 1968 I used to have a lot of friends, in London, sadly they are no more. But when the weather is good sometimes we talk on the phone.
One is a bit fat and the other one is fatter, we used

to call him fat bear," and he laughed. "He could not even run 2 meters, can you imagine, but was such a lovely fellow, chubbiest, I heard he got eaten by a crocodile during an African Safari in Rhodesia," he chuckled.
"He must have been tasty."
She looked at him speechless and in shock but he just stared at her and blew his pipe.
"What the hell Gunther that's not funny," she protested.
"Oh sorry about that I did not mean to make you vomit, I mean he was a chubby fellow, and funny," he said grinning.

Chipo breathed heavily, "um by the way, Gunther do you think you can show me, where I can find this Mutare hostel?" She asked politely.
A beep message flashed on Gunther's phone,
"Was ist das denn?" *(What is that now?)* he cried out in German.
He looked at his phone wryly and she looked at him eagerly. He bit his lips, his eyes wide open as he scrolled through the phone, gasping.
"Ehm, achso, ja, ja, so ein komischer Typ hat mir gerade die Adresse geschickt. Ehm...ehm Charlottenburg Wilmersdorf."
"Such a bimbo agent has just sent me the address," he rumbled. "Yah let's go it's not far from here," as he got up. She was astonished.
"Let's go, let's go," Gunther shouted. Her face was lit
with excitement, she could not believe her luck, as she gathered her suitcases, she thought to herself Germany is great, she had this big smile on her face.

At that moment, two women dressed as nurses approached them, looking joyful. One of the nurses was African and the other one looked, Arabian.

"Gunther oh Gunther my good God you nearly gave us a shock, we have been looking for you for ages, it's late and you need to take your medicine," yelled the Arabian nurse. Gunther stammered, feeling ashamed, "yah yah". "You met a new friend yah, I can see that," says the African nurse.
"She is very nice," he blurted out. "I need to show her where to go," as he starts walking. "She is lost, we have to take her to Wilmersdorf Mutare hostel, Mutare hostel," he repeated.
"Stop Gunther stop," says the African nurse, who later introduced herself as Sonia from Lagos Nigeria. She held his hand, "Gunther you are such a kind soul, isn't he?" And she winked at Chipo.
"Nadia, we need to get back as soon as possible, I got a date tonite. I am not gonna miss that for nothing," Sonia cried out.

"Come papa, tell mama how was your day?" Nadia tried to calm him down.
"Schippo is coming with us, I promised her that I would take her to Mutare hostel," he shouted and squirmed.
"Schippo" Who is Schippo?"
"It's Chipo! C.H.I.P.O," she corrected her, "and you are Nadia right, hello," she shook her hand. "Hello, nice to meet you,"
"You just landed?" Sonia asked politely."
"Since six hours ago I am here, Gunther was a very good host, an intelligent storyteller." Chipo replied kindly.
"That's great, Gunther you have been complimented," as she patted him on the back.
"Where are you from?"
"Zimbabwe," Gunther blurted out, "Zimbabwe," he yelled. "And I have to take her to Mutare hostel, Wilmersdorfer," he struggled to talk.
Both Nadia and Sonia stared at each other, somehow

they knew Gunther always got his way. "Where is this Mutare hostel Gunther?" Sonia asked.
Gunther pulled out his phone and pointed at the screen, "here, here, not far from here."
Sonia scoffed as she grabbed the phone, "alright then, we can drop you off Chipo. Do you want to use the Klo Gunther? Pipi machen."
Gunther shook his head, feeling embarrassed.
"Chipo is this all your luggage?" Asked Nadia as she dragged one of the bags.
"Yes that's all I have, it's all mine. Thank you very much for helping me out. I appreciate it, ladies. I am so stuck, at least I have learned a new word Klo, that means toilet, right?" And she giggled.

"Officially it's forbidden, we are not allowed at all to carry any strangers, because of insurance issues, but the truth be told, without helping you Gunther will not move an inch," Nadia narrated. "Let's go guys," she said as they dragged her bags towards the car.

"Gunther has dementia," whispered Nadia. Chipo's eyes widened with feigned shock, her suspicions had been confirmed.
"I thought something was not right upstairs, My uncle used to have dementia back home and we thought he had been bewitched, we used to call him Vahewuhewu," and she laughed.
"Bewitched that's crazy woweueu," Nadia repeated, and they both laughed, "almost every day he comes here because he used to be an air pilot for one of the biggest Airlines. He still thinks he is, he can forget everything else but not this airport, isn't it Sonia? Yeah one day he almost got through the boarding area, after telling the security officers he was late for work and didn't have time to put on his uniform," they all giggled. "Why are you in a hostel anyway?

Are you passing through or you thought this poor old man was an easy catch?"
"Come on Sonia don't be so mean. Just because you have your own personal controversial history, doesn't mean everyone is like you," Nadia confronted her. "She has her own strange stories, about how she got here, don't pay attention to her. She had to walk for two months through the desert and stayed 5 years in an asylum camp, just to come here and end up looking after old people," revealed Nadia.
"I lied to you, I flew oh, I came by plane, Emirates Airways first class," Sonia retorted and laughed.
"I Am here to study," Chipo jumped in. "But my agent somehow forgot about me, he dumped me"
"Is he German?" Asked Sonia.
"Yes," she replied.
"That's odd and strange, Germans never forget or mess up these kinds of things, regardless he should have been here or found an alternative solution. I hope he is genuine, you have a lot of fake people out there. Keep your eyes opened and be careful, not everything that shines is gold, you know what they say?" Chipo shook her head and stared at her in confusion.
"Don't get duped my sister, I beg, oh" and she smirked.
Chipo's heart sank, she couldn't believe what Sonia had just said.
'Germans are known for being straight-up business people. They are not corny,' she thought to herself.

"Come on don't scare her Sonia, don't listen to her Chipo, her own experiences are making her paranoid, she sees everyone as a conman, everything is going to be fine," Nadia assured her.
Suddenly Gunther started running muttering to himself.

"Oh no please Gunther," Sonia moaned, "that's what he does when he is ignored, he becomes jealous." "Gunther, please stop that, stop that," barked Sonia, as she ran after him.
Nadia watched them and laughed.

"How long are you going to be staying in a hostel?" She asked.
"Maybe 10 days."
"Whoa that's a long time, accommodation is hard to find in Berlin. I hope you have good connections, otherwise, things can get tough." She warned her.
"Is it that bad?" She was surprised.
"I know a lot of people from my country who have had serious problems with accommodation. I am from Iran by the way, they struggled to find a place to stay, it took them almost six months to find a decent place. You must have family members or good friends who are willing to help you and give you a lot of advice."

"Now I have you," Chipo said smiling. "Germany is not an easy country to live in, as most people think, you need to be in the system and have your documents in order, to enable you to do many things. Without these documents you can't work and you can't do anything and when you can't work, how are you going to survive, you need to pay rent and take care of yourself, especially a beautiful young lady like you, oh my goodness you are going to break a lot of German hearts. But you are lucky, you are here as a student. How long is your student visa anyway?"
"Uhh...um," she stammered "about 6 months and with an option to renew it of course."
"Be careful with that, I don't mean to scare you, but sometimes they might refuse to renew it if you don't follow certain procedures. If you have a student

visa you are allowed to work parttime, that is a few hours in a week and the money you get is usually not enough to cover your costs. And to make things worse if you don't attend your lessons, because you need to work a lot, to get more money.
It's another reason to have your visa canceled. I hear this from most former students who quit because they could not study and work at the same time. It's a dilemma, hey." Chipo stared at her stunned.
"You have to pay attention and be focused, once you are in the system the sky is the limit," she advised her.
Chipo gazed at her speechless, without blinking her eyes.

"Can you please put the big bag at the bottom," Nadia asked, as she opened the boot of the car. Sonia was strapping Gunther to his seat.
"A land of milk and honey, hey, everyone says the same thing, when we are back home in Africa. We are always fed with the wrong information, and we come here with so much hope and full of naivety, am I right Nadia?" Sonia shouted shaking her head. Nadia sulked, "don't worry stay positive," as she held her shoulder, "you'll struggle, that's expected, but I can assure you, if you stay focused, disciplined and you follow the German laws, the outcome will be very rewarding. Your parents will be proud of you. Whatever happens, keep on studying no matter how hard it becomes, because things can only get better," Nadia encouraged her.
"And don't get into Schufa," (*credit controlling institute*) shouted Sonia gigling.
"You can sit in the front Chipo, Sonia has to babysit our grandfather at the back."
"Oh man the more I talk to people, the more discouraged I get," Chipo grumbled.

"Buckle up, it's gonna be a lot of fun," Nadia yelled sarcastically. "Fasten up everybody," as the car sped along the motorway. Gunther looked like a big baby sedated in his seat, Sonia was chatting on her phone and Nadia was smoking a cigarette, as Chipo pondered about her future.

They pulled up to the Mutare hostel and Nadia offered her a business card, "hey when you feel like talking, or you need some advice, don't think twice about it, just call me up."
"But not for money or men!" interjected Sonia as she laughed," just kidding my sister, this is a free democratic country and you know what? We have equal rights," she added with a big grin on her face.
"Thank you ladies, I appreciate it and I'll definately keep in touch." Chipo said gratefully.

Chapter Three

She felt relieved when she realized Mr. Schneider had partially stuck to his word. He had paid for the hostel bill for the next 5 days, although on the phone he had told her he would pay for 10 days.

She opened the door to her room and nearly choked, music and smoke engulfed her. By the window stood a group of five young girls, smoking and drinking alcohol. They stared at her awkwardly, "hi your bed is right at the top," pointed one of the girls.
There were six bunk beds in the room, "is this room 235?" She asked doubtfully.
"Yes," they answered in a chorus.
"You have so much luggage, do you want to put it in a secure place? There is a safe room where you can lock up your bags, otherwise things could go missing." Said one of the girls.
"I think that would be a great idea, I just need to unpack a few goodies," she obliged.
"You smoke blunt, this one is quite good," says the pretty blonde girl.
"Nah, I am fine thanks, maybe later."
She pushed her bags into one corner and climbed up the ladder onto her thin hard mattress. Her body was weak, jet lag was beginning to kick in. She longed to lie down and take a nap. Because of the amount of time she had spent at the airport she underestimated how tired she was. Within a few minute of lying down, she soon fell asleep.

Only to be roused up with a jump, dizzy and woozy she nearly fell off the bed. The light-headed teenagers, with silly giggles, had kicked the door in, drunk and stoned, she stared at them with anger evident in her look.
"Sorry to wake you up, we are so high," said one of them, as the others tittered.
She glanced at her watch, her head was whirling and spinning, her vision was blurred. She had slept for 12 hours straight and her body was numb. She was in some kind of state of shock, thoughtless and confused. Wondering where she was.
She thought she was dreaming, her mind and body seemed to be all over the place, it had not sunk in yet, that she was in a foreign country. She found it hard to fathom that she was far away from home.
"Damn I miss sadza," she cried out loud.

She looked around the room trying to adjust her eyes, she caught sight of the other girl on the opposite side of the bunk bed staring right at her, she must have thought Chipo was a bit weird, she quickly turned away once their eyes met. She felt sore, her muscles cramped.
She waited until she was confident enough and slowly began to descend from her three-story bed, in search of a toilet and a shower.
It took her 20 minutes to discover where the loo was situated. When she finally found it she was shocked it was like a prison toilet, open for all. She gasped in horror, it reminded her more of the bush system. She felt nervous. At that moment, two ladies in a fit of laughter walked in. They went straight to do their business like she didn't exist. Little did she know this was going to be her home for a while.

She went back to her room, the place was filled with harsh snorting noises, it was stuffy and malodorous, sounded like a horse stable in trance. The wide ajar window did not do any justice, the walls and the carpet had been fumigated with a permanent terrible stinking odor. The positive part for her was that she now had access to WiFi, she could at least communicate with her family and friends back at home. She dragged her bags under suffocation and locked them in a secure room. She took her laptop bag and her phone and sat by the reception. She browsed through all the gossip columns, read most of the interesting stories, and updated her blog.

Then she searched for the address of the language school and discovered that she needed at least 30 minutes to get there. She had a chat with the lady at the reception about the transport system and was given a few options, either she could get a ticket on board or buy one by the ticket machines at the station. And if she was a student she could also buy a student ticket, but she needed to have a student identity card for that.

Chapter Four

The directions were pretty straight forward, thanks to google maps and her skills of tracking animals at the farm. As she stepped outside the hostel, the cold wind shocked her and reminded her she was now in Germany and needed to buy a warm thick coat.
She was awed by the overwhelming difference, the buildings were massive ancient solid, the roads were wide. She noticed Mercedes Benz and BMW cars being used as taxies," wow!" She exclaimed.

There were trams on the roads running along parallel to the cars. There were trains whizzing by on top of bridges and trams operating underground, five ambulance helicopters flew by, small trucks with rotating blades were being used to clean the streets, "Damn! This is a first-world country for sure," she whispered to herself.

Everything seemed to be so structured and well organized. She searched for the underground train number U2. Once she jumped inside she discovered there were no machines to buy a ticket as the receptionist had explained.
She looked around anxiously, everyone looked too serious, she was afraid to ask anyone and she thought maybe a conductor would come by.
Lost in her thoughts, someone tried to talk to her, "Fahrkarten bitte," (*tickets please*)

"Sorry I don't speak German," she replied shyly. She looked confused. "You don't speak German, uh, no problem, I speak many languages, can I see your ticket please?" The ticket controller requested. "I would like to buy one," she said confidently, taking out her purse.

He laughed, she felt all eyes staring at her. The young controller smiled, "you cannot buy a ticket inside the train, you must buy one from the machine, before you board, now you must pay a fine of 60 euros."
"What!" She exclaimed.
"At the next station please come outside with me," as he went on checking other passengers.
She was dumbfounded and embarrassed. As the train came to a halt, the young man signaled and yelled at her to step out. "Can you come with me please," he shouted, everyone just turned around and looked at her, something struck her, she was the only person of color around, she felt like a little wet chicken.

"Where are u from?" He asked her excitedly, looking at his ticket machine.
"Zimbabwe," she replied.
"Do you live in Berlin, you have an address here? I need to see your ID please."
"I don't have an address, I'm staying in a hostel." She answered nervously.
"Hostel!" He snapped. "Oh that's expensive, are you visiting?"
"No, I'm here to study but I don't have a permanent place yet."

He sighed and looked straight into her eyes and then he whispered, "in Berlin, you need to buy a ticket all the time, a monthly ticket is cheaper than a daily ticket. We people of BVG, Berliner Verkehrsbetriebe, are not here to punish you, you know, we are not so cruel, we always give everyone a fair chance. Today is your lucky day, if I ever catch you again, I'll make you pay twice. Now go before my colleagues find out about my pure kindness, you must thank your beauty for that."

She was humbled and unable to believe her eyes. "I can give you my number," she choked and he just laughed. Still surprised and embarrassed by the situation, she hurriedly walked away.
"Thank you, thank you," she trembled, as she blew a kiss at him.
"60 euros, good lord, that's a salary for a whole month," she deeply exhaled.
He was watching her as she moved towards the machines, she looked at him again and he pointed at the ticket machine while nodding his head, he seemed to be enjoying the situation.
Three of his colleagues had joined him by then, she just grinned back and bought 5 tickets, not knowing she could have bought a day ticket.

Finding the school wasn't easy, it was situated at the back of an old building in an area known as Nollendorf. When her name was called for registration she smiled, she wasn't sure about anything anymore. There were 15 students from different parts of the world. Their teacher was a short sturdy blonde old woman with a beautiful smile. She was very good at teaching and she loved explaining and expressing herself dramatically, using her long years of experience. Her voice was loud and clear.
She showed a lot of sympathies and was interested in
knowing about their cultures. Since Chipo had done a bit of the language back home, she was excited to hear a native person speaking, she had never come across such a hard, threatening language.

She wished she could eat bones, Mazondo. During a short break she got a call from Mr. Schneider, a terrible call. "Chipo are you already at school?" he asked politely.
"Yes I am," she answered candidly.
"Oh that's very good, please try to learn as hard as you can, after 6 months if you pass, you'll be able to enroll in a university, that is the process here, you need to finish your B2 course, and then you are good to go."

"I am on it," she said nervously. "How about my accommodation?" She inquired. "It's terrible where I am staying, we are six people in a room, it's noisy and smoky," she complained.
"That's why I called you. I just noticed there were some discrepancies on the letter my former secretary sent to you, she did not include the accommodation fee, so I am not able to offer you a place to stay. I am truly sorry.
However I'll give you a telephone number, that you can call, all you have to do is to tell him, the owner, that you are one of my students and he'll give you a place at a reasonable price. Chipo let me explain, you have to know something, I did what I had to do, to bring you to Germany. Some people are trying to study here, but cannot get a visa for different reasons. The fact that you are here, consider it a blessing. You can easily be sent back home and lose everything, be very careful and don't
trust anyone, don't even talk about how you came here, people are very jealous. You have made it, and stay away from the police, they can be very nasty. From now on, do what you have to do, you are a smart lady and believe me you will make it, on your own. Good luck." And he hung up.

She was in shock, she knew that her parents had paid for everything, including accommodation, with

their hard earned money. She just acknowledged and dwelled in no man`s land.
She had only 850 euros left between her and life.

Chapter Five

For the remainder of the lesson, she did not even understand one word, her mind was blank, she felt like a monkey sitting on top of a tree clutching a dead deadly snake, wobbling because of the venom running through its veins.

She had this dark cloud hovering over her head, it was as if she was hallucinating. Everything seemed to be moving too fast and out of control, she had no idea how she got where she was. She sat shivering on a dirty cab starring in the distance, trying to catch some trick sunshine with nothing on her mind.

"Hey, sistren, lovely to see a sista, enjoying the beautiful Berlin weater. You have just wowed me wit your trembling dance." Chipo chuckled as she looked up, a tall skinny dreadlocked guy, who could be Jamaican, wearing a decorated colorful woolen hat, with big headphones over his head, stood over her with a big smile on his face.

"You looking for someting goood my sista, to spice up your day," he said with a grin.
"I got all you neeeed, weed, ecstasy and looove. You are new here? Never seen your pretty face around dis area before. But you not police are you," he said gigling. Chipo scrutinized him, he had a small face with big eyes and a friendly smile. His lips were dry and burnt, he had a bottle of beer in one hand

and another one popped out from the back pocket.
A joint was perfectly placed on his ear.
All of a sudden he burst out singing in front of her.

"Whatever you going through,
no matter how hard it is,
Jah will always bless you, with a bit of spliff.

Make yourself high, be your own destiny,
Love is in the heart, for the whole world to see
Coz you are beautiful and you deserve me."

Chipo cracked up and giggled like a child, for a moment her worries vanished and continued laughing. "Yeah, my sista look how beautiful you are, when you laugh, when you smile. I am Jah's son I bring sunshine when its snowing, me wanna do you good, I got a nice drink and a spiritual spliff, here you wanna a sip of some of dis goood stuff?"
As he offered her his drink.

"No thank you, and thank you again for the beautiful song, you are very talented and funny. I like the words, I appreciate that you made me smile and laugh."
"Big up man Chamu, the charmer Rastafarian, all the way from Zimbabwe big-up big-up," as he fist bumps her.
"Wait a minute, you are from Zimbabwe?"
Chipo asked excitedly, her eyes wide open.
"Yeah man, deep down south H town Mabvuku baby," he shouted.
"Awesome! I am from Zimbabwe too."
Chamu exploded, "I knew it, you look like one of dem tin."
"Hallo wait a minute wat tin?" She yelled.
"Well you nice and shiny sista, clean, white teeth,

no dark marks on your knees." "Huh you can't even see my knees," Chipo giggled. "Kamusalad, kamu-Nice nice." She felt bemused and happy that she met him. She also felt a bit offended because he had already judged her.

(*MuSalad is a word used for privileged young girls who have never been to the ghetto and are spoilt, usually they speak English with an American accent.*)

Nevertheless, she felt comfortable meeting someone from her country.

"What a coincidence that we meet, just like that in a big city like this," she told him. "If it was written, it was written, What Jah wants Jah gets, Jah love ma sista, pleasure, pleasure I am everywhere."

"Saka unonzi ani iwe we?" (*What is your name?*) he asked in shona. She laughed.
"Oh my god, you speak shona, a moment ago I thought you were Jamaican."
"Uh tinotaura chirudzi chamai"
(*Uh, I can speak my mother language*)
"Ndodya sadza nemuboora zuva rese."
(*I eat sadza with pumpkin leaves everyday*)
"Oh you killing me, my God, you just made my day, "Ndinonzi Chipo."
(I am Chipo)
"Uh,"as he jumped up,"Hallelujah Chipo changu chandakapihwa naishe."
(*My gift from God*) as he beat his chest.

"Hold on for one minute please I need to appease the spirits," and he pulled out a long thick brown joint. As he lit it up and puffed, he violently choked from the inhaled smoke and gestured to her to take a pull, she was a bit tempted but she gracefully rejected it. He looked at her smirked, coughed, and scoffed. He searched for some change from his pocket and went to a nearby kiosk (tuck shop) without saying a word.

He brought back a chocolate drink, "a chocolate for chocolate, welcome home, home sweet home my sistren, let the vibes begin."
"So you have been around for a while, more like a pioneer,"
"Almost born here," he boasted, "me know who is who and they know who is me." Chipo was charmed.

They had a long and interesting conversation. What she didn't let slip was her full situation, she just told him she would be getting an apartment in the next few days. Somehow she thought the more you tell people about your problems the more they distance themselves from you. He turned up to be very kind, helpful, and was so much into his music.
They exchanged numbers and he invited her to one of his gigs the following weekend. She found out he was married to a German woman, and he had lived in Berlin for almost 20 years, so he knew a lot of Zimbabweans in Berlin and around Germany.
It made Chipo feel very comfortable, but he warned her not to expect any favors from anyone.
"Most people are more concerned about themselves and there is a lot of spite and jealousy in the society," he conceded, squirming. Chipo was amused by his character and actions.
"You have to trade carefully, Berlin is a beast full of temptations." He warned her. "Somehow I survived, not once but twice, stay away from dem drugs, work of the devil."
He lectured her about the dangers of abusing narcotics and gave her a few examples of his friends and people he knew, who had fallen prey to the famous Berlin nightlife. "Berlin is a techno city and

you know techno and cocaine, are brother and sista. Speedy and ecstasy that's the desert, they go hand in hand," he barked.
"Don't even try heroin," he looked at her sternly, "that's the biggest bitch," and he laughed. "Dat is the shit, oh man," as he swiped his hands. "A single dose and you are hooked forever, gone. I am talking from experience and believe me I am lucky to be alive, you see these marks, these scars," as he taps on his wrists, "I flew to hell and I came back riding a pig. Jah is real," as he blew a kiss to the sky.
"Tornado is one hell of a motherfucker, that dude, it's a miracle he is alive today. He was the talk of the town back then, big ass motherfucka, a bull-dozer of a man, smart, sharp tongue, quick-witted, had all the chicks at his feet. That guy used to run a successful club, throw parties, he had cash, big ass cars, but you know what goes up comes down. One day one of his girlfriends set him up with his other chicks and hell broke loose, Satan came down seething for his soul.
He lost everything, she kicked him out, to the point where he had to live in a homeless shelter, it was there where he got hooked up. He claims one of the junkies injected him with heroin whilst he was asleep, but I didn't believe him. De ting is, these shelters are large halls, with 100s of mattresses spread across the floor. They can accommodate from 200 to 500 people, packed like sardines, can you imagine someone who used to be 150 kg, shrunk to 60 kg in a matter of weeks," shaking his head
"It was so sad, I saw him one time coming out of the train, I looked away I could not see my brotha like dat hey, but as soon as he caught a glimpse of me he took off like a bolt of thunder. He ran away like a wild boar," as he mimicked a boar grunting, "he was ashamed," cracking himself up.
Chipo just smiled.
"You know what saved him my sista? This life we

are living Jah is great. You wanna know what saved him?"
"What?" She asked attentively.
"Jail," he yukked, "he was put in jail."
"For real, jail, no" she objected.
"Yes because in jail no drugs are allowed, they do random tests, and the only reason he was put in jail was that he started stealing to quench his thirst, to feed his habits. He would steal anything, but he wasn't good at it," he laughed.
"He kept getting caught all the time, he had lost so much weight. When he tried to outrun his pursuers, he would sway, stagger, and fall. His legs were too weak, being high on drugs he would run and wobble some times on the same spot and he would get caught.

He committed so many petty robberies and he continued to get caught. He would steal get caught, and he would steal again and get caught until the judge had had enough of him and he threw him behind bars. He was given 2 years, but I heard he requested to stay longer," they both laughed, "yeah coz if he was out, he would be dead by now."
"Thank Jah he came back to his normal senses, the Tornado as we call him, but the fact is, it's a very thin line, you can see it's very easy for him to fall into the same pit. This shit, once it's in your blood system, your whole body is contaminated, it stays lurking in the background and can be triggered by the smallest amount of any drug you consume. I pray that the brother stays safe. A lot of the brothers have fought the battles and they have lost. Can you imagine having no papers, work permits, no money, no place to stay, let alone have no woman? Oh no, let me not go there, a woman can be worse than a drug, let's not talk about that. A German woman oh man!"
"What about a German woman?" Chipo asked him.

He sighed and looked around, "let me smoke my blunt first," as he smiled. "When you have a typical German woman, my sista you'll know what stress is all about, the Nigerians will say, she'll give you Wahalla." And he laughed. "But don't get me wrong, there are some good apples. Not all women are the same but the ones I know, and those that my friends have come across hey," he scoffed. "You'll have to trade carefully even angels will have second thoughts. German men cannot handle them. There are too strong-minded, educated of course, and too independent. They don't bow down easily, they have a certain set of principles. They want to do everything by themselves. A German woman can build a whole house alone. Very determined, this is because after, the 2nd world war, most of the men were incarcerated so the women were left to fend for themselves. That's what made them strong, they love their independence so much to the point that, if you take her to a restaurant she wants to pay for her food and drinks. For me it's perfect because money is scarce anyway," he laughed. "But the problem with that is if you divide everything all the time, this is my own opinion, as a woman, you'll
miss out on a lot of things. Men will become lazy, they'll stop treating you like a lady. Because you insist on doing everything by yourself. I'll just chill and not put any effort into anything. Even in bed, that kills my libido, why should I satisfy you? When you do everything else by yourself. At home, I am facing fierce competition, from the other brother in the drawer."

"Are you sharing your wife? What about the other brother in the drawer?" Chipo asked confused.
"Why do you think dildos are the most sold items in Germany?"
"Not only in Germany, I thought they were sold more in China," Chipo objected and chuckled.

"Whatever but you know what I mean?, Come on, I'm competing with something unbeatable here, it's the same as challenging Usain Bolt," he scoffed, "a rubber with bumps and spikes that don't breathe and can go on forever."

Chipo burst out laughing.

"It's true every time before I do my thing, I'm always a bit hesitant because subconsciously I'm aware, big brother can be summoned to finish up the job. Sex is supposed to satisfy you like the food you eat everyday." Chipo smirked, "Ho ho wait, you are exaggerating right? I don't believe what you are saying, but what's wrong with self- satisfaction, it's a girls ting?"

"I don't know what's wrong with you women, these things make us men paranoid."

"I think you should speak for yourself, some men I am sure it's a pleasure for them," she attempted to school him.

"What would you prefer?" Chipo continued, "that I go and sleep with someone else who can satisfy me, when you are not around or I use big brother."

"Wait a moment, cheating is no go, people get murdered for that, he roared fiercely. But what you just said, that's a totally different thing, if I'm not around then it's fine, I'll support big brother, but as soon as I'm back, lock it up, not in the bedroom, and not in the drawer, somewhere far away in the cellar, basement," he gulped his second beer and burped.

"I have friends from everywhere some are single, others are married. Most are separated or divorced and they all have a story to tell. We discuss these issues, the difference in mentality, and the cultural unawareness is huge. It's horror, most of these guys are suffering silently, they cannot handle it. Don't forget you are coming from a world where the man is the head of the house. That means you do your things at your own pace, at your own time and then you find yourself in a different world. I am sure

everywhere else is the same, it's not only a German thing. I just have more experience with the women around here that's all. And as a husband you find yourself being delegated to, getting told what to do, how to do it. If you are not strong enough and you lack communication skills or you are not able to adjust and tolerate certain needs, you will go crazy. It's a new world order. Some guys work from 9 to 12 hours a day, hard labor my sista, after work they are afraid to go home. They would rather chill and smoke with me."
"And why is that," Chipo asked?
"Because as soon as they get home, as soon as they open that front door and she hears the keys clicking, she is already in her kinky underwear, Schatz, ich bin im Schlafzimmer, "(*Honey I am in the bedroom.*)

If you don't have money for viagra, then my friend start meditating, war is coming. The pandora box has been opened," Chipo laughed unstoppably, she felt compelled to interrupt.

"But what's wrong with having sex? Well if you are the boyfriend or the husband, then why not, no one wants sex 7 days a week anyway,"
"Oh-oh," Chamu nearly choked from his beer, he coughed and wiped his mouth.
"I am talking from experience my sista, the guys have no choice."
"How can they have no choice? How can they be forced?" She argued. He chuckled. "They have no choice because it's not a choice. If they don't oblige, they are accused of infidelity, she will scream and bang walls and threaten you. Even falsely accuse you of anything, yes! If you don't hit it she will feel like she is worthless. She will complain that maybe it's because she is not attractive enough and she will think you are getting it from somewhere else."
"Hold on, you said sex is like eating food, you eat

food every day right. So if she wants it everyday, what's the problem with that." He laughed, "but my sista I don't eat the same food every day, Some times every 2nd or 3rd day but of the same quality food, no problem. I'll eat the food gracefully and without an invitation."
"You are sleek, you are crazy Chamu, you mean son of a gun."
"If you don't comply with her demands that's when she will give you an ultimatum, I'll report you to the foreign office, I'll tell them this is a marriage of convenience and you'll be sent back to Nigeria," he scoffed. "My sister you'll start apologizing, thinking damn, I came here with a banana boat, I paid those smugglers 10,000 dollars, my family is depending on me, hey, you'll close your eyes and give her a nice fat kiss, you'll start massaging her feet. If she can cook, you are very lucky, usually, it's soup and bread with cheese," Abendbrot he added and they both laughed.
"You'll be a sex slave for the next five years until the German government says okay, my brother you have worked very hard and you have paid enough taxes and contributed to the society here is your permanent stay." Chipo belted out laughing.
"For real or you just bluffing Chamu."
"Uh uh, it's not a joke oh, you'll be blessed if she is 90 kg, usually, they are big heavy duty 150 kg and above."
"Hey!" Chipo exclaims, "Chamu, please."
"Ask around 60 years old women, they love them 20 years old young boys with boiling cobra blood, with enough power and spice ginger to execute the killer punch. Why do think Gambia is the most popular destination for older white women? Because the young guys are selling their choppers at the beach, the guys are lined up and the women move around shopping for the right product."
Chipo just Smirked. "You and your chauvinist slurs,

I can hardly hear you, you are corny," she shouted and said it sarcastically. "I could say the same thing about older guys with younger girls. The old men with bellies that are too far stretched to see their Willis."

"No no that's not the same thing," he bulked, "you can't compare that, their girls are models now, vivacious young and pretty and raring to go," he protested. "There is a big difference here, do you think it's easy to go for a walk with her, like that woman over there," as he pointed at some overweight lady. "Huh," he continued, "You have to put her in a wheelbarrow if you want to go shopping with her. For christ's sake there is no excuse to be like that. Hey, hey," he started shouting after her, "watch your weight, weight watcher is watching you," he clowned her. Chipo was not amused before she could say anything, he cut her off. "Try to go shopping with her, everyone would be staring at you, pitying you, that's when she will hold your hand and say, kiss babe." He laughed and rubbed his beard. "You will panic for a second and if she feels it, she will squeeze your hand and give you that dirty look, the paper warning eye."

Chipo thought he was drunk and high, she was a bit disturbed by his character, but she gave him the benefit of the doubt and allowed him to continue.

"Sometimes you will see a brother walking 10 meters ahead, she can't catch up with him, she is struggling to breathe coz she is too heavy, she can only take baby steps," as he trotted on one spot.
"Maybe it's better for her to coil and roll herself like a ball, it's faster that way," he burst out laughing.
"You are a mean man." "Sista it's not easy oh, the brother will just shout, I'll see you at home oh, whilst increasing his pace." As Chamu talked he

imitated the movements of the couples. Chipo had tears dripping from her eyes from laughing. "I have witnessed grown-up men seeking psychiatric help. One of my best friends gave a dog some milk and the next day it bit him. I witnessed it personally with my own eyes. He gave his childhood friend a place to stay after he was released from jail. He gave him clothing, fed him, gave him pocket money, took him for haircuts, so he could look sharp. He treated him like family, they would move around together, share secrets, they were like brothers, but guess what happened, when he was at work, the guy would rape the woman, and she was afraid to tell the husband. She didn't want to destroy their friendship and put her marriage in jeopardy until one morning he forgot his keys, he returned just after 5 minutes and he found the guy choking her on his bed. Bless him he didn't do anything stupid, he would be in jail for life. If it was me, I would have castrated him and shoved a knife up his ass. The woman became pregnant from the guy."

"Wow that's brutal, that's murder at it's best, but are you sure he was raping her, I detect some red flags in there."
"Well I heard soon after my friend left, she moved in with his friend. It never worked out though, now she is bitter with everyone. She became paranoid, angry with everyone. She couldn't find her balance. The rude boys know her as Killer T. No one knows what triggered that kind of behavior. But she has a history of picking up young asylum seekers, stay with them young boys for six months. After the little rabbit runs out of steam, she would just bring another bigger rabbit home and tell the other one to sleep on the couch," he said giggling. "Whoa! She is a savage and a rogue elephant, seeking destruction." Chipo chastised her.

"Coming to Europe is like going to the unknown, forget about everything that you have ever known or done. Here you gotta start again from zero. If you want to live in Germany, get your papers right, and follow the laws. You might think you are clever, but the law will always catch up with you. Don't take things for granted, whatever you do, whether you are moving into a new apartment, new job, whatever it is, make sure you get a contract or a signed agreement.

There is someone always wanting to fuck you up, for no reason. This kind of people have nothing to do, you see them looking out of the windows all the time, they get pleasure from seeing you miserable. When you come to Germany sistren," as he patted her on the shoulder, "you are not only coming to learn and work and seek refuge. Nah nah, here they'll teach you discipline, they'll instill some sense of responsibility. Because for every wrong you do, you'll learn the hard way, you'll be fined, reprimanded and punished. You'll pay dearly for it, through your nose. But there is a positive outcome to that, if you can make it in Germany you can make it anywhere else in the world. Hallelujah," as he rolled another joint.

"The law is king, you see that Hamburger take away over there, Fred Kruger, if the owner wasn't smart by now he would have closed down for good.

This place was dead, they tried all different types of businesses, nothing worked out and he came out with a brilliant idea, to sell high-quality burgers. From day one the place became a hit. Every day it was packed, then some jealous lonely beaver who lives on the 4th floor, can you imagine, got envious of his success. She called the city council and told them that the smoke of the burgers was tainting her clothes.

Everyone else didn't complain, only one single person, the council threatened to fine him and close

down the place, either he had to invest in some expensive chimney which would require approval from the authorities, or move somewhere else. But his German woman was a fighter. She went upstairs to this lady, grabbed her by the collar, and threatened to remove her fake nose. After that, she offered her a burger with chips and a drink every day. Now he has peace. The clothes don't stink anymore," he said giggling.
"So if someone wants to mess around with you they can very easily do damage. Law is law. Am I talking too much?" He asked as he saw Chipo checking her watch.

"No I am good, please go on, I'm learning a lot, very informative," she encouraged him. "I don't know if it's good for me though, because from now I'll be looking at people suspiciously."

"Nah once you have an apartment just go to the city council and register yourself. As soon as you exist on the computers and you get your anmeldung paper."

"Anmeldung, what's that?" She wanted to know. "That's your golden key to everything, without that you can't do anything, you cannot open a bank account, let alone get a contract for a mobile phone. I'll help you, don't worry, get a place first, that's why I am here anyway, consider me a gift from Jah," and he took a long pull of his weed and coughed while beating his chest. She let out a big sigh, she was left contemplating. Everything sounded heavy for her.
"Hast du 50 Cent für mich, Bruder... oder eine Zigarette?" A scantly dressed man asked Chamu for money, high as a kite struggling to stand.
"Ja, Bruder, wie geht's, 50 Cent nicht aber eine Zigarette, ja, du kannst auch zwei nehmen."

(*Do you have 50 cents for me my brother, a beggar asked Chamu. Yeah brother how are you, I don't have 50 cents but I can offer you a cigarette, take two in fact*)

Chamu saw the expression on Chipo's face. "You look like you are in shock, what's up with you? Haven't you seen a German beggar before?" And he cracked out laughing, "Oh oh oh you are in for a big cultural shock, wherever there are human beings, there is always going to be a lost sheep, people have different weaknesses you know, different experiences and sometimes it's not easy to handle difficult situations. Berlin is full of very poor people, junkies, drug addicts, homeless people, you will come across a span

of them, and of course a few lazy souls, hey I mean, well the social system here is quite good."

"We don't have a social system back home," Chipo added.
"He laughed Ha!ha!ha! Third world country," he began to sing, "Africa liberate Zimbabwe.
I wish Bob was alive man, Lazy asses get paid money for not working, for basically staying at home."
"Uh uh Chamu, I have never heard anything like that," Chipo was surprised, her mouth wide open, "really!" She rubbed her forehead waiting for confirmation.
"I have German friends, they are in their late 20s and they don't do anything. Their argument is always the same."
"And what's their excuse?"
He coughed heavily as she waited patiently for his answer.
"Welcome to Germany my sister. Look at it this way, if I go to work, I'll get paid maybe 1,100 euros and I have to wake up at 6 am and work till 4 pm by the time I get home it's probably 6 pm. And if I don't

work at all, I will get paid roughly 700 bucks, hey, that's a lot of bonds and I don't have to bother myself about getting up early or traveling an hour to get to work. The temperatures here can drop to minus 10 degrees, I will freeze to death man. I might as well sit around a fire in my hut and smoke a blunt and chill." He blew some smoke and smiled.

"Well it makes sense though, why work when you can get paid without working, but that also makes you lazy, I hate the word social, it sounds more like you are useless and you can't do anything for yourself," Chipo scorned. "In a way the system makes you lazy," she added.
"Uh yeah, but there is a lot involved, the amount of taxes people pay, that would even make you more lazier. Germany has one of the highest tax rates," Chamu giggled. "It's a catch 24," he shouted.

"It's getting dark," she said, Her mind was trying to figure out the way back home.
"Where are we?" She asked calmly.
"Am Arsch der Welt," (At the end of the world)
"Am Arsch der Welt, what's that?" She yelled.
Chamu pulled his joint again, "you are not very far away, you see the blue sign there, that's where you get your train U2. Try to come to the show hey, you will like it. It'll be blazing, help me to promote it, bring some people."
"How can I?" She shouted. "I don't know anyone here."
"Bring yourself then."
"You can count on me, I'll be there," she promised as she made her way to the station.
"Don't you just miss chewing ndzondora?"
(*Chicken feet*). She howled. "Nzondora," he repeated and laughed, "here we eat Döner with Tsatsiki," as he disappeared into the bushes nearby. On her way back, she tasted a Döner for the first time.

(A Döner is a typical Turkish delicacy, which is made of a round bun that is sliced into half and stuffed with chicken or lamb filled with different types of salads, vegetable, topped with a chili, garlic or yogurt dressing. Very cheap and quite tasty and it fills you up, though as a lady eating it, you got to worry about some side drippings messing up your make up.)

Chapter Six

As she opened her hostel room, she was met with an odor that you can only experience in a garbage bin. She stepped back and choked.
"What the hell?" She screamed, "damn girls this place smells like shit. Can't you let in some fresh air?" As she rushed to open the window. They were three Asian chicks, travelers, she gathered. Her new roommates, they looked at her in bewilderment.
She pointed at their shoes, one of them grinned, picked up the hiking boots and placed them on the window seal, "sorry about that, we have been on the road for three months, we can't even smell our own breath."
"Jesus Christ!" She exclaimed. "Please leave the window open for a while, a cat will suffocate in this stuffed room." She hissed.
She couldn't stand the stench so she decided to sit by the reception. Moreover, she knew that there was a better internet connection and she also wanted to talk to her parents in private. The video call with her parents lasted for less than 30 seconds, the video connection back home was bad.
"At least they had a chance to briefly see me and be reassured that I am alive and kicking," she thought to herself.
She talked for a long time with them on a normal call whilst on speakerphone. She did explain that there were some hiccups regarding her accommodation, besides that she told them she had started

her language course. Her mother let out a sigh of relief, "Makorokoto!" (*congratulations*)
Her dad advised her to use part of the 8,000 euros which by law they were required to deposit as security before applying for a visa. Chipo had almost forgotten about it, her nerves almost tickled her from excitement. She told them about Chamu and his gut wrenching stories, they laughed at times, but she could tell that they were also concerned.

"Be careful of these Rasta Pasta people, they are all junkies full of ganja, stay away from them, they'll disturb your studies." "I agree," the father added. "Don't forget you have a beautiful family here. If you need any help, we are here for you." Assured her mother.
"I'll always cherish that Mama," she nodded her head as if they could see her. After a long lecture her mother prayed for her and they wished her well. "Amen." They said in a chorus.
She was almost in tears. It was such a hard call for her, for she knew nothing she had said was true. She was startled by three giggling girls, grinning and laughing.
They were offering her some Chinese snacks.
"Now we are clean," said one of them. Chipo just laughed, "girls, I didn't mean it like that," she apologized, "I am sorry if I disrespected you."

"No it's fine, we were really dirty, five days without showering was hard for us."
"Five days! Oh my," she exclaimed, "that's enough, please say no more," she protested. They all giggled and nodded as they streamed out.
Chipo had received a couple of messages from her Zimbo connections in Germany. Most of their answers were quite similar, it was always, everything will be fine, don't stress yourself, get an apartment first, learn the language, and try to get a part-time job.

At that moment she visualized, she was alone and had to achieve her goals on her own. Her aim was just to get a place to live in and focus on the most important things, education and work.

She called Dana her best friend and partner in crime, immediately she almost forgot about her problems. They had known each other since junior school. Dana was full of life, you could put a rock around her neck and throw her into a sea full sharks and she would survive. What a hustler at such a young age. She told Chipo to forget about her Zimbo low life guys. "You are in Germany now, do what the Germans do, find yourself a nice blonde dude with thick lips, big blue eyes and a strong shaft," Chipo rolled on the floor laughing.
"And if they have any friends its even better, hook me up, show them my pics, the ones in which I look a bit slim. You know these white guys they like skinny bitches, they can't handle a loaded truck. I need a blesser oh, (*an older guy with money in a relation with a younger lady*) come on girl hook me up, at least mature guys don't bother you, they know what they want and they already have what they want, not these young guys still trying to get an insurance for their car, you dig me. I'm not worried about age, as long as he can take me away from this fucked up life. You are my last hope of survival, the only friend I have, my best friend, you can't let me suffer and hang like a dried rat," she moaned.
"Otherwise you'll have to send me money, talking about money, can you please send me some Nike sneakers, the latest ones."
"Dana are you mad? Where will I get the money from? I am not even working, I have to depend on my parents, I told you this guy duped us dawg."
"Chipo please use your head, you are now in Europe, Germany, if I was there, I'll have my own house within six months, no time to sleep, you gotta

hustle hard, send me some iPhones, make up kits or perfumes I can resell them for a profit." Chipo just laughed and said, "when the time comes I'll not forget you my dear. How is Joe anyway?"
"Uh! Who? That dude, eish! He is struggling bro, at the verge of getting dumped," they both laughed. Joe was Dana's longtime boyfriend. "By the way did I tell you, that nut head Mavis is pregnant, she is now a small house (*a side chick*) Can you believe it, the guy has two wives, but he is loaded," Dana gossiped.
"Oh my god, she is only 18, how old is the guy?" Chipo inquired.
"I don't know, who cares, she now lives in Borrowdale man, one of the most expensive places, in a big ass house."
"Whoa!" Chipo was surprised.
"Yeah I heard this guy`s eldest daughter is the same age as her."
"Really" and they laughed, "beep beep beep," and the phone cut, that was the end of their conversation.

Chapter Seven

Chipo was admiring herself in the mirror with a smirk, She wasn't impressed by the small pouch building up, her hair needed some attention. She twisted and turned as she watched her hump.
"Not too big, not too small. I am sure I can turn a few heads and maybe make someone fall in love," she convinced herself.

Among her friends, she was the quietest person and the teachers used to like her. She wasn't known for getting into trouble, it was always someone else's fault. She thought about the first time she consumed alcohol. She was nearly kicked out of school. If only her mother had not pleaded with the headmaster, without her father knowing about it.
She had insisted and lied that she drank a glass of wine thinking it was the newly promoted apple juice. But this time it was different. Dana had convinced her and two other friends, to meet up with some boys from another school. It was a Friday and they had an allowance to go into the city until a certain time. Dana had gushed about these cool guys the whole week, and she really wanted to see one of them. Mavis decided they should buy a bottle of Amarula. They passed the liquor around among themselves drinking from the bottle. The guys turned up late, they were initially supposed to meet them around 2 pm, but they only turned up 2hours later and the school gates would close at 5 pm.

They were 30 minutes away from school and kind of tipsy. As soon as the guys appeared, Chipo and her friends forgot about their worries and started partying. They danced and played music in the guys` van under a big fig tree. Chipo had her first kiss, she was nervous and was sweating all over. But she felt lucky and blessed. The girls were very much attracted to the guys. They were in a jovial mood, carefree attitude, that they didn`t notice their headmaster's car pull up behind them.

They had bottles of alcohol lying around, blasting hiphop music, hanging around with weed smoking, bandana-wearing boys, who looked like gangsters, and to make things worse, Georgina, one their friends was caught in an uncompromising position. Dana who was outside, at the back of the van grinding to the beats collapsed as soon as she saw the car.

"Oh shit, we are done," shouted Lewis as he jumped into the van leaving Dana on the ground. "Your headmaster man, we done brothers," he whispered. "What do we do?" Chipo spoke softly. Everyone just melted. Mavis was too drunk to realize what was going on. Mr. Mutambara was a towering figure, he must have been 2.20 meters tall, maybe the tallest headmaster in the world, usually they come short and fat. As he swung the van door open and leaned forward, the car almost tipped over.

He had to double bend to pop inside. Mavis burped with nervousness, "Oh hi, it`s you," she shrieked, and then she threw up missing him by a droplet.
He didn`t flinch, his face was folded like a lion, ready to crush some bones.
"There are few things I don`t like about my job," he barked, "but by and large I enjoy it," he said with a smirk. And began shaking the van.

"Get out, get out, get out of this stupid Matata Kombi," as he banged on it.
"Get out of this car and get into my car right now, now I said," he screamed.
"This guy must have been once a sergeant in the army," the boys thought. One of them made a sudden movement.

"Stay where you are, big man unless you want a thorough beating," he roared. The girls quickly slipped out like little ducklings. Dana had gotten up, it was as if she had seen a ghost. She was staggering and had dirt all over her.

"One thing that I know and I can predict quite good ladies, you are all going to get a hiding," he rumbled, as he got into the car.
Dana choked, "Sir, I can explain, it's not what you think," she stammered.
He gave her the Godzilla stare, "Young lady, under the existing circumstances it is probably prudent to keep your mouth closed and just listen," he retched and cleared his throat. "Pass me my Mazoe drink underneath the seat, somewhere at the back," he shouted. Mavis trembled as she searched for the drink. But there was only a bottle of water underneath her feet, and the bottle of Mazoe was empty. She froze, "there is only water sir, I think the Mazoe bottle is empty. Here sir, should I open it, Sir, eh no more Mazoe, Sir," she fumbled for words and stuttered. "Huh, shut up and just give me the water," he paused for a moment, "who drank my Mazoe he asked furiously."
The girls were confused, they just looked at each other and shook their heads.
"Little cherry thieves," he called out and grabbed the plastic bottle, squeezed it until it was flat, and threw it out through the passenger window.
He gave a heavy sigh and clicked his tongue.

"One thing is disturbing me though, Chipo," he chuckled. "Chipo," he said wagging his finger in the air. "I reserve my doubts, huh Chipo, I am flabbergasted, totally convinced these three bullied you into it, huh Dana you dragged her into this, into this disgusting, inhumane, barbaric, gothic behavior, am I right Chipo? I know I know," he nodded his head and stepped on the gas as if he was in a rush to thrash them. Even the car felt his anger. He leaned forward and hugged the steering wheel. Stepping hard on the fuel pedal opening the throttle as the blue Nissan Pulsar flew past other cars.
They looked like dolls packed at the back seat, whilst he sat alone in front. Try to picture that.

They were so silent and still, a mosquito could have bitten them a thousand times, sucked all their blood out and they wouldn't have moved an inch, that's how scared they were.

"Gosh, this guy, Mr. Mutambara was like a spirit, he was known for appearing in the least expected places, maybe he had been following them. You could never do anything without him not finding out. It was as if he had bugged the whole school," they thought Chipo felt relieved somehow she had been exonerated, she was relieved. But as soon as they were in his office, Mavis turned the tables against them, she twisted and burnt them one by one. She wanted to save herself, so she divulged all, she narrated everything.
"Sir, since I enrolled in this school I have never been in trouble, my grades are good, my behavior is recommendable. If only I had followed my heart, I would not be in this kind of situation. You know my father is a pastor, a well-respected man in the community. He brought us up in a Christian way and we go to church every Sunday. I had never tasted a single drop of alcohol until Chipo suggested it.

She bought a full bottle of Amarula and forced it on me. Dana is like the snake, Sir, that lied to Adam, she convinced me under the disguise that we were only going to meet one guy, to pick up study material. I had no idea that she was setting me up with some drunkards, uneducated street kids.
As naive as I am, Sir, and because of my stupidity I just followed her blindly. I have no idea what got into me, I apologize, Sir, for my behavior. I don't ever want to have anything to do with these three, Sir," she abruptly and harshly defected from their side.

"Where did the weed come from?" He asked in a gruff voice.
"Georgina should know better, Sir, I saw her rolling a joint," Mavis replied calmly.
"A joint, what is a joint?" she remained silent.

"Well young lady as much as I appreciate your honesty, you know how the saying goes, if you move around with crooks, automatically you have become a crook too. It's a pity you chose to follow your head instead of your heart. Next time you'll know better, it's a life lesson learned. Your judgment let you down and there are consequences for everything. I want a full report, from every one of you, I want you to write me 10 pages in a detailed explanation of what transpired. If I had to make a hasty decision right now, you'll all be expelled. I'll hold my judgment until I read your testimonies and after that I want you all to go home and come back with both of your parents," he concluded in a deep harsh voice.

Dana started sobbing, Mr. Mutambara chuckled, "Cry me a river young lady, now who gets to be whipped first," as he took out a bamboo stick from underneath the table and swung it, testing its flexibility in the air. What a cruel way to punish a kid. The girls never talked to Mavis again and Chipo passed all her exams with distinctions.

Chapter Eight

It was the 4th day in Germany and the owner of the apartment had not called her back.
She had left five recorded messages and had to pay extra for the other 5 days to extend her stay. She wasn't bothered about it, there was still 8grand in the bank. She begged the receptionist to move her into a room with two single beds. The area she was living around had become quite familiar to her and the surroundings were easily recognizable. She knew her way around, so when Camisa one of her Spanish classmates suggested that they should all go to the weekly student party, she didn't hesitate. The club was called Watergate, like the name it was close to the water. The place was packed, steamy and dimly lit, long drinks were expensive.
"7 euros for one," she gasped as she read the drink card.
"A bottle of water and soft drinks 4.50 euros, ouch! beer and shots of tequilas 1 euro, that's me, you can't blame me for choosing the latter," she shouted and beamed to her friends. Not that she had to spend any money. Somehow her classmates Camisa and Abu were competing in buying shots.
The feeling was awesome, almost everyone spoke English. They danced, sang and got wasted. Abu the charmer had pinned one chick in a corner and Camisa was flirting with some Caribbean hunk. Chipo got a tap on her shoulder, as she spun around, she was met with a huge harmless kiss, for a moment she

was in shock, but it felt good and she went for it. It was dark and the disco lights made it even harder to see. Through a twinkle of light she noticed it was a girl. She tried to push her away but the girl held her firmly.
"It's my birthday," She screamed, "one for you and one for me, take this," as she drowned a tequila, and placed another kiss on her forehead and staggered away. Camisa stared at her like what was that, but Chipo just gulped the shot and started dancing. She heard a couple of bangs on the door.

"Time to check out , time to check out," a lady shouted. She lifted her head half-dead, a sharp pain ran down her neck, she had slept fully clothed with her shoes on. She was in pain, a monotone sound buzzed in her head. There was vomit on her sheets, she was disgusted and mortified. When she looked down from her tree bed, her head spun, she was dizzy, she felt as if she was wearing a VR going downhill. Her body was weightless and her vision blurred. A short woman stood by the door, grinning.
"Too much alcohol last night hey?" And she laughed, "drink lots of water, but you must check out now, I need to clean up," she shouted smiling in a Spanish accent. Chipo remembered she had to change rooms and just nodded her head.
"Five minutes, five minutes," she repeated.
She noticed it was already 11 am and had missed her lesson. Her heart sank, she was angry and shook her head in disapproval. She murmured to herself "I promise this will never happen again."
Her new room was far much better, only two separate beds. She slept the whole day, only to be awoken by her phone ringing.
"What a gwan," came out a loud voice, it was Chamu. "You still sleeping, what's wrong my sister? You'll miss the boat if you sleep too much man, get up and prepare yourself for the concert tonite. I will

put your name down on the guest list, no need to pay. It's Friday and Berlin is on fire TGIF bless you."
"What-what?" She stammered, "Is it Friday? No, it's Thursday," she confused herself. Ha!Ha!Ha! Chamu laughed, "gimme some of that weed you are smoking man," he rumbled.
She soon discovered she had slept the whole of Thursday, missed two lessons.
"Damn," she cried out, she was so muddled, so disoriented. "I'll be there, I am just relaxing," she lied.
Chipo scrolled through her phone, there were 15 missed calls, "never had so many calls before," she moaned. All her German Zimbo friends had called at least twice each. It was as if they knew she wouldn't answer. Mr. Schneider had also called and written her a message. The owner of the apartment had been waiting for her for three hours, she reckoned that she had missed the appointment.
"That sucks," she yelled. She tried to call him back there was no answer.
She took a long cold shower, her mind raced to the day before. "What happened? How did I get home?" She tried to trace her path. "How did I really get that drunk?" She asked herself but nothing made sense.

She called Camisa. "Hey Sipoh, you alive I was beginning to get worried, you not picking your calls. Where are you?"
"You never called me," she objected.
"I did a lot of times, with my Spanish number too, check your phone," Camisa replied.
"What happened that night?" She asked in suspicion, "I got no memory of nothing man," Chipo said.
Camisa was laughing. "You just went crazy man, from 0 to 100, like a plane. I tried to talk to you, to calm you down, but you pushed me away and left the club."
"Really, was I that drunk, Oh Gosh!" She retaliated.

"Yes, you ran and jumped into a taxi."
"Was I alone?" she asked hesitantly.
Camisa laughed again. "No, with two guys."
"What?" She shouted.
Ha!Ha!Ha! "I am just kidding, you must have taken some crazy drugs, maybe the girl you kissed left something in your mouth."
"But was I alone?" She insisted.
"Of course! You were alone, hold on did anything happen that I am not aware of. Uh oh," she shouted excitedly.
"Did you wake up next to someone with a disfigured face?" she belted out laughing.
"Camisa, this is important man," she was getting frustrated.
"Ok cool, you left after you quick froze that tall guy, you stood him up on the dance floor. You left him scratching his head with confusion. He didn't know what hit him," she continued.
"He was bothering me the whole night about you, he wanted your number."
"What tall guy?"
"The one you were making out with," her heart stopped.
"For real Camisa?"
"Oh man, you don't remember shit, look in your photo gallery, you took lots of pics. He was kinda nice though, what's up girl," she yelled.
"Damn Camisa I really messed up hey."
"No you didn't that was a cool night man, one of the best nights ever. I took his friend Markus home, yeah babe, hot, hot. What's up with you, are we going out tonite or what?" She shouted.
"Let me get back to you," Chipo said quietly.

She quickly checked her gallery, scrolling through a lot of weird photos, and for sure she had had the time of her life, they were some disturbing pics.
"How could I kiss such a handsome guy without

remembering?" She was angry with herself. He was a typically German guy, tall, heavy biceps, big chin, blonde. She was wowed with pics and smiled widely as she browsed through.
"Not bad, hey," biting her lips. "Dana would love this," she cried out.

Chamu calling popped on her screen. "Yo," she answered, "Oh man, big up, Jah love, got news for you, one of my lady friends is coming through attending da party, you should meet her she is well connected, knows the whole of Berlin. Whatever you need? She will hook you up."
"Sounds good man just what I am looking for right now, networking," she yelled.
"Don't be late sistren? Peace out," and he hung up.

She went by the Donner place, filled up her tummy, and made her way to Yaam.
"I just love google maps, with a touch of a button it all pops up," she said silently.
She was looking super-duper, as Dana called it.

Chapter Nine

According to city info, Yaam was a well known reggae venue. Many popular artists had performed there and the place was close to the water where the owners had created an artificial beach and some outdoor food markets. It was divided into three different music rooms and was quite multicultural.
A lot of dreadlocked guys smoked weed and danced happily. Some were playing drums, others listening to a beatbox. As she headed for the club building, she was met with a few unwanted greetings and suspicious looks. One or two guys offered her a joint, which she politely declined.

After a short walk she heard the unforgettable horselaugh. "Hoy koi hoi koi" immediately she knew it was Chamu. She followed the laughter and came across a group of guys in a circle. They all turned around, when they saw her approaching.
"How much you want sistren?" A tall skinny guy asked as he walked towards her.
"Nah nothing, just looking for my friend Chamu, I thought I heard him laugh."
"You what, looking for Chamu," he looked surprised, "Hey Chamu," he yelled. "Hey, Chamu Chamu, why you always getting the good girls man, look, man, she is hot, hot man, she is hot hot, when she jigs you, oh man you gonna go bomboklat man." Chamu starred at her high and confused, he couldn't recognize her.

"Chamu it's me, Chipo," she yawped. Suddenly he grinned. "Hey man, me I am thinking who is this top model, who wants Rasta, Mi Naah Look at you, then I remember, she is too skinny man, she can't wine it like Spice, my sistren welcome," as he hugged her, "Hey yo, hey this is my sistren, live and direct from Zimbabwe."
"Whoa, in Zimbabwe you got such nice tings oh," as one of the guys stared at her, with such hungry eyes.
"No wonder why Bob Marley wanted Zimbabwe liberated," shouted the other guy and they all laughed. "My set is in 10 minutes man, let's go in, let's go," Chamu bellowed. He looked so different, he was dressed in Jamaican colors with a white cloth tied around his hair creating a shape like a huge cone on his head, that replicated a beehive. He looked the reggae part, she could have mistaken him for Buju Banton she wondered to herself, only that Buju was in jail.
They were let in through the back door. Once inside, the place was jam packed, the smell of weed was in the air. Chamu whispered something to her, that she didn't really understand because it was too loud and he disappeared, leaving her confused. One of his friends offered her a drink, but she was a bit skeptical. She walked towards the bar squeezing herself through the crowd. She was about to order some water when someone touched her shoulder.
"That's on me boss," he shouted, at the barman totally ignoring her. She stared at him as she turned around, it was a German guy with cornrows grinning at her God given assets.
He whispered, "whatever you like is on me, in my country we don't allow a beautiful woman like you to buy her own drink," Chipo was astonished and she blushed, she had heard German guys only approach you when they are drunk. This guy had so much confidence and guts.

"Whoa," she thought to herself. "Two Desperados please," the guy hollered at the barman.
"Um uh wait, hold on, hey barman, make it a bottle of Vodka with some red bulls," he boasted.
"A bottle of vodka," Chipo thought, some rich kid maybe.
"You drink red bull don't you," he asked her.
"No," she answered.
"Well it will be your first time then," he said smiling arrogantly. She just grinned back, he pulled out a bundle of cash and paid for the bottle, giving the barman a 10 buck tip. He seemed to like the attention he got when he carried the bottle around.
Chipo caught a glimpse of a few ladies observing them and she felt special, "drip, drip," she smiled. They pulled up to a hidden table, somewhere in a dark corner sat five black guys looking thirsty, their eyes wandering around. As soon as he put the bottle on the table, they brightened up, gave him fist bumps.
"My dawg, that's how we do it," screamed one of them.
"And this is how we roll, he uttered into her ear."
"These are my boys, we grew up together, me gonna wala wacka tonite oh," he purred to one of the guys. Chipo was taken aback.
"A white dude speaking pigeon English, damn he must have lived in Nigeria for a long time," she thought. She got worried but felt hopeless, she was attracted to him.
"Even Dana would have carried her load and walked away," she laughed.
"Stay away from Naija boys," Dana had warned her. The other guys didn't pay so much attention to her, as they were busy massacring the vodka. One word she learned very fast was "Prost," (cheers).
"You must look into someone's eyes when you say cheers," he protested.
"Why?" She asked.

"It's a German thing, otherwise, you'll have five years of bad, bad sex, but not with me though, that shit don't work on me," he bragged. The music was great, the vibe was tip top, they were playing some of her favorite songs and Chipo loved dancehall.
She was astonished at how well this dude could go down. They were whining and grinding and then suddenly he backed off.
"I'll be back in one minute," he pleaded.
Chipo was left standing in the middle of the dance floor alone.

"What the hell man, no respect," she complained to herself as she turned to walk away, he immediately grabbed her hand.
"Sorry about that, I just saw someone who owes me some money," he shouted. "Yeah 25,000 euros and guess what, he just gave it to me, yeah," grinning.
"Tomorrow we are going shopping. I am taking you for a spin, you are my date now, worry about nothing, we got money to spend. I got it all in check," he quipped.
"Come on I'll show you around the club," he literally dragged her. They went outside, to the back of the club. It was designed more like a beach, Caribbean style.

"Holly Molly," it was chilly but Chipo didn't complain. He bragged a lot about himself and she thought it was part of having money. She was dreaming, he could maybe buy her lots of stuff, pay for her school fees and her rent. She let her mind run wild.
"I bought my latest car 2 weeks ago, I love it, Mercedes Benz ML, in fact, I only drive Mercedes Benz, my father is crazy though, he has five different Porsches in different colors."
"Wow!" She exclaimed, as she rolled her eyes and finished her drink.

She thought to herself, I finally got a young blesser. "It's a bit cold out here," finally she complained, "should we go inside," as she walked away.
"Hey chill a bit, my charm will warm you up, just gotta say something. I don't want you to think I am being pushy, or forcing anything on you, I kind of like you in a different way, that's all. When I first saw you, I liked you, I don't know why."
"If you don't know why you like me, then why do you like me."
"You know that itch on your nose, when you smell something good? Let's just spend some quality time together with me and you and see what happens. You got nothing to lose, if it works it works, if it doesn't work, it doesn't work. We could drive around, show you the city, go for a swim, eat popcorn or some ice cream at the movies, you know, the usual. Sip some Champagne, go shopping, put a smile on your face, and maybe if you are lucky, I'll give you a massage." As he licked his lips.

She thought he was going for a kiss but he didn't. "Thank God, I am not ready for that," she blushed.
"I can drop you off later at your place, you don't need to take the train, it's cold, too many thugs outside, are we cool."
"Alright, that's fine with me," she agreed.
"Shall we go back inside," she persisted. He put his arms around her, and kissed her on the forehead. Somehow he knew how to stamp his authority, how to claim his prize.

"Don't worry about the guys inside, they all work for me," he boasted. "Whatever I say they do, it's called building life babe, I got my shit in check." She caught sight of Chamu on the other side, she had almost forgotten about him, "hey that's Chamu, the guy I came to see."
"Which one?" he asked.

"The one with a white piece of cloth on his head, standing next to the lady in a red dress."
"Uh that one, forget about him, he has nothing, he just likes to talk talk talk, he is a runner, he carries bags for other Deejays and smokes too much weed, you have to be careful, I heard through rumors he is a pimp, drugs women and steals from them." He got her scared. She was stunned, confused before she could say anything, he pulled her away. At that moment Chamu saw her and was gesturing at her to come over. She pretended like she didn't see him. She was doubting herself. A bit shocked by what this guy had told her.

"Chamu doesn't look like a pimp," she said to herself. She was surprised at the sudden change of plans, all of a sudden they were in a hurry to leave the club. He called his boys, Chipo trotted along and they left Yaam. One of the guys had hidden the bottle of vodka in his jacket and they were drinking it like water.

"Did I tell you, I am Marko," Chipo nodded her head as if she knew. He didn't drink while he was driving, Chipo admired that. "He is disciplined and responsible," she thought.
"Let's pass through Surprise," he suggested, little did she know it was a name of a club. It was almost 4 am. Surprise was a popular African club.
Once they were inside she actually thought she was somewhere in Africa. They were playing African music, full of African people dressed in African attire. It was packed, sweat was dripping from people's faces.
"The air condition must be broken or maybe it was a trick to get people to drink alcohol," Chipo wondered. They made a streamline until they were right at the back. There was an extra room for VIPs. The security made way for them. Marko and his group

were quite acquainted, they knew almost everyone. Chipo thought it a bit awkward as they were jeered while walking past a group of girls. Some of the ladies rolled their eyes and scoffed at them. Marko kept his head down as he pulled Chipo along. Most of the tables in the VIP room were filled with bottles of Hennessy, Whisky, and Vodka. People were having a good night, as she looked around something struck her, there were older white guys with young black women and there were younger black guys with mature white women.
Chipo thought about Chamu's stories, she was getting a bit paranoid about it.
She became very observant. Most of the white women were a bit overweight and a lot of younger guys were all over them. These Gogos (*grandmothers*) could whine it, they were dancing and shaking their bodies, it was quite amazing to watch.

As usual, Marko was everywhere, chatting with whoever, randomly he would just pop his head, checking on her. Chipo made her way to the ladies room, the atmosphere was vibrant, lively, a couple of scuffles here and there, but the security was very agile, quite busy actually.
You could tell they were a lot of ladies of the night, sticking their bums, on anything that crossed them. The place kept getting fuller and fuller, no one wanted to go home. When she got back from the loo Marko had bought some spiced up West African pieces of meat, they were so tasty, she didn't realize how much hungry she was. The spices made her even drunker. He was really doing his best to impress her. She could tell he was well known among the females in the club. That made her even more attracted to him.

"I used to organize events before, I brought in a lot of artists from all over the world, Jay Z, Sean Paul,"

he clarified when he noticed her suspicions.
"Really that's sound, dope man, cool," she was excited about it. The thought of meeting a big American star made her cozier towards him.
She was dazzled by his ways, he was easygoing, very confident, and very communicative. Chipo stopped short of taking the next bite when she noticed her purse was half opened, her ghetto instincts kicked in. She snatched the bag from the chair.
"Oh no my phone is gone," she yelled.
She took a deep breath, Marko took notice.
"What's wrong?"
"My phone is gone," she told him, "thank God I have my money in my jeans pocket."
"No, no way, we were here the whole time, there is no way anyone could have taken it, check your bag, maybe you forgot it in the car," he cried out.
"You must have dropped it somewhere else when was the last time you used it?" He growled whilst searching everywhere, his buddies too, they were looking under the chairs, tables, in between the couches, questioning some people close by, but no one had seen anything.
"I'll get you a new one tomorrow, don't worry," he assured her. She was depressed. "Oh all my numbers, my contacts," she shrieked.
"Hey listen don't bother yourself about it, I am sure it's in the car, we'll find it let's not spoil the night."
She just smirked. "My phone is gone," she yelled.

"Rule number one, never leave your bag unattended in a club or bar or anywhere," she remembered Dana's words. She knew that very well, but she was in Germany with a German dude. She didn't want to be the spoilsport," Chipo thought to herself.
"One more round of tequilas," Marko suggested.
"You know your number off your head, I can try to call it to see if it's ringing," asked one of the guys.
"Nah, it's a Zim number not working here just the

WhatsApp," she replied. By the time they left the club it was almost 8 am, she had never stayed out for so long. All of Marko's friends had disappeared without a word. He dropped her off and promised to check on her later in the evening. She was dead asleep within a second.

Chapter Ten

She woke up with an ass in her face, the place was smelling of weed, rock music blasting.
"Hey what the hell man," she jumped up pushing her away.
"Hey hey relax relax, I was just trying to wake you up, you were screaming in your dream, I did you a favor."
"You did me a favor by farting and putting your ass in my face, are you crazy."
"Oh sorry, that was just for my fans, you know I need to be creative."
"Delete that shit or we gonna have a problem right now," as she advances towards her, hitting her palm with her fist.
The other girl's face became red. She had tattoos all over her body as she was wearing a tank top, she was big and a bit scary, but she got scared of her, Chipo had a short temper though.
"Ok cool, calm down," cried out the other girl, she showed Chipo the video and she hit the delete button. "What's up with you?"
"Are you crazy you don't do that to people you don't know," she declared. "Who are you anyway?"
"Well I paid for this bed," she blurted out. Chipo just turned around grabbed her towel and bathing items and stormed out. They were five other girls taking a shower, she hated it, group bathing, toilet sharing was never her thing, it was hard for her to take a dump. She wondered what kind of meat she had

the previous night. The spices were burning her ass. "My phone is gone," she said quietly, it made her even more depressed. "How can I be so stupid, I am sure one of those black guys took it, maybe I forgot it at the Yaam, or dropped it in the car." She was just angry with herself while showering lost in her thoughts. She found herself laughing out of the blue, the girls bathing opposite her, were all clean shaven.
"These chicks look like shaved chickens," she giggled. "She had a thick black bush, one would get lost in there," she observed herself. They must have thought she was crazy.

When she got back to her room, she found her new roommate with two glasses of Sekt, sparkling wine. "Hi again, my name is Maike," she sounded so sweet, "I guess we started off on the wrong foot, I didn't mean to upset you, but since I'm going to be here for the next few days I thought we should make up, let's have a Prost. What do you say?" She was right in her face.
"Nah it's too early for alcohol for me."
She longed for Matumbu. (*Grilled intestines*)
"But it's 7 pm she insisted."
"Really oh my god I'm losing track of time damn, what day is it today?"
"You drank a lot last night hey. When you came in this morning, you greeted me and passed out."
"Oh for sure I don't remember that part, on second thoughts," she took the glass and made Prost, "Prost," she repeated, Chipo found Maike to be quite nice and a good talker, she sounded intelligent, they were almost the same age. She was weird, unpredictable, and very interesting.
"So where are you from?" Chipo asked her after a while. Ha!Ha!Ha! She bounced her head side to side, with a big smile. "I try not to think about that, I am from everywhere, I used to live in Bonn with my

mum and dad, but when they separated I moved to Hamburg with my mum and stepdad."
"Wait a minute, the four of you were living together?"
"Its a complicated story," Chipo rolled her eyes.
"I can see that." They both laughed.
"Seven years ago, I ran away from my crib, I was fifteen then," as she puffed some smoke.
"For real, why? How is that?" Chipo asked curiously.
"Complicated," she says again, they laughed again.
"You traveled a lot, do you always travel alone?"
Maike chuckled, "I have been to a lot of places, most of the time alone. I can't stay in one place for too long, it's as if I am running away from something."
"Maybe your shadow," Chipo teased her.
"How about you?" She asked Chipo. "This is my first time outside Zimbabwe and what a difference. You guys have it easy here."
"Is that what you think, you need to travel around, unless if you are comparing with Zimbabwe."
"Tell me something, what's the worst thing you have ever done in your life?" Maike asked her.

Chipo took a deep breath, "the worst thing, that I have ever done in my life, ooh let me see, uh I don't know, smoked weed I guess."
"Ha!ha!ha! That's not a bad thing," she screamed, "I mean something adventurous."
"Hold on let me think, uh now I know, one night I wanted to go hang out with my friends, so I tried to sneak out of the house, I got wedged, my underwear got hooked on the window panel," they both laughed.

"I was left suspended, hanging in the air and to make things worse the dogs wanted to bite me, they thought I was a thief man," they both laughed.
"I was lucky my brother's bedroom was right next to mine and he helped me up. My parents never got to know about it, but I had to buy my brother a pair

of Jordan sneakers, for him not to squeal." "That's nothing out of the book though," she dissed.
"And you, what was the worst thing you ever did or experienced," Chipo asked curiously.
"A lot she laughed, I'll need at least one week to explain," she cleared her throat, "the simplest one is this, Umh...but you have to look at me," she suggested. And then she opened her mouth revealing her split chopped viper tongue.

Chipo screamed and jumped, she quivered in shock. Her eyes had popped out, she thought she was seeing a devil in human form.
"Oh my god what the hell, are you alive? Why did you do that to yourself? Gosh it must have been painful, oh gosh," she exclaimed.
Maike chuckled and laughed hysterically, she was thrilled by her reaction.
"You should've seen your face," she cried out.
"Damn girl, holly cow, you find that amusing, you scared me to death man." Maike continued laughing like she was possessed.
"You freaked me out man, Why did you do that?" Chipo asked inquisitively, she was very curious. She had never seen anything like that in her life. But Maike kept on laughing, after a while of choking, and wiping tears, she gathered herself.

She looked at Chipo and said, "I might look 22, but inside I feel like I am 50 years old. That represents my fucked up life, how fucked up my world is. Doomsday is coming," she yelled.
Chipo was spooked. "Tomorrow we have a photoshoot at the East sea."
"In this cold, are you serious?" "Yeah, everything we do is too extreme. I am a member of a group of special people, we are about 5000 of us in the whole world. And we do extremely things." "Extremely things like what?" Chipo asked frantically.

"Well anything that normal people don't do, we do, body modifications, extreme piercing 99% of our bodies, sharpen our teeth, look more like a vampire, corset piercing."
"Jesus," yelled Chipo.
"Lip sewing, eyeball tattooing, body branding," Maike continued.
Chipo was having goosebumps.
"Taking walks in freezing temperatures, You know, we walk naked in the snow." Maike bragged. "Anything not for the faint-hearted we do," and she chuckled. "And why do you do that? Do you get paid for it?" Chipo asked nervously.
"Nah no money is involved, just to cover expenses.

This group is very special, most of the members, if not all have been through a hell lot of difficulties in their lives."
"Hey," Chipo listened attentively. "I can give you a couple of examples, a friend of mine was abused by her whole family. The father and brothers sexually assaulted her." Chipo was at a loss of words.
"Is that a true story."
"Yeah it's all real, and she didn't have anyone to turn to, except to run away, after years of abuse. She was only 14 years old then. And now to get rid of that part of her, she cuts herself when she showers."
"You mean like cutting herself?" Chipo asked in disbelief.
"Yes she uses a razor blade, she slashes her hands, legs, all over." Chipo looked alarmed, wide-eyed, shell shocked.

"If I tell you some of the stories, you will have nightmares, you will think I made them up."
"That's some deep shit man. If that's for real, now I am getting worried, I am very anxious and worried about you. What's your story?"

Chipo confronted her. Some more Sekt please," as she filled her glass, "my life is fucked up, I am messed up and I know that.
My stepdad had been abusing me since I was 13, and every time I told my mother she didn't believe me, she thought I was jealous of her relationship, that I was angry because she had left my dad. So the abuses continued and I kept complaining until she sent me to live with my uncle for the summer holidays. I relayed everything to my uncle, at first he was very understanding, but not concerned.
I liked him because he allowed me to drink whiskey and smoke, you know, do things my mum wouldn't allow me to do. He had so many friends, and we always had guests turning up in the middle of the night. It was cool, I was having the time of my life, I didn't want to go back home.

One day I passed out, I woke up and my uncle and his three friends were having sex with me, disguised as jokers. The next day he pretended as if nothing had happened, he told me I had a terrible nightmare, that I was hallucinating and seeing things that were not there. I was confused, I did not know what to believe, I went back to my mum, I didn't say anything after two days a piece of condom fell out while I was peeing, and the abuses at home continued," Chipo cringed. "When I was old enough I made my move, drugs became my best friends, and trust me I don't give a fuck about this life. Inside me I am a zombie, cold, heartless." In the streets I lived, I have been gang-raped, but I feel nothing, I just put on my headphones and listen to music." Chipo was almost in tears. "I don't know what to say, I am sorry to hear that. It's just unbelievable. I mean your uncle, that didn't happen right, your stepfather, I mean your mother would have noticed it right." "Usually yes but I guess she chose not to, cursed family, I call it" Maike decried. "And so for me to forget and wipe my hands clean of the past pain, I had to separate myself. I got my tongue cut into half and it makes me feel so much better, but I am not done yet, I want more modifications."

Chipo gasped. "Eheh chakafukidza dzimba matenga. (*What you see from the outside in certain households is not usually the reality*).

Chipo was not convinced, "but uh," she stammered, and then there was a knock on the door.

Chapter Eleven

"Knock knock Chipo, are you cheating on me?" Marko shouted as he popped his head inside. "Hallo," and grinned. "I brought you some food, I heard your belly rumbling from a mile away, let's eat up and go for a ride."

"KFC, oh that's my favorite, without chilly I hope," she mumbled excitedly. "Nah its a mixture of both I didn't know your preference. Food is food right.

"I appreciate it, thank you," as she smiled and grabbed the package.

"Hi there Ms. Tattoo," looking at Maike while rubbing his nose. "Let's have a bet if I am wrong I'll give you a piece of chicken."

"Oh yeah go ahead," Maike responded.

"Um, I bet you have piercings everywhere, a red one in a particular spot, don't worry I'll not say your little secret, but you know it," as he laughed.

"Marko chill out, be nice to a lady," screamed Chipo, hitting him on his back. "Just kidding I bought a lot of chicken, please feel free to dig in," he offered her.

"I don't eat meat, I am a vegetarian but thanks anyway," Maike replied calmly.

Marko scoffed, "Well, there is some coleslaw, grass and carrots, the usual rabbit food."

"Nah it's all good. I am Maike but you can call me SB."

"SB stands for shit bag," he wailed up.

"Nah it stands for small balls," and she cracked up.

Marko sulked, "Maike Maike Maike Maike," he yelled

sarcastically. "My gracious pleasure to meet you."
"Chipo take a guess." Marko whispered into her ear.
"Nah I am eating I can't talk," as she chewed a drum stick.
"Lost and found property," as he dangles her phone in front of her.
"Oh no," she was so flabbergasted and she jumped on him.
"Thank you, thank you so much. I was so depressed, so lonely without my phone," she gave him a tight hug.
"How about a kiss on the cheek?" He demanded.
"Yeah you deserve it," as she was about to plant a kiss on his chick, he turned his head so quick and she ended up kissing him on his lips.
"You dirty," she scolded him, "that's a trick from centuries ago," she belittled him.
"You taste like salted water," he laughed while lea-king his lips.

As they drove Chipo was overwhelmed by the beauty of the scenery.
Marko showed her lakes and touristic attractions of Berlin and then they drove for hours towards the North Sea. The Mercedes Benz he was driving was short of being impressive, but the beauty of the landscape made up for all the other inconsistencies.
"Germany is a beautiful country," she marveled to herself. They drove through the countryside, past ancient gorgeous villages and then they came to the sea.
"Wow," she expressed astonishment and admirati-on. "I have never seen such beauty, blue endless water," she whispered to Marko. She could not hide her excitement.

Marko parked the car right in front of the beach next to a restaurant.
Only a hand full of people were playing in the water.

The beach was so wide and stretching out of sight. There was a group of kite surfers fighting against the waves, Chipo felt goosebumps all over her body, it looked scary.
"I've never been to a beach before, Zimbabwe is a landlocked country, we only have lakes and rivers. I love this but I am not a fan of water, in fact anything that I've no control of gives me willies and makes me shiver."
"Oh yeah, like what?" Marko asked. "Things like sky diving, canoeing in the open, bungee jumping, eeish that's scary," she rambled with confusion. Marko was just nodding his head and getting pleasure from her nervousness. Gusts of wind became strong and the kite surfers were rushing out of the water. It became so vicious, Marko wrapped his arms around her and led her into the car. The wind was extremely strong that the car was being swayed from side to side.
"You see what I was talking about," Chipo shouted. "Can you imagine being in the middle of the ocean on a boat Nah Nah," she moaned. She had never experienced such a sudden change of weather. Marko was ecstatic.
"The water is coming back he shouted with joy."
"What do you mean?" Chipo asked curiously.
"Just watch in 5 minutes the whole beach would be flooded. Wow we are lucky to observe this Chipo. This is so great, usually, it happens before a Tsunami or a storm."
"What?" She was frightened.
"No no don't worry," he calmed her down, when he saw the fear in her eyes.
"In this part of the world, we got all that shit in check. Our Tsunami warning systems are top of the range," he assured her. "If you are in an Asian country and the water recedes, then you better start running," he said with a grin on his face. "The waves can get up to 30 m high."
"Oh, damn, no way," she pleaded, "we should get

going then," but Marko just kissed her on the cheek and rubbed her hand. "Chipo everything is good, calm down. This is normal, in the morning the waters recede, goes back into the sea, and in the evening like around this time it starts coming back. It's amazing hey?"
"Maybe we should go and sit in that restaurant, it looks more solid," as the wind became too strong. "And it's on higher ground," Chipo added visibly afraid.
Marko laughed again. "Now I know what makes you scared. This is nature at it's best my love."
"Uh nature, what nature? Unoda kuti ndife panoapa? (*Do you want me to die?*)
Let's go to the restaurant," she complained. "If you want to see nature, go to Hwange National Park," she giggled. They ran inside the restaurant and sat at the bar. The place was full with holidaymakers, drinking beer from heavy big mugs.
"People celebrate everyday here," Chipo wondered to herself. After some time she realized she was the only person of color around, when she noticed an old couple observing them. They were looking at them and smiling every time she turned around.
Marko noticed it too.
"You know Germans are like that sometimes, most come from the villages and have never come across an African princess before. So when they see a white handsome guy like me, with a beautiful African princess, they are in disbelief and full of admiration.

All they can say is, what a beautiful picture," he preached. "That's bullshit, most probably they are disgusted," she laughed. Marko excused himself, he was gone for a long period. Chipo continued refilling her glass and through the reflection of the mirror she caught a glimpse of men who were watching her. She sat up adjusted her sitting position and posed using her body language to show that she was approachable. The alcohol was doing its magic and the flirting was definitely working. As she played with her lips she winked at a mesmerized victim. The man almost hid under the table. She felt more confident and smiled cheerfully as guests passed by. Men nodded their heads and the women simply smiled back or turned away. She whipped her hair and sucked some olives salaciously in lieu of sipping her Martini.

"Du siehst aus, als würdest du aus der Karibik kommen." (*You look like you are from the Caribbean.*)

Her show was abruptly distracted. She slowly looked over her shoulder and stammered.

"Umh... hallo I am sorry my German language is still in the garage at the moment. It still needs a bit of panel beating, please say your name in English," she quipped. He smiled and quietly said, "I hate flirting with disaster and then end up getting all washed up without achieving any results." She looked at this gentleman speechless, he was beach elegant, Marco Polo attire had a jumper around his neck and he was wearing Hugo boss shoes.

"Are you from the Islands, you look very much Caribbean," as he penetrated her eyes. She laughed aloud. "Me from the Caribbean, why would you say that, am I suppose to be flattered, but anyway it doesn't matter. You wanna know where I am from?"

"Yes if you don't mind," he responded.

"It's a place very far away from here and to be exact it's 7,986 kilometers by air, not far from the Indian Ocean," she retaliated.

"Oh yeah, is there a clearer hint," he urged her. She sighed, "We share borders with five other countries including South Africa."

"Uh I got it," he jumped in, "Botswana."

She smirked "Do I look like I have a big ass."

He tilted his head checking her out. "Nope you don't, then that makes you," as he pouted his mouth.

"Aaah Madagascan." "Oh please, you going further away, I am from Zim."
"Zim, Uh Zimbabwe," he said confidently, "I have never met anyone from Zimbabwe, that makes you very special then. Is everyone as beautiful as you are?"
"It depends on your taste."
"I want to go to Zimbabwe too," interrupted one of the guys.
"Hi my name is Guido, don't listen to everything he says." He is a good talker."
Chipo was blushing, fascinated, If she was white she could have turned red. She couldn't stop flickering her eyebrows.
"And I am Morris, I apologize for my friend here. He is kind of cuckoo, you know what I mean," as he took her hand and gave a kiss. "I assume you are just passing by or are you living around here. Must be very cold for you," he laughed. "I have a summer house in Spain," he continued.
"Really?" she giggled, "that sounds cool must be fun, I just moved here actually this is my first week in Germany."
"Oh," Morris reacted, "you are still a virgin," and he lets out a loud laugh. She just smiled. "I am here to study."
"Oh yeah what are you going to study?" Insisted Morris.
"IT."
"IT, that's very good, good choice I can give you an internship, you could come and work for me then," declared Guido. "Nah not a good idea he is not a good boss believe me, I know this guy, but my company could do with someone like you, smart, beautiful, very communicative and we offer company cars," challenged Morris. "Uhhhh...but what kind of cars?" Guido burst out laughing, they've Ford focus. He continued giggling. "Morris please you can't put a girl like that in a Ford Focus, look at her, she

deserves better, the least car you can offer her is a Porsche."
Chipo was loving it, she did not know what to believe. The guys were full of praises and compliments.
"You guys must be very good friends, so who is the good cop here."
"Ehm.. nochmal drei B52, bitte." Guido ordered. (*One more round of B52 shots*).
"Sie hat etwas," they spoke among themselves, "sie hat echt einen richtigen Knackarsch, geil, oder? Ich könnte sie die ganze Nacht nehmen."
They howled out laughing.
(*There is something about her, the ass looks tight, I am sure I can clean her up the whole night*)

She was aware of the conversation, but she could not follow or figure out exactly what they were saying about her.
"It's impolite to speak in your language when I am here," she challenged them.
"No no his wife just called," snitched Guido.
"Nah Nah," protested Morris, "I am divorced. I was married but not anymore, I said to myself I'll never marry again. But now I am looking at you and I am having second thoughts," and he giggled. "Thank you that's nice of you," she replied politely.
The barman brought the drinks, they were three small long glasses with some kind of liquor inside that was on fire.
Chipo gasped, "Oh my my, what is that?"
"This is what we drink for breakfast," Morris boasted. "Only when it's cold outside" sneered Guido. This is Kahlua, Baileys, and Captain Morgan rum," as he pointed at the different colors, "Kahlua is just coffee. It is really good, I'll demonstrate for you," as he picked up a drinking straw.
"You take a straw, but you must be very quick otherwise you'll get burnt. So here we go."
He dipped the straw in the burning glass and sucked

out all the liquor at once. "Whoa!" Chipo exclaimed in surprise.
"You want to try, we can drink together," suggested Morris, "you ready one two three and suck."
Chipo loved the taste, her head spun for a few seconds.
"What a shot, what do you call it again?"
"B52 like the B52 bomber," smiled Guido.

She almost forgot she was with Marko, by the time he came back she was sitting around a table with ten strangers. Guido and Morris were great at interacting, it was so natural for them, the evening was amazing. Almost everyone was drunk, Marko bought a round of drinks as a way of introducing himself. He felt intimidated by Guido and Morris they were just too good. They had an answer for everything, and were successful professionals, they could speak Spanish, French, English, German. They had traveled all over the world together and could tell so many stories about their adventures. Marko was quiet most the time, he knew Chipo had only him to depend on.
"Hey Chipo," Marko mumbled, "we might have to spend the night here, my head is terrible, I think I drank too much. It would be too dangerous to drive, don't worry I have already secured a room, with two beds of course," he grinned. "We'll leave early in the morning so you don't have to miss your class."
Chipo just nodded her head, she had no other choice and she was drunk.
"Lass uns ping pong spielen," (*Let's play ping pong*) Marko shouted as he got up. Ping pong is a drinking game. The worst game Chipo had ever played. You had to throw a small table tennis ball into cups arranged in a pyramid way filled with beer on both sides of the table, anytime a member of the group sinks the ball in the beer cup, the opposition team has to drink a beer. Chipo drank so much that night

and did a lot of unforgettable things. It was a night of firsts and a lot of firsts. She woke up the next morning with a heavy hangover. Marko had played with her coochie till dawn she wondered if he had used a condom but was too embarrassed to talk about it.

Chapter Twelve

Mr. Müller gave her a surprise visit at the language school under the guise that Schneider had instructed him to check on her, yet he wanted to take her to the new apartment.
She thought it was strange that a landlord would pick up a tenant even though they had not agreed on any terms. He didn't talk much other than, telling her he was doing her a big favor. He was a short frail old man with tiny cold eyes. His smile was fake, there was nothing real about him.
On their way to the hotel he called Mr. Schneider on speaker phone to confirm he had picked her up.

"If it wasn't for Schneider who was calling me day and night I would have given away the apartment," he said. "But he pleaded with me and still we couldn't get hold of you, you are very lucky. A lot of people were dying to move into this apartment," he boasted.
She told him she still had three nights left at the hostel, but he told her not to worry.
"It's wise to move in immediately, the hostel will refund you your money, I'll have a word with them." He assured her. They drove to her new apartment, the place was further out of town. She needed at least an hour by tram and then 20 mins by bus from her school. It was a huge wide dilapidated building with more than 500 apartments. The entrance hallway was filled with full letterboxes, there were papers all over the floor, the place was filthy.

"Here we are," Müller finally said something. "You can move out whenever you want, but I need at least two months warning usually it's three months' notice by law. You'll be required to pay 400 euros in rent and three months' rent as a deposit. Is that ok for you?"
"1,600 euros," she quickly calculated silently.
"The place is furnished, you have everything that you need in an apartment. All the utensils, beds, blankets, Tv, cupboards are all available. It is a fully furnished apartment," he repeated.
"One more thing, you'll be sharing with one other person. A young guy, he is a student just like you from Syria." Chipo was a bit taken aback, he had not told her that before. She just nodded her head.
She was terrified of Müller, his eyes were small and too hallow. He showed no feelings what so ever and all she wanted was a place to stay until the storm subsided.

The next day she came back from school tired and hungry, only to find her bed had been pushed to one side and another single bed had been added. A girl named Amara from Kenya had moved in. No one had asked her about sharing her room. A one bedroom apartment had been turned into a four-bed apartment. Amara didn't seem to mind, she was sitting on the bed doing her makeup, while munching Cashews.

"Mueller told me, you were bored, all alone and you didn't have enough money for the room. He also said you needed company," Amara revealed.
"Did he say that he never said anything to me," Chipo replied.
"Let me hear what he has to say about it."
Chipo called Mueller immediately, he told her, he thought it was a good idea for her to have someone around since she was new. "People can break into

your house and steal your things, once they realize you live alone. So many people have stayed in that room, I have lost count and sometimes the tenants lose the keys. It happens a lot or it could be worse you can get robbed and raped. This is a dangerous city," he warned her. "And after all, I think Amara is a good person, get to know her, she is quite lovely. It wasn't planned I agree, it was just a spontaneous idea, for your own good." He yelled.

He said that he had met Amara in a bar the night before and she had begged him for a place to stay for a couple of days. He went on to say that all other tenants share their rooms and 400 bucks for a room was too cheap. He told her she could move out anytime if she wanted to.

"This is Berlin," he jeered her. "Your new roommate is paying me paying 500 bucks," he went on.
"This is a rip-off, this room is not even worth 200 bucks," she shouted and he hung up.

Chapter Thirteen

Marko had not called for a week since their seaside fling. She tried to focus her energy on her school work and familiarizing herself with the city. There is one thing she loved about the transport system, the buses, the trains, the trams were always on time. She could live on 10 euros a week, food was very cheap, she fell in love with the Aldi supermarket which was a few meters away. Berlin City has a very rich history. Chipo would slip into tour guided groups and listen to the narratives.
There were a lot of amazing places to see in Berlin, Her top five places were.

1. The Berlin Wall is an 87 miles long concrete barrier that divided East and West Berlin, the fall of the Berlin Wall occurred in 1989 and it was almost completely dismantled, very few segments of the wall remained today. The largest section can be found on the East Side Gallery, although small sections are dotted throughout the city.

2. Brandenburg Gate is probably Berlin's most famous landmark, the gate is a symbol of the German capital, it's a huge ancient Roman structure, with carvings of the Roman goddess's victory, driving a horse drawn chariot. Most major outdoor events are held there.

3. Charlottenburg Palace was the summer getaway

for the queen of Prussia, one of the most beautiful museums and Berlin's largest royal real estate.

4. The Reichstag is the famous German parliament building. After it was destroyed by fire in 1933 and again by the bombings of the 2nd world war, it was rebuilt into a stunning piece of architecture, particularly the remarkable roof terrace and the dome.

5. The Tiergarten is a huge park expanding to 630 acres. The name of the park translates to „Animal Garden" because it served as a hunting ground for a few selected Germans during the 17th century. It's very close to the famous Berlin Zoo.

Amara was a weird woman, one day she could be very communicative and the next day she wouldn't even greet you.
She looked like she had so much shit going on in her head. She seemed focused at times and then she would display an I don't care attitude. Her mind was distorted, she acted as if she was hiding a huge secret.
Then again her immaturity free spirited millennial mentality would captivate her, leaving her mumbling and being rowdy under the influence of alcohol. She tried her best to isolate herself and to mind her own business. Maybe she was afraid she might say the wrong things.
Very often she was on the phone talking secretively and calculating figures. Chipo had no idea what she did or what she was up to. Sometimes she would say she is working, then she would say she is studying, but she was always home. One good thing about her, as she wasn't fussy and nothing seems to bother her.

Chipo got back from school one day and Amara was nowhere to be found, no note nothing she had just disappeared, without even paying her rent. That got Chipo thinking she felt she was in the wild wild west, where each dog is for himself. She thought deeply and scrutinized her situation. Trying to fine-tune her objectives. Money became her number one focus, she blamed herself, she thought she was too naive, too laid back. "I think my focus is on the wrong ball," she murmured to herself.

The next day, when she got back from school, she found Müller fixing something in her room. He told her there was a gas leak, the whole place might explode, if it wasn't done that night. He was working and drinking whiskey at the same time.

It was almost midnight and Chipo was tired but he just didn't care. He would disappear in the cellar and reappear after a while, telling her about how rich the immigration situation had made him. The government had paid him five million for five years to host the Syrian refugees.

"I am filthy rich" he boasted, "I can buy you anything, Russian girls 20 years old, your age they love me, why can't you? If I go to BBC, Blonde Boobs club right now," he shouted. "They'll surround me like Berlusconi, they'll go down on their knees and we make Bunga Bunga parties. Tits, asses, everywhere 10, 000 euros will give me the respect I deserve. I can help you out, I can take care of all your needs, your family in Africa too, I know you people are very poor and you need the money. Are you a black muslim?" Chipo didn't respond.
"I feel sorry for you, God has punished you twice, zweimal bestraft," he repeated in German. "Make a choice young lady, this opportunity comes once in a life-time. Money is no problem," and he threw a bunch of notes on the bed, Chipo blinked, but remained calm, hoping he doesn't take the money back.

He told her dirty old man sexy jokes, showed her his tongue skills as he burped and saliva dripped from his mouth. He was drunk, Chipo calmly displayed her disgust towards him with her facial expressions. He gave up, staggered and sat on the bed, falling asleep immediately. Within a second he was snoring like a rhino.

Chipo waited and observed him until he was in a deep sleep. She smiled and rubbed her hands before running through his pockets. She removed the watch and took out all the cash that was in his wallet, amounting to 1,340 euros. That night she slept butt naked, with one eye opened. She watched him helplessly early in the morning, scared as a chicken as he embarrassingly ran out of the room. She sighed and slept the whole day.

Chapter Fourteen

After about a week she had another roommate called Susie. She was the opposite of Amara. Typical African woman, with all the resources perfectly in place, and she, was hungry and raring to go to achieve success. She had these big wondering eyes, it was as if she had just been let out of jail.

"Chipo you are always looking clean and fresh, who is buying you all these perfumes, I like your style girl you are very clever. I bet your boyfriend is a top model. Is he German or Swedish? There is no point in going out with these African guys, they have nothing to offer, except to treat you like a housewife. Some of them have no permanent residence here, they are also looking for papers. It's like two blind people trying to lead each other," she ranted and chuckled.

"You'll go nowhere, you'll crush oh. Here we are equal, you do yours I do mine," she said and burst out laughing. "Don't waste yourself, use what God gave you, that thing there is black gold, that's your passport to the world of riches."
Somehow Chipo did find affinity in her words and in her as a person. Susie was rude, wild, impatient, very impolite and a direct shooter.

"I am here to make monie, I need monie oh, I've to support my family. What am I gonna do with a black guy again," she declared. "You need to get that paper oh, me once I have the paper I am gonna scatter everywhere. One day I'll wake up with Bill Gates lying next to me, make him my babe daddy," cracking herself up.

She was fun to be with and Chipo took some of her words very seriously. They were talking and laughing while cooking in the kitchen, Susie's accent and her use of words was genius, she had a funny way of speaking.

"My sister you laugh," she would say, "life in this Deutschland is very very hard ooh. I was five years in an Asylum camp, three years I was working in a slave camp."
"Slave camp, what the hell," Chipo interjected, "that's some bunch of gibberish right."
Susie Scoffed, stared at her and let out a burst of high pitched laughter, shaking her head.
"You know nothing ooh, we Africans we are cursed, we will die suffering. Some of these bearded men, who claim to be men of God, hey, they are the most ruthless people on earth, they will shit in your mouth, whilst they are eating their food and still ask you to pour them water. I've seen it all, nobody can tell me anything. I saw people, little boys, young like this getting shot in the head for fun, killed, gone for nothing. I witnessed men, big men getting kidnapped, raped, beaten up like children, and sold as slaves. Women, we women we are just sex tools to them, they experimented on us, what they can't do with their wives, they did it with us. If I take you to a brothel right now, more than half of the men are foreigners, they pray every day, but look at how they treat their women.
So if they can treat their women like shit, how about the ones who don't belong to them. You know how I came here, you've no idea, you read every day

a boat has capsized, hundreds killed, thousands drowned it`s all true, it`s not fiction O. Let me pour myself a drink, and drown my sorrows. Come let`s sit down and drink now ."

"Tell me your tales now," Chipo insisted.

"Can you handle it," Susie scoffed, Chipo just pouted like a baby and nodded.

"If I tell you oh, don`t cry. You see, Nigeria is not far from Libya now, when Gaddafi was alive things like this never happened ooh. But since they slaughtered him, you know they killed him because of this oil now, oil is monie, everyone likes monie. No one wants to die poor, In Nigeria if you have no monie, you have no voice. So me, my sister and I," she poked her chest. "We took a plane and entered Libya with valid visas ehe, so we then looked for these people, everyone knows them now, they help you to cross to Italy by boat ehe, the smugglers," as she wiped her mouth with the back of her hand, chewing nuts. "So we made arrangements with this guy, one short man like that. He told us that we should wait for him around 20 pm in the evening now, at a certain place. This area was dark and there were no street lights. We reach this place and we find 20 other people waiting, it`s business now, this guy comes with an open truck.

We all squeezed into this truck. He said we would pay him once we got there. We wanted to take the boat, to cross to Europe, this guy was driving like crazy ooh, he didn`t care. It was dark and dusty, you could not even see the person next to you. He was driving for a long time, if you fall off, people would shout, stop stop, he didn`t care, he didn`t stop. Some women had kids with them, you`ll just hear a scream, oh my son has fallen off, please stop please stop and sometimes some of the mothers would jump after their kids.

The driver wouldn`t stop. May their souls rest in

peace. The driver continued driving, by the time the car stopped we were all dusty and coughing, our throats were dry. We looked like zombies, we couldn't see anything. We found ourselves in an enclosed compound, surrounded by men with small pieces of rubber hosepipes and huge dogs. They just started beating us up oh, they didn't care they thrashed everyone up until we couldn't even cry, we were so scared. One bearded man with a shotgun told us, we all now belong to him. Hey, we were shocked, we thought they just wanted to steal our little belongings.

"You are all my slaves, I have bought you all from your master, the driver," he boasted. He gave this driver monie and he drove off.
"If you try to run away, you'll be shot, you'll die and the dogs will eat you." this bearded man threatened us. It was hell on earth, during that night we were sexually abused, both men and women. They did it in front of everyone they didn't care. Those people, I tell you, they are worse than pigs.

The next day a couple of us including my sister were dragged outside and sold to one rich businessman. He wanted people to work in his factory, he made us sign some papers that we had agreed to work for him and he would pay us 150 dollars a month. For one year we worked there. He was kind to us better than the other master, he gave us food. In the factory we had everything there, we were not allowed to go outside. It was a huge factory with an open ground. There was a little super shop with everything inside, you would get food, clothing, soap on credit and he would deduct it at the end of the month. After all the deductions you would be left with about 80 to 100 dollars. Do you know what it's like to be deprived of your freedom? I shared a room with my sister and you had to befriend the guards. You give them what they want, ehe you know now, they would do you small favors. After one year, we had a choice to stay or to leave. We told the owner we wanted to leave, we had saved enough money for the smugglers. He told us he would pay us the rest of the money in the evening and after that, we had to leave the compound. Evening came and we got our monies, we took our small bags. I think there were about eight of us. We walked about 100 meters from the gate, two cars approached us from both sides, a group of men jumped out and started beating us. They robbed us of all the money we had, we were left bleeding, bruised, and poor."

"Oh my god," Chipo cried out, "for real?" "My sister now it's only a story," she retorted, "but when it's happening, you'll think you are in a dream, some of the people with us went back to the compound and started working for the same man again. But we decided to soldier on and of course, the owner of the business set us up now. It was obvious. We walked for miles in the dark, we were prepared to be raped anytime. We finally met one woman, just like that, we begged for employment. She gave us work and paid us 200 dollars a month
but we were not locked up. We could move freely. After almost two years we had raised enough monie for the boat, to cross the Mediterranean sea now. We gave these boat guys monie, but they said that the boat was not finished and we should wait until the next day. Little did we know that the boat was still being built. As we waited we were shocked, bodies would just wash ashore, my sister."

"This is a movie, right? This never happened," Chippo said in disbelief.
"Hey, it's a horror movie, while you are waiting to board, a dead body would just float like that.
I saw more than 500 people being packed in one

wooden boat. I saw boats made of huge round plastic bowles like tube boats, fitted with a small scooter engine. When our own boat was finished to my shock, it was a round plastic tube oh, the smugglers did not enter the boat, they instructed another Somali boy to direct it, and gave him a compass, this guy didn't have to them pay monie oh.
We were about 80 in a place meant maybe for 30 people. Days came and went but we can't reach our destination," as she sipped her whiskey. "People were falling sick, you had to shit into the sea, in the open, in front of everyone. You just had to stick your ass out, and let everything out, it was horror my sister. Mothers were throwing their dead kids overboard. You look into people's eyes, you see hunger, you see death. Now I am here, chopping, eating. I have reached Deutschland oh, Germany praise the lord almighty. This is the promised land. Now you want me to sleep on my fat ass, my nyashi. Instead of making monie, I'll use what God gave me now. Me I don't joke, gimme three months even two you will see, you cannot tell me what to do," she scoffed. "Me, I've seen it all, I've done it all.
By the grace of God we reached shore, sand beaches, we didn't know whether we were in Italy or in Spain," they both laughed.
"Everyone just jumped out and scattered, started running like wild mice and we were disoriented. We were like ghosts, from The Pirates of Wakanda," as she laughed. "You should've seen these white people's faces at the beach. They thought we were zombies, they were running and screaming away from us. Some just stood there and laughed at us. It was chaos, survival of the fittest. Me and my sister took off in one direction, we ran like Tom and Jerry," Chipo's mind was in disarray.
"All I remember is that we tried to stop a number of taxies, but no one would stop. We looked like mad people," she was laughing. "Uh, these people

man, no one would stop, just one old man, I think he thought we were prostitutes. Our clothes were in tatters, he stopped and we just jumped in without saying a word. Please just drive very fast some people want to kill us, please drive, go, go, we were shouting and crying.
The old man was confused, he wanted to give us a lecture. I grabbed him by the collar and choked him like that, I told him if you don`t drive you are a dead old man. He drove ooh. We told him to take us to the nearest African restaurant or a bar. This man god bless him, he saved us, I will never forget that man."
"So were you in Spain or Italy?" Chipo asked eagerly.

"Uh wait now, I am coming," Susie said laughing, "at first the language was confusing oh, me I don`t know the difference between Spanish or Italian, I said to the man Italia or Spanish,
and he said "No, Tunisia."

"Oh no, Tunisia?" she burst out laughing. "Italy my sister was a dream," Susie said giggling. "But here is where it gets interesting, the old man, was an Italian courier, he took us to his guest house, we chopped food like scavengers, bathed, scrubbed ourselves like baboons. Every two days this old man Antonio would ferry to and fro, from Italy to Tunisia with his goods, I am sure he is mafia. After a month of staying in his house, he smuggled us to Italy.
The first thing I wanted to eat was a Pizza Margarita," she laughed. I could write a book about this oh, make a movie about my adventures. Thank God that`s why they say, every cloud has a silver lining. Now they have two kids."
"Who?" Chipo gasped, "The old man Antonio with my sister now. Hey, we don`t play, we are here to slay, this man was given to my sister on a golden platter, like plantains, he was sent from heaven.

But for me, I said my own is not here, God has other plans for me. I wanted to reach Berlin, Germany. I stayed in Italia for a few months at Antonio's house. He has a big farm, with goats and chickens. After three months I found my way to the city of Cologne. There is an amazing church, called Cathedral, The Dom. While I was waiting for my babe, my beau, my boo," she chuckled, "my guy now, to come and pick me up, at the main train station, The Hauptbahnhof, so that we could travel together to Berlin. I heard "Ausweis bitte," I turn around, four policemen with greyhounds, big dogs were behind me, "hey" I said "oh god why have you forsaken me, I just collapsed," she roared with laughter.
"Oh what can I do? To cut the long story short," As she poured her 5th glass of Jim Beam, which was almost empty.
"I had to seek asylum. I just put my hands up, I am a political refugee, I am a political refugee, I shouted and yelled."
Chipo was tearing up from laughing.
"I was taken to a place around a town called Braunschweig, hey, I met people who had stayed there for ten years. I said to myself my life is over, oh, there was only one bus, the whole day, the place was dirty. I thought I am back in the slums of Lagos.
They were people from all over, different countries, multicultural. It was like mixing, goats, cattle, with sheep. You would find chicken heads, intestines thrown all over the floor, and to make things worse we didn't get money from the government. We used to get food vouchers, I came to a point where I did not even have a single cent in my wallet. I went for almost two years without getting in touch with any of my family members. You know what we used to do, we would get these vouchers, buy a lot of water, go to the camp pour the water out, return the empty bottles and get a refund. That's the only way we could have some euros in our pockets but some

smart guys would sell the vouchers to willing clients for half the price. A lot of people became junkies. There was nothing to do, you couldn't work. You sleep, you wake up, drink cheap alcohol, and stay drunk. People were getting mad, crazy.
I remember there was a guy who started barking like a dog, every time he saw the officers he would bark at them, woof like a big dog." They laughed.
"Hoow hoo hoow, he would bark all the time until one of the officers took him to a doctor. They thought he was crazy. I heard the doctor gave him a letter out of pity that he should be released, under the mental health program." They laughed hysterically.

"You had to do what you had to do. Another lady pretended to be mad, but she was unlucky, they put her in a mental hospital, with real crazy people. After two days she was fighting with the nurses, she wanted to be released, they thought she was too aggressive and put her in isolation for five months. When she came out, she had become disturbed, I heard she is moving around, picking up trash and talking to herself."
"Wow, that's sad, life can be cruel sometimes," yelled Chipo, shaking her head.

"It's hell out there, you will only know it, if you find yourself in that situation. One Ghanaian man formed a church, now he is rich, he is taking away all the small monies from those poor people. When you are desperate that's when you need God the most and that's when false prophets take advantage of the hopeless.
I said to myself, where I have come from, is too far to go back, nothing is going to stop me. Hang in there Susie, not my real name by the way," she cracks up.
"So how did you get out of this mess" Chipo was impatient. "It so happened one day I am minding my

own business, I was just wondering around and this big car stops behind me. Maybe he saw the ass, it‵s big now ehe, got it from my mama," as she smiled. "I cursed this person, I was in my own world, and I hear a voice, excuse me, sista, sista, I turn around and this black guy comes out of the car. I nearly fainted, the guy was fine oh, driving a big car like that.

A black successful guy here in Germany. I nearly preached, but I played cool, pretended like it was nothing special. My heart was already screaming to my mind and soul, I was shaking with excitement.
I had no control, my body sold me out, I was already wet oh."
Chipo giggled.
"You laugh, I said to myself, this is a sign from god oh, it‵s now or never.

From outside I was as calm as a gold digger, I knew what I wanted now. He tells me he is looking for someone called Francis from the camp. I asked him "why?" He said he has a job for him. My antenna activated, are you sure he lives in this camp, I asked him again.
Then I acted as if I knew him, I just wanted to get into his car.
"Maybe I know him ooh, a bit dark and short," I had no idea who he was, so I said I would take him to Francis. I got into his car, my sister, I said to myself, this is where I belong. I don‵t know what expensive perfume he had on, but it turned me on. Babe Susie started twitching. I asked politely, "what kind of job you do sir?" He just smiled, he told me, "I work for nobody, people work for me."

"Hey!" I shouted and praised him. "Man like you are destined for greatness, everything you put your hands on becomes yours. That was brutal, oh, I whispered to myself silently and when I looked at him from the corner of my eye he was nodding his head like a king. I knew this was the right time to attack, while he still feeling himself. It's hard to say no now, when you have just been worshipped. You will feel obliged to demonstrate your powers. I said let me give him more. "Such a man as you should never be seen associating with flies like us, it takes the shine away from you. Let us the mosquitos suck the blood and feed you, while you sit in your golden chair, with your diamond crown on your head."

He stared at me, from top to bottom, me I just smiled, and put my ass in his direction, pretending like I am facing outside through the window.
He nearly had an accident now, I had to control the car, I rushed and grab the steering wheel," she chuckled.
And after rolling out my sweet tongue what does he do, He pulls out 200 euros from the dashboard and gives it to me. I nearly collapsed. I had never seen a 10 euro bill before.

"Buy whatever you want, just don't become a junkie and die in this stupid camp." He told me boldly.
I stammered, "Uh uh, boss, uh uh boss" I said, "this Francis you are looking for, I don't think he still lives here. I heard that he was a thief he stole some money and ran away. He was an alcoholic anyway. Why don't you let me do this job?" He looked at me and giggled. "Are you a hard worker, can I trust you with my monie?" he asked. My eyes opened wide.

That was the beginning of my freedom, I could have opened my legs on the spot, waaya." They both laughed so loud.
"Enough for today oh, me I feel like eating pepper soup now," as she got up, leaving Chipo dying for more stories. "Uh let me bring it to you now, just

sit and continue with your rise from the dead, I am enjoying this oh." Chipo protested. She had a lot of questions in her mind, she didn't know what to believe and what not to believe. Everything seems so surreal, so scary and exciting at the same time, exciting in the sense that, it sounded like a cool movie with a happy ending.

"Don't be too naive Chipo," she shouted from the kitchen.
"You have no idea Susie, you think I came in blind, with no negative expectations whatsoever, you are dead wrong oh," and she slapped her ass.
"Don't touch that thing oh, it's for the bosses of bosses, you can't afford it" she said as she tasted her pepper soup. "Whoa just like how mama made it."

Chapter Fifteen

The German language is not an easy language to learn, really complicated. Chipo needed extra lessons, interacting lessons, so she joined a group called (GLBC) German learning booze club. The name said it all, but it was surprisingly a helpful group.
After getting drunk everyone spoke German. She met with different German speakers from different professions and different backgrounds. As she began to integrate, she learned and noticed a few things about Germans. They only talk to you if you talk to them, unless of course if they are drunk. When most germans are drunk they are the friendliest people ever, but once they come back to their senses it's as if you have never met.
They are like programmed robots, they retreat into their own shells. You would interact with someone whilst drunk and have great chemistry, but the next day if you bump into the same person in the street, they would pretend like you never met. They would be so shy, they even want to turn back or cross over to the other side. And if you meet the same person, the same evening, they'll act like you are their best buddy.
Chipo was spending a lot of time with Hayet her German Eritrean friend, she would tell her about German mentality, characteristics, and weird stories she had heard or encountered.

"In German most things are done by the book, if

you are supposed to open the door with your right hand, then it must always be your right hand. If you happen to be unlucky and you break your right hand, that means you can not open the door anymore."
"Really!" She exclaimed. "A typical German person will argue with you, he will tell you Nein, nein nein so geht das nicht. (*It doesn't work like that*)
You must only use your right hand, and when you demonstrate that you can also use your left hand and he sees it with his own eyes, don't think he is going to admit it either, no! He will turn around gurgling with embarrassment, no apology offered. He will awkwardly try to justify himself, by saying something like, that must be new technology." Chipo laughed.
"It's true because usually when Germans are taught that something works in a specific way, it has to work accordingly. They are perfectionists, no substitutes permitted." Chipo listened in disbelief.

"If it happens that you invite a German person to your home and you offer him food. He will politely refuse, but when you put the food in front of him, he will eat and finish everything, even lick the plate," she said it laughing.
"And if you don't offer them, they'll starve silently and never ask," she scoffed.
"Uh they have never been hungry," Chipo added shaking her head.
"Germans hardly beat around the bush or cut corners, they are straight shooters. They'll give it to you as it is, if it's a No, it's a No with no sugar coatings on it, it's straight to the chest, no feelings, no remorse.
They don't do it deliberately though, it's the only way they know. I once offered a German guy a drink in a bar once, and he asked me what for?
The barman had to explain to him it was because

of my birthday, that's when he let out a big smile and showed me how thirsty he was." Hayet explained. "He didn't want a free drink," Chipo yelled. "Wow, you can't do that in Zim, you'll get broke, she chuckled, the guys there will even start to nudge you for more, if you are a slow drinker."
The one time I have witnessed Germans really happy was during Carnival, everyone is wearing a costume, there is no boss, no employee, you are all the same."
"Is it like the mind-blowing Brazilian Carnival?" Chipo asked excitedly.
"Maybe even better, but you need to go to the city of Cologne for the best captivating party."
"Oh yeah?"
"But be warned don't go with your boyfriend, you know what they say, why take a tree to the bush?"
"Um sounds very interesting."
"It is, it's a lifetime experience."
"What else do I need to know?" Chipo craved. "Why don't you get yourself a German boyfriend and find out."
"Do you have one, I mean my boyfriend is too neutralized, he is too far gone, he doesn't consider himself to be German."
"One more thing, it's not easy to crack a random joke, if you don't know the person, you can't just pull one's leg if they are not used to you. They would look at you as if you are crazy."

"Isn't it like that everywhere else, um maybe not," Chipo said thoughtfully. "Well that's their loss for missing out on good laugh," she continued. "That reminds me, Boris the big dude, you know him, he is part of the group. He once said to me, Chipo you are too nice, you smile a lot, sometimes people might think you want something from them. And I said to him, but this is who I am, I can't fake a smile, he just smirked, and said I was going to have a hard

time making friends. He said a real German person would never invite me into their home, unless they grew up with me or they can really trust me and usually that take years, he warned me. I told him in my country we just turn up and there are no door bells, so we shout, I stuck my tongue out at him and he rolled his eyes." She said laughing. "I have heard that before," Hayet suggested "but I think that kind of mentality was developed during the cold war, when the KGB used to use the beautiful Russian women to seduce the German commanders to get information.
In Berlin things are a bit different, if you go towards Bavaria that is the southern side and Nordrhein-Westfalen that is the Cologne side.
The mentality and dialects are very different, from region to region. Most people that live in Berlin are not original Berliners, they all came from other towns and cities.
"How would you characterize Zimbabweans?" She asked curiously.

Chipo was caught off guard. "That's a hard question, no one ever asked me that before, but in general I think most Zimbabweans are logical thinkers, a lot have been Europeanized, Westernized and Africanized so now I think we are all over the place. The one thing that stays the same though is our own 2nd natural wonder of the world, the Victoria Falls, popularly known as The Smoke that Thunders.
That should be on your bucket list, I believe before every living human being dies, they need to visit that place, let alone take a jump into the devil's pool," she bragged.

Chapter Sixteen

Time flies when you are having fun until the landlord calls you or in this case until a long lost friend leaves twenty messages on your mailbox. Marko was very apologetic, he had gone for almost three weeks without calling her. He went completely off the radar. He told her he had a terrible experience the same day he dropped her off. Because someone had bumped into his car and there a scuffle with the guy. Police were called and when they ran his name they realized he had an outstanding warrant of arrest for something that happened five years ago. So he was busy sorting it out and the stress was just too much for him.

He picked her up and took her to Macdonald's for lunch. He looked different, his attitude was not the same as before. He was totally the opposite of the Marko that she had first met. He looked disheveled, lost, and worried.

"What's up with you?" She asked him, as she tried to break the ice.
"Oh man, I think this time I messed up. I went too far. My reaction was not professional. Look at me now I created a perfect storm for myself. I fucked up badly, I shouldn't have punched him. Because of this bullshit, I did, now they are looking into my finances and all my accounts have been frozen."
"Whoa for real, damn that's a perfect storm for

sure," Chipo added. "It must have been something serious then?" She added.
"Nah not really, it's just that, the German system sucks sometimes. But I will sort it out, no worries."
"Well you should start by getting a haircut, you don't look so charming. You left me in the cold hey, with no winter coat," she joked. "You gave me a cold shoulder, I thought maybe I am a skunk, I stink or something," she complained.
"Nah Nah, I didn't mean to do that, I should have found a way to contact you, but hey, I am back and I will make it up to you," he said smiling.
"I definitely hope you do," Chipo said staring at him.
"You like surprises, don't you?"
"Why?" she asked.
"Because I have been thinking a lot," Marko continued, "and it's a step to the next level. I believe what I am about to do is the right thing for both of us. Come with me let me show you something that you will like."
"Uhh huh, last time you said the same thing I had a hangover for five days."
"Well, I had the time of my life," he bragged.
"It was a good thing I went away for a while I was beginning to fall in love, with myself, before I fell in love with you. I have reversed that angle, that way of thinking. It's the other way now."
"You got a strange way of thinking buddy," she smirked and shook her head.
"I want you to meet someone," as he took her hand.
"As long as he is not a drug dealer," she teased him.
"What made you say that?" He snapped. Chipo just shrugged it off. He let out a quiet chuckle and walked in silence.

They walked for a few meters and after going a couple of stairs they were at his apartment.
"This is where I live," as he flew open the door. "Okay at least you have a Macdonald's like a neighbor," she

mocked him. "You should have just said it. I wasn't going to protest, I can take care of myself, no need to trick me."
"Maybe but I have my own way of doing things, you like it?"
"What am I supposed to like? it's a typical guy's place, big TV, PlayStation, that's an old version though," she chuckled, he wasn't impressed.
"Just kidding," she added. She had expected something a bit spacious, well furnished since he was always flushing a lot of cash.

"I live here alone as you can see, I moved out recently from my parents so I took over a friend's apartment. Well, I am also a bit clean and I love cooking," he elaborated.
"I mean there is enough space for two people. You don't have to be paying rent or live in that filthy apartment of yours, with strangers. It's all yours for free, for as long as you want."
She was caught unaware, "and there is also a bathtub, we could have bubble baths, you'll get a massage every day after school. We'll watch movies and eat popcorn together," he tried to impress her. She was excited although she had her own doubts. The offer on the table was unbeatable.

"No expenses," she thought to herself.
"What's the catch?"
"What do you mean? There is no catch, I mean it, I really mean it." He was acting a bit shaky.
"Well don't be so nervous, I am not going to say no if you actually mean it. But hey be cool, take it easy and we should do it step by step. I still have to hold on to my side of the agreement with my landlord," she told him. "He still has my deposit, it's a lot of money for me. I am not as rich as you, how will I get it back. I need to give him at least two months' notice."

"Two months living in that dump, as you called it. Nah, I won't let my woman do that, don't worry about the deposit. Leave it to me, I will handle it. Tomorrow I will call him up and we will find a solution."

That same day they drove to her place, and packed all her stuff. Marko did all the carrying and the loading. He was hissing and cursing the place and berating the landlord.
"This place is not meant to be inhabited, a fucking pigsty. This landlord is a criminal, he should be in jail," he grumbled. She was sure she had made the right choice. Marko could help her in a lot of things, in improving her language skills, getting around the complicated German system, and she liked him.
She had never lived with a guy before so she was looking wryly amused. Her good friend Susie was not around so they were out within a short period.

Their first night together was very romantic, very relaxed, cozy, he told her a lot about his life, repeating himself at times. He talked about his adventures, places he would love to visit, and told her about the countries he had been to. She found out he had no more contact with his father.
Chipo didn't dispute it, contrary to what he had said before.

"How did you sleep, any nightmares in your new palace my darling?" She winked at him as she sat on the table and said. "Snug as a bug in a rug."
"I guess that means beautifully, I am glad because it's the beginning of greater things to come."

"Do you usually talk so much in the morning."
"I am just excited by your presence, this house hasn't seen a female companion for a decade."
She giggled, "that's a pure white lie and you know it.

I saw some blonde hairs in the bathroom and some hairpins," Chipo said. "Huh, really, oh, I got female friends you know."
As he walked away.

He went on to make breakfast and drove her to school. When she was done with her course, she found him waiting for her outside by the gate. She felt joy and content. She became very relaxed and started planning for their future together.
She called Müller and told him exactly what Marko had instructed her to say.
She told him the place was damp, the bathroom was full of fungi and she was allergic to it. She lied that it was making her sick and that she had slept overnight in a hospital.

Marko grabbed the phone from her and he had a long grueling back and forth conversation with him. He then called one of his friends and they went to Müller's office while she stayed behind doing her homework.

Chapter Seventeen

She was woken up around 2 am, Marko came in drunk and loud. He was carrying a bag of food and a bottle of Hennessy. He looked as if he was on drugs. "Chipo my love oh darling, I missed you so much. Come here, oh I know I am drunk and I smell and I am late. Oh man I hope the food is not cold. So sorry I didn't call you earlier on. Am I late, am I? Yeah, yeah I know but it was not my fault. You know Dino, my friend whom I was with, he won a betting game 2,000 euros, yes and he just went berserk, out of control. I brought you something to eat. I hope you are starving and guess what I got a bottle, of some tasty liquor," as he slurred.

Chipo observed him in amusement and in astonishment.
He started to dance and to sing, then from nowhere he just threw himself to the couch and began to sob. He was acting like a little child, looking for love. The real person in him came out. He was telling her about his life, his achievements, and his goals. He was schmoozing her up. She was clueless, she felt genuine compassion for him. What started as fun turned into a period of self-regret. He divulged some deep family secrets, his mother had secretly given him away as a baby, to a British family while his father was in jail.
Chipo was overwhelmed with pity. She thought deep down he was a lonely person, who longed for love

and wanted to be loved. He had tears running down his cheeks and then he did something unexpected. He got on his knees and declared his love for her. He told her he could not live without her and he had loved her the first time he had seen her in the club. She was smitten, from that night on, she was prepared to do anything to defend him and to stand by him. He had opened and showed her his heart. He had exposed his weakness like a dog's belly. She felt honored that he had trusted her and she felt compelled to do the same. She wanted to divulge all her secrets, but after a while of cuddling with him, she thought better not, it was his day.
She hugged him so tight before tugging him to bed.

He overslept the next day and she had to find her own way to school. She was putting a lot of effort into her learning. She could now hold down a decent conversation and she wanted to start looking for a job. So that she could cover some of the expenses since Marko's accounts were still frozen.
Overnight she had become the breadwinner. She managed her accounts to accommodate Marko's needs. She would give him money for rent, food, fuel, and finance their partying habits.

She found out Schneider had only paid for three months for her language school. Although he had stated that he had paid for six months. The 8,000 euros in the account was dwindling very fast. She searched for Schneider's office, she wanted to give him her piece of mind. He had so many bad reviews on the internet, people were complaining from all over the world.
She went there unannounced, only to find out he worked alone from a tiny room. It looked as if he actually lived there. He was very surprised and embarrassed, but not apologetic. The packed room was filled with files. He could not recognize her, he actu-

ally thought she was seeking help and he was ready to sell her some fake dream.
She was so disappointed, she wondered how many people he had scammed, and no one had done anything about it. Mostly it was out of fear, that they might get deported. So a lot of students were prepared to struggle than face the humiliation of going back home.

Chipo's parents had paid an extra 150 euros for her to open a German bank account in Zimbabwe back then, she discovered he was not aware of the fee, his agent in Zimbabwe had manipulated them.
He made it clear that he had done all he had to do according to German law.

"Prices of school fees change all the time," he yelled. "I was also duped by some of these organizations, I have brought thousands of students from all over the world, and not once have I betrayed anyone, check my record," Chipo just smirked.
"I saw the reviews."
"Those are jealous people, my competitors," he moaned.
She became aware that she had to find her own university place. Yet he had disclosed that she had been accepted already, on the last email he had written. When she confronted him, he told her the University went bankrupt and gave her a list of other Universities around Germany to apply to.
It was very disheartening and depressing for her.

On the other hand, Marko was becoming more and more consumed in the nightlife.
Nothing he said was adding up. His accounts had been closed for the past four months. She had been footing all the bills since then.
Marko assured her he was working on something that would bring in a lot of money, in excess of about

120,000 euros in a couple of weeks. But he needed three thousand to finance it.
They talked about her stay in Germany, he suggested it would be easier if he marries her, then she doesn't have to pay so much taxes when she starts working. And also she would be able to work full time and go to University whenever she wanted. She thought hard about it, she was prepared to do anything to make their lives easier and to keep him happy.

"Once I do this big-money deal, it'll be enough for our wedding," he assured her.
Chipo had to lie to her parents that she wanted more money since she was not yet allowed to work and that she had started university, which required her to buy a lot of books, and that she had to pay student fees and a whole lot of other garbage. In reality, she was just propping him up, financing his unaccountable businesses.

During her two weeks break, after she had given him the money. Marko suddenly started partying a lot. He wanted to go out almost every day. He would take her shopping and for an exclusive evening. They went for a romantic weekend at the Tropical Islands. That is an indoor swimming paradise, with sliding pools, whirlpools, a man-made artificial jungle, and hotel rooms.

Chipo felt true love. He had blissed her up, she was totally in love. It was just too good to be fake.

Chapter Eighteen

Whatever business he was doing, seemed to be lucrative. He was constantly on the phone and was always in a happy mood. One day after a hard night of partying they woke up late. His phone had been constantly buzzing for hours.

"Someone has been trying to call you the whole time, is everything ok?" She asked politely.
"Yeah I know, why are you looking at my phone anyway," he fumed.
"No, I didn't, I don't need to," she shot back. "It was just disturbing that's all, maybe you should put it on silent mode."
"Yah I know sorry about that, someone has been bothering me for the last couple of days, he wants to borrow money, but nah I am not giving him."
"Well why don't you just tell him straight up then," she suggested.
"Well, yeah, but it's not that easy, he once helped me out, so he still thinks I owe him a favor. After all, we don't even see eye to eye anymore, he knows what he did, he should just leave me alone."
"Huh that doesn't make sense to me," Chipo scoffed, "that just doesn't make any sense," she repeated again and went to the kitchen.
"You want some eggs and bacon?" She shouted annoyed.
"Um no, I'm not hungry, actually let me go and deal with this situation, I'll be back in about an hour," he

jumped out of bed and stormed out of the house. He came back late in the evening, drunk.
"Oh man, my life is gonna kill me, life is just too good right now. My business is starting to go well, all is moving according to plan," he yelled excitedly. "Drink something with me my love," as he poured two glasses of cognac. After a couple of glasses, they found themselves in a club, surrounded by familiar faces. The joint was packed to the deck, and it was a Sunday.

The place was smokey, the music was loud and it was hardcore techno music. Marko gestured to her to follow him. They went up the stairs and on every turn was a locked door with a security guard. They found themselves in a room with a big table and about eight people were sitting around it.
She got to meet the owner of the club, Craig C, he was like a zombie, tall, blue eyed, skinny, blonde long haired guy. He looked like a dead man walking, expensively dressed, with a stuffed nose, but very gentle and calm.

She chatted with him a bit and when she turned around, Marko was busy snorting cocaine. They were ten lines of dope and a golden small pipe on the table. The ladies were snorting it too, like it was thin air. Alcohol kept coming, everyone was high. Craig C the club owner offered Chipo a line, at first she hesitated, but she didn't want to be the odd one out. She grabbed the small pipe, leaned forward and pulled a line. She then tilted her head backward, inhaled, whilst pinching her nose, just like how the other ladies had done it.
She did not feel anything immediately, after a few minutes she took another pull again. Marko seemed not to mind, he had pulled at least five lines. She found herself in a dark room, she had no idea how she got there. She could hear people making

out but she could not see them. The moans and groans startled her. She smelt breath and felt hands all over her body, suddenly she shook the zombies off and managed to free herself, staggering as she searched for the door way. The whole place was like a merry go round, she had no idea where she was. Everything seemed to be stagnant and then from nowhere something would change. An angry Marko grabbed her by the hair.

"Where the hell have you been? I could not find you anywhere." He screamed.
Chipo just stood there and stared at him laughing. By the time they got home, it was 5 pm Monday evening. She woke up at 8 pm on Wednesday evening. Marko was nowhere to be found. She had no memory of anything, her clothes, stuff in her purse were scattered all over. She drank at least two liters of water.

The following day she went to school, she had started on her B2 course. Which is the formal requirement course before you can start studying or do any traineeship. Marko had not been home for three days and had not even called her.

In public, she did put on a brave face, but in private, she punched walls and cushions in frustration. And for some reason, she never felt compelled to call him.

She carried on with her business, went to school with bruised knuckles and met her friends for coffee. Susie had certainly changed, she was all about style and Chanel, beaming, as usual, she laughed as soon as she saw her.
"My Zimbabwean friend," she shouted, and gave her a big thick kiss leaving a stamp of lips on her cheek. Chipo could smell the strong breath of alcohol.

She admired Susie, she was a fighter and a hustler. When she talked every part of her body moved, her hands, legs, hair, boobs, anything that can move would move. She was as loud as a broken farm tractor.

Chipo felt like cowering under the table when Susie laughed, she had these sudden thunder bursts of laughter which made everyone stare at them.
"What do you think about my earrings? Its genuine gold, you like the ring? Huh? 20 carat diamonds, fur coat original Burberry since 1958," she would boast and crackle.
Chipo was just in awe, "glasses Prada, shoes Versace," she mimicked her.
"Who wears Prada?" She shouted, "the devil," they said in chorus and chortled.

"Chipo when you are finished with whatever you are doing, school, swimming, whatever," she said, "and if you need a break from reality, call me I'll hook you up, its all about the dollars please babe, I want you to be successful." She begged her.

"But you Zimbabwean woman, sometimes I fear you," she erupted.
"You fear me," Chipo said, surprised. "You the Susie fear me small Chipo, Ha!Ha!Ha! That's a nice joke, tell me one reason why a war machine like you would fear me?" She urged her.
"Uh you," shaking her head, "you are dangerous oh, like a live wire. Don't you know a fly can kill an elephant. You forgot the way you moved out, of that house, overnight hey, like a real Nigerian. You didn't even leave a love letter."
"Uh, that I can explain, What's the second reason?"
"Uh Chipo," she squeaked, "how you handled the landlord, he was so scared, poor old man he gave me one week to move out, after what you did to

him." Chipo was puzzled, "but I didn't have a fight with him, I mean he still owes me my deposit money."

"Nah don't lie I heard something else, I heard you sent some boys and they dealt with him," she insisted.

"That's bullshit Chipo disputed her claim."

"Anyway not my business, now to the good news," as she rubbed her hands together, "I met this man you know, very rich man oh, he owns hotels and buildings and some houses. The man is loaded, doesn't even know what to do with his monie. I am sure he wipes his ass with a bundle of cash, he has no wife, no kids just himself, nutin."

"That must be sad and what a punishment, you've all you need in life and yet no one to share it with, so when he dies he leaves everything to charity." Chipo felt sorry for him.

"Cut that bullshit, take your remorse somewhere else, he is living the life he chose. I mean I met the sister, she has or should I say had the same mentality, she is extremely successful, very rich too, now she is almost in her 50s and no kids. The funny thing is, she actually wants a family but she thinks its too late."

"Why didn't she have kids at a younger age?" Chipo asked.

"Well when I asked her, she told me when she was growing up she wanted to be successful, so she only focused on her career, she wasn't family oriented, and now that she has everything she realizes she is not happy. I told her it's not too late oh."

"Yah sure these days there is technology," Chipo interrupted her and continued "technology rules, women are giving birth well in their 50s.

"Forget about technology, I have Nyanya Docas in Lagos who can give her kids without sleeping with a man. That celebrity woman gave birth when she was almost 70 years old oh, how do you think that,

happened, Nyanya Docas now," she said proudly. "Nah I wouldn't support that, by the time the kid is 20 years old, you are in your 90s, Nah that's not right," Chipo disagreed.
"The guy is genuinely compassionate, very caring."
"Uhhh so what's the catch, I felt that one coming."
"Wait now," she hushed her. "He has special needs, a bit weird I should say, according to my morals." Chipo listened excitedly, "uh huh, so what happened, tell me."
"Get me another Hennessy, I have upgraded you know," she scoffed, "days of Jim beam are gone, that's for builders, the taste is too thick, scratches my throat. What do you see when looking at this photo?."
"Hey wow! Is that him?"
"Yep."
"Surely he knows how to dress, a gentlemen, an executive, I like his looks. He is handsome and you can see the richness in him." Chipo stated.

Susie gulped her drink, "forget about that one, do I eat beauty, I need monie oh," she muttered.
"You know how much I used to drink, now I drink three times more, at least two bottles of Vodka or whiskey a day. I have Champagne for breakfast, I brush my teeth with cognac. When I pee, I pee Viceroy," they both laughed so loud.
"I am going insane, I can't function with neutral blood, my spirit makes me do things I do. These weird unholy, satanic activities can not be accomplished with a sober mind."
"Whoa you must be going through hell, but it seems like it's worth it though, look at you, you look like a decorated heaven peacock, you belong to the oscars," she uttered.
"Forget about that one now, do I eat Oscars," she shook her head and cleared her throat, "but this is our secret don't tell anyone oh, it would be very em-

barrassing if his workers had to be aware of it. He is a popular citizen, a well-known person around the city, does a lot of contributions, charity work."

"Who can I tell? I don't know anybody," Chipo assured her.

"The thing is I have never had, such good sex, he is a workhorse, he knows how to treat a woman. Of all the sex I have ever had, he is number one. His tongue is so sweet oh God, I swear with Palm wine."

"So what seems to be the problem then? You get laid, you get good sex, you flood, you burst up."

"Chipo let me finish the story first." She sighs!

"So one day he calls me to his house for dinner."

"You don't live together?" She was inquisitive.

Susie just smirked, "No never. He gave me my own place now, so I go to his house, we drink, drink, drink, guzzle two bottles of vodka. After that, we had amazing sex everywhere, in the kitchen, in the bathroom, on the couch, on the floor, on the ceiling. We take a break, we drink again, then he says to me, Susie can I share a top secret with you, of course, darling you can share anything with mama," I replied, "why not?" Then he disappears somewhere in a hidden room, he calls me over, I am wondering where the hell he is. "Susie daddy is waiting," I hear loud strange music. I run around looking for him.

"Naked," Chipo twisted her lips.

Susie ignores her, "Then I discovered there was a secret room behind one of the bedrooms. He is naked in the middle of the room holding a leather belt with a dildo in the middle." Chipo roared with laughter.

Susie just stared at her and took another quick sip.

"Sorry about that," Chipo apologizes, "please continue."

"Uh, so he commands me to chain him to two pillars in the middle of the room, as he leaned forward on

a wooden block, like that and he instructs me to put the belt around my waist, with this big black dildo, with rubber spikes on it."
"Hey, my sister you are mysterious, venturing into the unknown," Chipo exclaimed.
"But the belt was too tight now, look at me, my waist is mama hippo," as she admires herself.
Chipo cannot constrict her laughter. "Oh shit what was the dildo for?" She mocked her. "I am curious I just want to know."
"Chipo do I need to take you to the river and show you how to drink. The reflection is right in the water. Why do you look puzzled Chipo? It's obvious, he wants me to wear it and jig him now."
"Oh shit," Chipo exploded, "dirty mother fucker, I thought he wanted to uh, oh okay, so you um, oh" she cried out. "Holy cow, but didn't you say he enjoys making love to you?"
"Yes he does, but he also wanted me to do him."
"Whoo, whoo Dear Lord wash us with the saliva of Moses and let the sea swallow the beasts of the earth, let your children dwell not in the unknown, but in the natural light of heaven," Chipo was rhapsode.

"Stop that crap now."
"So did you do it, were you in the seventh heaven?" She raptured. Susie scoffed, "finish your drink now, you haven't touched your glass since I started talking," she responded. Chipo was laughing her ass off, "were you standing or kneeling," she teased her again.
Susie sulked, feeling offended "it'll be your turn soon," she yawped.
"But on a serious note is that normal," Chipo whispered.
"What is normal? And what is not? There is always a first time for everything, I had never done it before," she replied.

"So you did it then," Chipo confirmed.
"Its obvious, the evidence is right in front of you, with the help of two bottles of whiskey, I was paralyzed with shock. I drank a bottle of whiskey in one go before I did it and another bottle after I did it. The problem now is, he says I do it so well, he wants it every night."
"Wow! Susie you are in demand, you should open a private Spa. You must be a murderer in bed," and they cracked up.
"I think its a psychological problem, I found out he was abused as a kid by a relative, I guess that's why he is like that."
"Is he gay? Why are you asking all these questions, I have no idea, all I know is, he bought me an apartment and I am building a house back home," as she drowned her glass.
"Oh, my sister, I feel for you oh, have another drink, a bigger challenge awaits you ahead," and she squealed with laughter.
"Nah tonite I am not going back there ooh," they both giggled.
"Show me the photo again." Chipo requested.
"Forget that one now," as she drained her drink one more time.

They had a good laugh, if you saw them you would think they were sisters. Susie rolled her eyes as the phone rang.
"Talk of the devil, that's his own personal assigned ring tone," as she pulls it out. With a high pitched adjusted voice, she answers the phone. "Hi darling, you miss me already, I am with a friend of mine, I once told you about her, yes from Zim, I'll tell her, did you get my watch? Really, oh you are such a darling, no need, I'll catch a cab, I am working on it, I need to do the theory test first, yes, see you later, love you." Chipo was playing with her eyes and lips, whipping the air with her hand, making fun of her.

“I‘ve started weight lifting, I need to keep my shape in check. You see he is calling me, he knows what he is missing. I am becoming a perfectionist at it. I am more German than the Germans oh, Lord have mercy on me.”
“There is nothing you can’t handle Big Su, just close your eyes and go in blindly.”
“It‘s not easy oh I‘ve to go, prepare yourself for the cold, winter is coming. Sometimes you have to do what you have to do. It‘s tough out there, my little princess, be safe and live life, don‘t let life live you. This world we are living in is for the lunatics, the unpredictable, choose your own destiny, don‘t let anyone bully you. Here take this,” as she placed bills of 100s in her hand.
”All this for me wow! Are you planning on pimping me?” As she held the money, with a grin on her face. Susie winked at her.
“I like you, check on me, from time, time, I might just collapse and die oh.”
“No, you won‘t, I still need you alive, but do take great care of yourself,” Chipo yelled.
She lit a cigarette, picked her coat up, and leaned towards her, “let me go and find out about my hubby’s many dalliances before he reveals them nonchalant to the birds.” She blew a kiss and disappeared, leaving her stunned and questioning her own morals.

Chapter Nineteen

Something fishy was going on, Marko had not been home for a week, but sometimes she could feel his presence. She could tell that he had been there, taken a shower, drank some juice or changed some clothes, but still, he never bothered to call her. She wanted to talk to him about her deposit before she inquired with Mueller. She tried to concentrate on her homework but something was bothering her at the back of her mind, she could not wrap it around her head. There was a loud aggressive knock on the door.
It made her jump and shatter a glass. She tiptoed towards the door, peeped through the peephole but could hardly see anything. The person had blocked it. She heard a baby cry and thought it was someone lost. She flung the door open and she got struck on the side of the neck with an umbrella. This chick just bulldozed her. Chipo was in total shock, her animal instincts kicked in, she grabbed a bottle of Hennessy on the table and swung it at her, missing her by an inch and breaking it on the wall. The other woman was frightened, she realized she had met a mad person, her eyes bulged out.

"What the hell you fucking bitch, you trying to kill me?" She screamed.
"You stuck me first and who the fuck are you?" Chipo shouted, breathing heavily, ready to fire the next bottle.

"My kids want to see their dad, where is Marko?" she yelled Chipo became incapacitated. The other woman noticed the look in her eyes, and she knew she had no idea about anything.
The kids were relaxed they didn't panic it's as if they were used to it. They came out of hiding when they realized the firing had ceased.

"You didn't have to hit me," Chipo spoke sotto voce. "What did you think I am Cameroonian it's in our genes," she boasted. "And after all the last time I was here, the other chick hit me first, so this time I was prepared, and I am willing to go to war," she intimidated her.
"Which other chick?" Chipo asked politely. She scoffed, "you think you are the only one, did he tell about his other four kids?"
"Four kids" she shouted surprised, "whoa," she was in shock, she thought she was getting crazy. "Four kids," she cried out. "Yes with three different women," she tortured her mind. Chipo felt her legs give way, she was becoming weak, crippled, almost about to faint. But she could not cry, the milk had been spilled. She was told stuff, she had heard from others and that had happened to others, but never did she think that it would happen to her.

"I started dating Marko out of pity, when I first met him, he had nothing, absolutely nothing. I met him at a very low point in my life. He was going through a lot and my mum had just kicked me out of her house. I moved in with a friend of mine, bless her she is such a kind soul. My mum was crazy man, alcohol got the better of her though. Rest in peace mum.
Marko was staying in an old caravan he had found dumped by the roadside. He lived like a junkie, no heating, no running water nothing. The guy was a junkie, but he was a smart junkie. Somehow he got

to know my friend and he would come to the house to clean and throw away rubbish. Sometimes she would send him to run some errands for her, for a few coins. After a few months we discovered he had moved into the cellar without us knowing. He had managed to get a spare key cut for the main door and every day in the middle of the night he would sneak in and sleep.
But the cellar was very damp. I found him sick to the point of death. I called an ambulance, they took him in and kept him for about three months. After he sobered up a bit, he got a job making burgers, and every time he finished work he would pass through my friend's place with a bag full of chips and hamburgers.
He tried his best to stay clean, but as soon as he had money in his pockets he would disappear for a few days and return once the money was finished. But you know love is blind I fell for him. Being in a relationship with him was the funniest thing ever.
He was very unpredictable, he would just turn up with a bunch of stuff, money clothing, flowers I mean he knew how to spoil me.
But he just had a sick mind, I guess it's how he was brought up.

"How long do you know Marko?" She wanted to know.
"About five months," Chipo replied.
"Five months okay, but I was here last month in the morning and I saw a German girl, I hope he didn't scam you too as he did to others."
"I lost 12,000 euros coz I trusted him." Chipo's heart sank, her mind went blank, she bit her lips but said nothing.
"He wanted to buy a car and sell it for a profit, so I took a loan for him, the car never came. He said some Gypsies had sold him a Mercedes Benz with an engine of a VW," she giggled, "now it's funny, back

then it wasn't. Can you believe that stupid lie, well I did in the beginning? I mean that's what he said, he was my boyfriend and my hard-earned cash was gone just like that. Only, later on, did I find out he had lost my money when he made a bet with some drug dealer, oh man," she cried out.
"I heard this dealer kidnapped him for almost two weeks, a few months ago."
Chipo's mind was racing with anger, she couldn't think straight.

"Shiva my former best friend lost 6,000 euros, well she was a bit stupid, she still is. I mean she sent him to withdraw 100 bucks, gave him the card, and the pin number.
When she was asleep, he would secretly withdraw some money without her knowing, can you believe it, stupid bitch."
Chipo took a deep breath, she felt betrayed.

"Jana the bitch, my Russian ex-school mate, cute though, she lost 7,000 euros I think even more. He got her involved in a loan shark business, they would borrow someone 500 bucks and get back 1,000 bucks a month, so I heard. It worked well for a while, but she got too comfortable, and I heard they gave three guys 2,500 bucks each, and these guys just disappeared.
He told her he got scammed and that the three guys had left town, only for one of Jana's friends to bump into Marko with the same guys in a club spraying Champagne, spending her money. The friend took a pic of them and sent it to Jana, there was a big fight in the club, if you look at Jana's left eye, she cannot properly open it. It's always twitching," and she giggled, "yeah that's Marko for you.
He is well known around here, you don't invite Marko into your home, everyone knows it, it's like leaving a voicemail on Little Rome's phone, telling

him you are away for few days. He will break into your house steal whatever is available including your voice box."
"Who is Little Rome?" Chipo inquired, "Never mind, he will steal from you and buy you new shoes and help you to find the robber" and she laughed. "I hope you didn't lose anything yet, get out while you can, nothing good will come out of this. The guy is a drug addict, a gambler, a liar, sometimes he wins, most of the time he loses and he owes a lot of people big-time money."
"I am surprised there is still furniture in this place before I left two years ago I would come back home from work and find the whole place empty. It happened more than three times. I would leave this house, run away, but you know I would always come back. I stayed because he is the father of my kids. Its a pity, but it's like that, when he is good, he is the best guy you wanna be with, but that's very seldom. I hope I didn't hurt your feelings or your neck," as she saw Chipo rolling her shoulder.

"But sister you are violent too hey, where are you from? I think he has finally met his match," she grinned.
"Let me introduce you to your step kids, this is Chris, Christopher his firstborn four years old, and that's Dorothy, two years old. Shiva has also a two year old boy and Jana a one year old girl and I am Sonia by the way. Welcome to the family, you not pregnant are you?"

Chipo just stared at her, "Well Marko is a breeding machine, one touch you are gone. Where is he anyway?" As she looked around the house.
Chipo exhaled, "I haven't seen him for a week."
"Oh really he must be at the drug house, did you give him any money, he usually comes to my house twice a week because he has to pick up the kids

from kindergarten. But this week he never showed up twice, neither did he call me, damn I hate it when he does that." She said it aloud.
"Well, that makes the two of us, I haven't seen him for a week too," Chipo quipped.
"Damn this guy, he will never become mature, you think he overdosed?"
She asked her curiously and sarcastically. She told Chipo all of Marko's secrets, the crying, the opening up, it was all a show, a ploy, she told her he did the same things to all of his girls.

Chipo was exasperated she gave out a loud sigh. "Can you do me a favor?" She asked her politely.
"I need a bit of your help here, I have been exposed, my weaknesses have been exploited, my kindness has been abused. My brain is messed up right now. I have pain in my heart, I am shattered, do you understand that? I have been fooled, taken for a ride, so this is what I want you to do for me," she said with a stern face.
"Please don't tell him that you were here or that we have talked, it would be very helpful to me that's all I need from you. Can you do that?" As she screamed and punched a cupboard.
"Sure I can," Sonia felt Chipo's anger, she nodded her head and stammered, "you have my number, just call me," and she dragged her kids out.

Chipo's mind floated in the air like a spirit was carrying her around. A heavy load had been removed from her shoulders.
She had been set free and was lost and exposed in a jungle full of wild scary animals. It was now a dog eat dog world. She felt transformed, and she could not afford to be weak or to lose. She took a long shower, cried, wept, tears flowed down her chicks, her nose ran. She let out and left all her anger in that shower.

She shook violently as she soaked and all her anger was washed away. After a while she sat on the couch silently, she didn't want to believe any of it, she didn't even want to look into her bank account or let alone even see her bank card.
She poured herself a glass of cognac and drank it quietly in deep evil thoughts. She had to scheme a way of at least getting some of her money back.

Chapter Twenty

Chipo felt lonely and powerless, she called Susie for comfort and guidance. Susie was drunk as hell, she was mumbling and stuttering.

"Heeyhey, my Zimbabwean princess, me me gonna enjoy life oh. It's a Friday night now, are you out and about?
Are you making that monie?"
"Susie I got a problem, can you talk, are you alone?" Chipo asked her.
"You don't believe what this guy just did to me oh, me I do everything for him. You know that now, I am a workhorse. But now I think he is getting carried away, he needs a thorough bashing. You know what he just did?"
"No I don't, what did he do?" Chipo asked already irritated.
"I walk into the house and I find him shitting with the door wide open," Chipo giggled and rubbed her face in annoyance.
"I need to teach him a lesson," she continued, "I'll call you right back."

Chipo was shaking her head and laughing as she sipped her drink. She looked up to the ceiling and let out a deep sigh of weariness.
She knew that it was a Friday and at some point in time Marko was going to come home, for some fresh clothes.

She prepared herself, she dressed up and felt gorgeous, ready to go for a party. She had also cooked a nice tasty traditional meal. The music was playing not too loud and she sat in partially darkness sipping her Hennessy. The door flung open and Marko walked in. "Where is my woman? He called out. "I can smell her, where is she?"
"I am here my love," Chipo replied calmly.
"Oh, yeah there you are, I know where you are, right there, there she is." He talked as he staggered towards her.
He was wearing new clothes and he looked really good. There was no sign of pretense on his face, he was a real professional, Chipo thought to herself.

"This is scary if he can pretend so good, he can even murder someone." She murmured silently.
"Look what I brought for you, this is what I've been up to my darling. Working hard yeah, no time to sleep as he rubbed her nose. He pulled out a large stack of cash, her eyes glazed, "this is real cash, the money you gave me, the returns are starting to return," and laughed feeling proud of himself. Chipo didn't know what to make of it, she just sat quietly grinning at him. He gave her a kiss on the forehead, his breath stank.

"You didn't miss me did you, not even one missed call, you didn't even call," he repeated.
"Well I knew you would be busy, I didn't want to disturb you, but that doesn't mean I didn't miss you.
"Did you miss me," she asked in return. Of course my love, I missed your beautiful ass," he replied grinding himself on her.
"Should I give you some food, I cooked your favorite?"
"Nah I am good, I ate already maybe later" his face was unreadable.
"Let's have a drink together, you look good, good

enough to eat, what's the occasion." As he ran his hands on her neck, she twitched a bit.
"I am afraid you too sexy for me, you don't want kids right now do you," Chipo asked sarcastically.
"Umm kids, kids are nice but we can wait, we got so much time, at least until you finish your university. You don't want little chipmunks running around everywhere, and who knows maybe I am sterile, incapable of producing any fruits. Big business is coming up, just have faith in me, soon you will get all your money back."

She observed him and listened to his lies, she wanted to interrupt him and tell him she had all the implicating evidence against him. But the lies were just too good, she paused thoughtfully for a moment and suddenly it kicked in, she might actually end up benefiting from the lies, if he lived up to them. So she let him bubble and float in a sea of happiness, just the kiss on the forehead made her cringe, but she held on.
"A lion that roars and roams like you, incapable, I doubt it."
"Tonight we party," he cut her off "we need to celebrate this good life, it's too quiet in here," he jumped up and pumped the volume. He walking into the bedroom bouncing.
"We back babe, we back in business, it's on yo, we going all the way up, up," he shouted.
"You are winner Marko," she echoed, as she peeped through the door, to see where he was hiding the money.
"Are you sure you don't wanna eat," she repeated.
"I ate already, the only person I wanna eat is you right now," as he walked out butt naked.

Damn the hardest part was getting nailed, while knowing you are not feeling it. Chipo surprised herself with her resilience and calmness.

As they lay on the couch, Marko was breathing heavily and he said, "You know what babe?"
"What?"
"I think I am gonna go back to loan sharking business, I can make a hell lot of money out of it." Since that day Chipo started smoking heavily.

Chapter Twenty one

It was the only way to cool her nerves. She felt as if she was in a movie acting, nothing was real anymore and nothing mattered except herself. It was all a game, she reassured herself all the time to remain focused.
They went to a club, the usual gang was swirling around. She was in such good spirits it scared the shit out of Marko. He could not figure out why and kept asking her if she was ok.

"This is what happens when you disappear on me," she whispered in his ear. She drank anything, she flirted, chatted and smoked. It was a new day.
She hooked up and mingled with some tall blonde snorting girls. She invited them over to their table. She was now networking, she needed to be close to some of his closet friends. They watched her in amazement as she interacted with different people. They looked at her suspiciously as she hugged and teased them.
"Consider me your wing lady tonight boys, I can hook you up with any chick you want. Why don't you try me Dino," she boasted, just show me any girl you want and I'll bring her over. We cool right," as she bump fisted them. From the corner of her eye, she could see Marko with an unpleasant look on his face and she decided to spice things up.
"Hey Dino," as she leaned on his shoulder tipsy, "You look like someone I could really like, I don't know

why, but I just like you, as a bro, you know what I mean." Dino was uncomfortable with the situation. "But you know what, I'll tell you something, if you ever fuck me up, I'll cut you up and make you eat your own balls, I'll summon my witch doctor, my aunt from Malawi, to turn you into a chicken."
He snapped and started shouting, "What's wrong with you man? Are you crazy? Don't play with witch craft." And he pushed her away.
She just chuckled, "oh don't tell me, you are scared, come on bro. I can out drink you in one go, you are a pussy."
His face beamed, "keep dreaming on Lady Gaga," he scoffed at her, "I got a Germany made tank of a stomach" he exaggerated.
"How long do you know Marko, huh can he drink like you?" She changed the subject.
"Why are you asking that now?" He wanted to know.
"Just like that, it's love I guess, he is your buddy right."
"Yeah since childhood man, almost twenty years."
She knew they had come a long way and were very tight. That night didn't end well, Marko took offense at her in flirting with his friends and in talking to one guy who was not part of their crew. And unknown to her this particular guy was now dating one of Marko's ex-girlfriend.
He dragged her away from him and she was pushing and yelling in response. "Let me go, What the hell is wrong with you?" She screamed.
"You can't just flirt with anybody, you are a fucking bitch. You trying to disrespect me, do you know who that guy is? That guy will drug you and rape you."
She was taken aback by his rage, she had never seen him angry before. She realized he was easily intimidated and she never knew he was so jealous and insecure.
"I did nothing wrong, my purse dropped and he picked it up for me that's all," she shouted.

"You dropped it on purpose, you did it deliberately," he fired back, "you think I am stupid. I am gonna choke you and put you to sleep," he threatened her.

Dino jumped in and kept them apart. But the security had already been notified and they were both thrown out of the club.
That was a major turning point in their relationship. They didn't talk again that night, they lay on the bed like strangers. When she woke up the next morning, Marko was nowhere to be found.

After lunch she called Chamu. He had a terrible cold, he was coughing and sniffing, his voice was horribly bad. She told him she needed a cellar to dump her bags until she found a new place. He was happy to help. Since it was a Sunday she could not do much, she went on Facebook, combed through Marko's profile. She wanted to know as much as she could about him, but there wasn't much to learn. He was like a ghost, he left no trails behind, His profile was squeaky clean.
She finally had the guts to check her bank account and for real Marko had cleaned her out, there was only 84 euros left. She blamed herself, she was too embarrassed to tell anyone about it. She checked to see if the money he had hidden was still there. When she saw it, it gave her some peace of mind. She had to play a smart game, he knew too much about her, regarding her visa situation. She needed to renew it within a week and she had not been to school in ages. There were a lot of things he could do to threaten her.

Chapter Twenty two

She dragged one of her suitcases down the stairs and met Chamu and his friend BJ by McDonald's.

BJ was a big fellow, smartly dressed, wearing a cowboy hat and a white coat. He did look more like a pimp. She wondered why Chamu had brought him along, maybe it was because he had a car, she thought to herself. BJ bought them burgers and drinks, while eating he said to Chipo, "eh Chipo you see, Chamu has told me a bit about you, I know you are a new arrival, fresh from the pond."
"Not so new anymore, I know my way around," Chipo answered.
"You see, you are smart, some people have been here for years, they don't know how to find their way around the city."
"It is a big city," she responded.
"Anyway, my point is, eh... this guy you are hanging out with, eh... Marko I know him pretty good. He is someone who is not to be messed with, he is always up to no good. Him and his clique are notorious bad boys of this hood.
They have been scamming unassuming young beautiful ladies like you for a long time. And somehow someone is always falling for their stupid wicked tricks. They are about five of them, Marko, Dino, Jerry, Frank and this Somali boy, Saiid.
I am sure you have seen that they are always together, they grew up in the same neighborhood,

they are like peas in a pod. I am not aware of your situation, but if you need any help let me know. You are moving out right, trouble in paradise," and he chuckled. Whatever you do with him, make sure you have some form of proof. As long as there is evidence that criminal activity has been committed, I'll gladly help you out. I got reliable contacts around."
"Proof-like what?" Chipo asked.
"Well eh, any form of evidence, contracts, recordings,
pictures, videos anything that proves you are on the right side."
"Thank you for your advice, I appreciate your concern, however, what I really need at the moment is a cheap place to live in, just for a short period of time. It would be cool if I can get a part-time job too," she said. "Any type of job will do for the moment, yeah anything just to have some money in my pocket. Do you also know where I can get CS gas." She concluded.
"Oh oh who are we dealing with here Chamu, we got a gangster in the house," BJ let out a dirty laugh and added, "I should warn you, whatever you do, make sure there are no witnesses," he dragged his words, "otherwise, you are in big trouble. Most people in Germany know the consequences of violence, so no matter how angry someone gets, only very few stupid, dim ducks, would actually dare to hit or inflict injury on anyone. The smart ones would engage in guerrilla warfare, hide, hit, and run. But then again, cameras are everywhere these days. Some will intimidate, instill fear in you and if you are weak, they can take you to the cleaners. I am talking about normal people, not the mafia."
"You have Mafia in Berlin," Chipo interrupted him, it made her feel worried and excited.
"Oh yeah there are big mafia family groups and they are in charge and in control of a lot of businesses, in certain areas. This is Berlin man what do you think,

this is where the 2nd World War ended. You are aware of the history of Berlin."
"A bit," she answered.
"Good then you should know once upon a time, Berlin was divided into two, you had the Russians on the Eastside and the British and Americans on the Westside. When the wall came down not everything came down with it. But you don't need to worry about that, they are just normal people as long as you don't mess with their businesses. A majority of them are really cool honestly speaking."
It sounded like a movie to her, in fact the more he talked the more she wanted to absorb.
"It does not matter which country, which place you are in, you just have to know which way the wind is blowing, you need to understand your situation, and deal with it accordingly." Chamu started coughing and complaining of chest pain. "Let me go smoke a blunt man," he cut in.
"Sista, don't worry, this is BJ, the Mayor himself, you are in safe hands here, Abaaay," he shouted and he left them giggling.
"Your brother is a mad man, I like him, he does his thing you know, respectful and is a peaceful guy. Anywhere back to our case, on a serious note, look here," he said as he almost whispered. "Chamu is not aware of a lot of things that I do, he just asked me to help him carry your suitcases. But when I saw you I thought hey, she has so much potential, she looks talented and smart. I don't want him to know anything about my stuff, we all have our own secrets in this world. Eh, I am not going to beat about the bush, I am into drugs, hard drugs cocaine, that's the reason why I didn't finish my masters."
Chipo was startled.

"Most girls that work for me are all doing their degrees in various disciplines.
People need to survive hey if I take you to a brothel,

I can assure you half of the girls working there are all university students. They have no choice, I mean it's not like they are going to do it forever. Only to pay for their bills and when they feel like it. When they have raised enough money for their studies, they'll stop and find their own way in life. But some will continue, of course, money is too sweet, it's all about a good life"

Chipo stared at him, wishing he knew what she was thinking. In her mind she was saying, "does this mother fucker know who he is talking to, does he know how I was brought up, do I look like some dirty cheap whore, he has the guts to be so open and direct, do I look like a tart to him, like some of those girls."
She was angry but she had a smile on her face, she needed him to carry her suitcase.
"You can make at least 10,000 euros in one trip," he continued, "it's just pick and drop, as easy as that, you could be making 10,000 euros every two weeks."
Suddenly her eyes popped up.
"But no rush, when you need my help and when you get stuck, when you think you can't go any further, gimme a call. I am the real deal, I will hook you up. And if you are as smart as you look, you might end up owning your own business. You like that don't you?" He said it as he got up, without waiting to hear her answer and he went outside to smoke.

Once again she was left stunned. "Out of the frying pan and into the fire," she chuckled.

Chapter Twenty three

She was beginning to think that to survive in Europe you have to be involved in some dubious things. She went back home and called Mueller. This guy was 24/7 available, she told him to hold on to her deposit because she might need a room.

He laughed, "I don't ever want to see you and your little wannabe gangster if I ever see that little punk, that freak face thief of yours again, I'll burn him alive. Are you trying to scam me, what deposit are you talking about huh, you are lucky I didn't go to the police? Huh maybe he didn't tell you that I gave it to him." hahaha he laughed. "If it wasn't because of the gun I would have beaten them both with my bare hands. He ripped you off yah, I knew it, he is a scam. He didn't tell you that I gave him back the money, did he, hahaha, you got what you were looking for and he hung up."

She was struggling to concentrate, she was so lost. It was as if she never knew Marko. She had five missed calls from Camisa. When she called back Camisa insisted that she should join her in a popular cocktail bar for a drink. She was emotionally drained and felt so depressed. She thought it would be refreshing for her to leave the house for a while and forget about her problems. They hugged, joked and laughed but she could not share her nightmares with her.

After a while a familiar face joined them, it was the guy she was made to believe she had kissed at the Watergate club, well she had indeed kissed him.
"There is my surprise for you," Camisa shouted, "he has been bothering me for months, I had no choice but to bring you guys together. I hope I did a good deed."
"You won't regret it Camisa, you are a darling," he told her.
"So Schippo, call me don't be a stranger girl, I love you guys, I got my own date to take care of. If you don't like this man, just tell him and he will leave immediately.
Don't worry about the drinks I'll take care of that."
She blew a kiss and was gone.
"Great friend you have," he said in a husky voice,
"I never formally introduced myself. My name is Lionel my fans call me DJ Lionel. You can call me whatever you like."
"Oh okay, you are a DJ? Are you famous? What kind of music do you play? What kind of a DJ are you?" She bombarded him with questions.
"To answer all your questions, yes, and yes I play everything, mainly charts, I can play anything."
"That sounds cool," she cleared her throat. "How much did you pay her? No worries but um let's do things our way, the normal way, not this guerrilla warfare."
"I am listening," he said politely.
"We could change numbers and then call, have a proper date," she suggested. "What do you think?"
"Yeah sure that's fine with me," as he took out his cell phone.
"It's just that today is a bad day for me. You seem to be really cool and nice, but I can tell, I am genuinely sure you meet a lot of girls during your gigs."
"Just business," he answered.
"Today," she went on, "uh there are certain things I really need to sort out, and it's urgent, a matter of

life and death." "If you need any help let me know, I have plenty of time on my plate." He offered.
"Before you finish your prepared speech, can I just say something?" He insisted.
"I understand you are an independent woman, you like to do things your way, but uh I had, uh kind of organized a little surprise for you, I mean if you don't like it, you can go but it's worth experiencing it."
"A surprise, she suddenly becomes awake, "what kind of a surprise?" She demanded to know." I love surprises," she added.
"Just be a bit patient, good things take time to happen," he assured her. She found him very sympathetic and understanding.

He looked at his watch and disappeared behind some walls. The music stopped playing and two guys came out of the kitchen with a cake and he started singing Happy Birthday to her. The other guests stopped what they were doing and joined in. She had completely forgotten it was her birthday and Camisa had told him about it. At that moment Camisa walked in with some of her school mates, she was overcome with joy. They had so much fun and drank a lot of cocktails.

DJ Lionel offered to pay for everything.

Chapter Twenty four

She carried some of the cake with her, and when she got home that evening she discovered that the locks had been changed. She could not get into the house. She had been locked out, It was as if she had been ice slapped by an angry Orangutan.

She was homeless, she tried to call Marko but he was not picking up. She sat by the stairs with her head in her hands. She called again, the phone was ringing and he was declining it. After trying a couple of times, he picked up the phone. She tried her best to be calm and controlled her temper. The tone of her voice was measured. "Oh, Marko um, I've been trying to get hold of you, my key is not opening the door. I,ve no idea what happened. I just got back from having drinks with my school mates, and then I don't know, something is wrong with my key I suppose," she stated.
"Nope, your key is good, I changed the locks," he chuckled, "I'm eating right now I'll call you back," and he put the phone down. Her anger flashed in front of her, she saw Marko dying with her own hands. She had never been mistreated like some piece of shit in her life. He turned up four hours later, around 3 am. There was no apology, nothing, "this is not a hotel," he barked, "you can't just come and go as you wish. Let me know next time when you go out to see your other boyfriends," he accused her. "I have decided from now on, we only share one key,

my key," he bullied her. "I don't understand your actions, what have I done? What other boyfriends are you talking about? Are you going crazy?"
"This is my place, my house, I make the rules if you don't like them you can leave," he yelled.
She realized where he was going, he had made up his mind. "Marko if you don't want me here, it's fine with me, just gimme back my money and I'll find my own place."
"Yes your money you'll get it, just not now, but very soon, that has nothing to do with this. As long as you are living here, you cannot go out anymore without my permission." She could not believe her eyes. "So now I'm a prisoner is that what you are saying, you think that would work."
"As long as you are living here. We play by my rules, my house."
"The least you can do is apologize for your actions and wish me a happy birthday, that's not a lot to ask for," she begged him. He looked at the cake, sort of confused, and rushed into the bathroom. She wished she could have recorded the conversation on her phone but the battery was almost empty. He slept on the couch peacefully and she had a sleepless night on the bed.

She had a terrible nightmare, she dreamt when she was at Masoro, Gokwe some village shopping center in Zimbabwe. She was having a drink with some friends and there was a lot of partying and dancing going on.
Everyone knew the last bus would come at midnight and once you missed that bus, you had to walk through a congested path full of night-walkers and ghosts. She got up to go to the bathroom and while she was in there, her dream jumped to another location she found herself surrounded by demons and evil spirits. The strange scary creatures were fighting to enter her body. She was defending herself

and pushing them back with her sword, but they were too many of them and the bigger ones would strangle and devour the smaller ones. As she ran through the woods, a huge devil grabbed her long garment, It was about to enter into her body, when another bigger devil slashed it's head off, during the commotion she rushed towards a ball of fire that appeared from nowhere, as the devils closed in on her and were about to pull her back, she sprung into the ball of fire, and found
herself back in the toilet. She was startled when she realized, the party had gone quiet, out of panic she jumped out of the toilet confused and afraid that she might miss the last bus. When she got out, the whole place was eerie still, it was pitch dark nothing moved, she was the only person existing in that area. She wondered how she was going to get home. She looked into the direction towards home, it seemed as if the shadows of darkness were stalking her. Then there was a sudden gust of wind, a blistering movement of what appeared to be a cyclist went by almost impossible to see. As she tried to figure out what it was, a very tall headless human-like giant with wooden legs strolled by holding a golden sword that was dripping with blood. The creature was so tall its body stretched into the clouds, a cold chill ran up her spine, "definitely not of earthly origin," she muttered. The giant stopped and turned towards her. She froze, peed in her pants as the giant approached, it leaned forward and lifted its sword, she screamed in her dream and woke up sweating, her bed was wet.

She was now basically a prisoner, she could not go to school. And if she did she would have to wait for hours before he came back. One time she was forced to sit the whole night with old drunk men in a 24-hour bar. Her disdain and hatred for him grew each day. She could only leave the house when he was leaving and follow him wherever he was going. He would park the car and leave her sitting inside for hours. At some point the car almost got towed away. When she went looking for him she was nearly in tears, only to find him gambling in a betting shop around the corner. The time to renew her visa came, they asked her to bring an attendance confirmation from the school, her Anmeldung, to confirm her address and her bank statement, to show that she had the 8,000 euros in her account. She had none of those and she knew she had hit a barrier.

When she got home around 4 pm Marko was nowhere to be found and he was not picking up his calls.

She checked his friend's Facebook accounts and one of them had posted about going to a party that day. She went and sat in a hotel bar so she could use the internet and keep herself warm.
She bought a liter of water, some bread rolls, and a small bottle of Jägermeister from the Supermarket since hotel prices were too high. She had to eat and drink secretly out of her bag. She was not dressed for partying and she wondered if they would let her in the club. Her mind had been made up, that this would be the last time he would ever disrespect her ever again. She prayed that she would find him in that club and that she would hurt him badly. Around midnight she chatted up some guys and they helped her sneak into the club because of her attire. She was tipsy and drunk with anger.
He had shown his disregard for her and she had nothing to lose anymore. She just wanted to hurt him, break his leg, or stab him. She lay in waiting, hidden in a darkcorner, where she could see who came in and who went out without her being noticed. As she observed the entrance she started having seconds thoughts.

If the police were called and she was caught she could be deported. She had two choices either she was going to accept being treated like shit or swallow her pride.

She decided to put an end to it. And putting a stop to it meant intimidating him, instilling fear in him as BJ had said. Around 3 am she was almost giving up when Dino walked in with 2 girls, one of them was Sonia, Marko's baby mama.

"Bitch sold me out," she snarled. A couple of minutes later Marko joined them. She sat there waiting for them to be comfortable. Her bottle of Jägermeister was almost empty, she grabbed an unattended half-full bottle of beer from the table and drank out the beer.

She was so high and full of anger. Alcohol and anger are the worst enemies. She observed them with such intensity of a lion preying on Zebra, she was like a soldier waiting to attack her enemies. As she marched towards Marko and his crew, somehow Dino spotted her. He ran to warn his friend.

Marko startled got up and charged towards her. He thought he could scare her away, but Chipo was determined.

She was snarling, hissing, and clawing, people thought she was mad. Marko smiled as he approached her as if nothing had happened. He raised his arms about to hug her. She whacked his head with the beer bottle, he was caught by surprise, blood splattered on his clean white ironed shirt. He sprung at her as she was about to strike again. He tried to choke her but she dodged. Marko was taken aback by her speed. As she swung again Dino jumped in and blocked the 2nd strike, using his body by coming between them. Dino's big body saved Marko from further beatings but he took all the punches.

"Hey, Marko, this is embarrassing man, take your woman home, take her home, we don't roll like this man," Dino shouted. The crowd started to gather

around them, the DJ stopped playing music and the security was approaching fast. The women in the club were looking at her in shock, they had never seen such violence.
"Wow I wonder what he did to her," someone from the crowd yelled.
"Hey let her go she is a woman, you woman beater asshole" shouted some girls. She was surging forward, desperately wanting to batter and whack him. She was acting like a giant scorpion fighting with both hands and feet. As she attempted to crawl on him the hulk security guard picked them up like toys. They were thrown out of the club and she was still seething with anger. Dino was holding her from behind, as Marko walked a safe distance towards the car. She was dragged into the car uncontrollable, hysterical and he was a raging bull. He kept hitting the steering wheel promising her that he would end her life that day.
He drove so fast like Lewis Hamilton and as erratic as Verstappen. All the while punching the dash board and going through red traffic lights. He was cursing and fuming, giving her that dirty look, that murderous stare. Dino sat in front but kept his eye on her. He was ready to prevent her from throwing any punches. He was a busy man that night. She was not backing down, "You have messed up with the wrong woman, I am from Zimbabwe and I'll deal with you, I'll murder your ass." She screamed at him.
"What?" He braked so suddenly, the car screeched and stopped in the middle of the bridge. He went around the car and pulled the door open, blows began raining, it was blows for blows. He dragged her out, tried to lift her up, wanting to throw her over the bridge. Dino tackled them both to the ground.
Chipo found herself free, she ran back to the car and took a jack underneath the seat, as Marko approached in full speed from behind she slammed the

jack right into his face and he fell backward. Dino froze in shock, he was stunned, blood poured from Marko's face. "Unoda kuita zvekutamba neni, handisi mwana wamai vako, nhasi ndokuuraya."
(*Don't mess around with me, I am not your mother's child, I am going to kill you today*)

"Shit this bitch is crazy yo!" Dino rumbled and added, "the police will be here any minute Marko, if you don't control yourself, this means jail man, you know what I mean, Let me drive man."

Marko lay there for a few minutes his eyes wide open. "Are you okay buddy? Get up we need to go before the police come, give me the keys let me drive."
"No I am good," he shouted as he got up.
"Are you sure homie," Dino insisted.
"Damn you, I am gonna kill this crazy bitch," Marko screamed hitting the steering wheel. He struggled to put the key in the ignition. He was seeing stars, he must have been concussed. His driving was wayward, as they came towards McDonald's, he slowed down to turn into the road that led to their apartment.
Marko had recovered, out of anger and frustration of being beaten by a woman, he threw a full beer can that hit her around her eye. She shook and with animal instinct she thrust her leg out and ended up hitting Dino by mistake who slumped onto Marko causing the car to swerve and hit the pavement, taking out a few bicycles in the way. She plunged for his neck and choked him against the headrest from behind.
"Hey, stop, stop you'll kill him, this is not good," Dino was shouting nervously. He got out of the car and pulled her out.
"I'll fucken eviscerate you, skin you alive bitch," she screamed as she struggled with Dino.

"This shit gotta stop man let's chill man, relax people," Dino was in panic mode.
"We'll have the police all over us man," he was trying no to yell. "Come princess let me take you home, we can talk about it tomorrow," as he dragged her away. All the time his eyes were looking around to see if no one had seen them. And for once Chipo saw fear in Marko's eyes, he knew he had messed with the wrong person.
Chipo wanted to inflict as much pain on him as possible. Marko knew his image had been tarnished, but he was arrogant, he wasn't going to let a chick slap him around.
"I want you out of my house, you ungrateful bitch." He shouted after them, blood running from his nose. Dino had to force her into the house.

"Look here what you are doing is too dangerous for you, if the police come, you'll be in big trouble. You know what I mean. You've made your point, so chill. Marko is too terrified of you, I've never seen him like that, let's talk tomorrow," He tried to calm her down.

Chapter Twenty five

She barracked herself inside, she put a table against the door with empty bottles on top. She was scared he might return and invade her later. That night she didn't sleep well, her eye was swollen, her head was aching.
"My worst experience ever, Where do I go from here?" She blurted out. The next morning she looked into the mirror and felt ashamed. She chuckled and shook her head in disgust at the thought of the events of the previous night. He had brought out a side of her that she never knew existed.
She talked silently, assuring herself that everything would be alright.
"This is it, I am on my own now. I am not a failure and I'll not embarrass or disgrace my parents. I will achieve my goals no matter what it takes."
One thing that was definite in her mind, regardless of any consequences she had to create a life for herself and maintain a perfect picture with her family.
Her phone was full of text messages of threats and intimidation.

After two days she became aware that Marko had been observing the apartment. She was worried if she went out of the house he would switch the locks. There wasn't much food in the house so she knew her days were numbered. She was stuck and she had missed her deadline with the foreign office, so technically speaking she was now an illegal

alien, caught in an awful cycle. Marko engaged in the habit of turning off the lights from the electricity box situated outside, just to piss her off.
He would continuously ring her doorbell until she had to disconnect the wires. She wrote him a message that she needed her money back. She told him, she knew he was given her deposit money and until she got all her money back she wasn't leaving the apartment. Marko had deployed his cronies to constantly dial her number, her phone was continuously ringing without any response. Randomly an unknown person, would just savagely bang on her door. She was getting threats from all directions, throughout the day. She sat on the couch weighing her options. She wrote down the names of people she thought might help her.

She decided to give BJ a call. "Hi, how are you doing, are you good," she faked it. "I am calling because I wanted to find out, if you managed to find a part-time job for me?"
"Oh my bird, my little bird, my little bird I've been waiting for this call for a long time man," he shouted.
"Why don't you jump onto the golden bandwagon, you know you could become very good at it. It's a trend all beautiful women are on it. Follow it before it's too late, everyone else is doing it." He started laughing. "You are a vey lucky girl oh, why don't you come over for some drinks and you will never need to work again. Make hay while the sun shines little bird. This chance comes once in a life-time and little bird let me warn you, once the ship sails, oh oh, you will have to run after it like the wind and the price to pay would be unaffordable."
She found it hard to figure out his way of talking. He continued, "stop sitting on that dirty spiked fence, the grass is greener over here, hey Joe pour me some champagne and order some steaks,"

he commanded someone. "Don't go down in flames like those stupid junkies, fortune favors the bold. You know where to find me, The Pearl VIP babe, champagne on ice," he blows a kiss and he was gone. She sneered and roared her eyes. Fortune favors the bold blah blah she repeated after him.

She took a deep breath and then called DJ Lionel.

"Hi there, I am sorry I did not call you sooner, a lot has been going on, hey listen, I hope you are good."

"Oh yes yes I am very fine, I am so happy that you called me." He said excitedly.

"Yeah I am glad you are, uh listen I am looking for an apartment, yeah a place to stay. My apartment here, the toilet just fell in, yeah old building, you think you can help."

"How can I help?" He asked curiously.

"I just said it, she scorned."

"Oh," he burped.

"Well, uh I will need to put my belongings somewhere safe for a couple of days. I got a few bags, do you have big enough room, like a cellar."

DJ Lionel sounded lost, "You have no place to stay oh, that's too bad, what are you going to do.

Chipo was sulking, "I just need a place for my stuff that's all."

"Oh yeah we got so much space, the whole cellar is empty."

"Cool that's great when can I bring my stuff over then?"

"Uh-huh" he paused, "um hold on a moment please uh, can I call you back my mum is not around right now, I just need to confirm with her first."

"You live with your mum, are you under 18," she ridiculed him.

"Um yes, no I also stay with my two younger sisters."

Chipo was pissed off, "Ok I will catch up with you later," and she hung up frustrated. Big baby," she mocked him. She then called Susie, but she told her she was of no fixed abode. At any point in time she could just pack her bags and leave. Camisa was next, but she was out of town.

Chapter Twenty six

It turns out Chamu was always her last hope. He brought her some bread and peanut butter. She was left with only a backpack, stuffed with a few essentials needs, comprising of perfumes, lotions, a pair of blouses, and decent shoes.
Chamu seemed not to be bothered by nothing. For him it was just another day. He had seen it all and he understood the saying, "every dog has its day."
"There is always a light at the end of the tunnel my sista, come and stay with me, for a couple of days. My woman would not approve of course, but hey I can't leave you on the streets. Anyway, she is not available the whole day. I am sure we can find a way. I have helped a few people before."
Chipo felt at ease. At least she had one option but there was something that always bothered her about depending too on him. At the back of her mind she thought Marko would come around and make things right but she was dead wrong. The guy never flinched, not even a single call came through.

The last text message she received was a bombshell. Marko wrote to her, "You keep on talking about your money, the cocaine and drugs you took, the alcohol you drank, and all the parties you attended who paid for it. You think it was for free, nothing is for free in this world. If you are not out of my house in two days, I will report you to the police and the foreign office. Your time is running is out. Pack your shit and leave, I was never in love with you bitch, do I look crazy?" She was frightened out of her wits, cold sweat ran through her back. The mention of police and the foreign office made her shiver. Marko was starting to show his true colors. She had no more choices, she became unnerved, panic-stricken and she would jump at every sound she heard. Getting deported was her worst fear.

The tone of the text message made her very cringe. She was fearful and ready to vamoose, like a mongoose. But her head was her worst enemy. She was stiff-necked therefore she decided to play with his mind.
She wrote back, "What are you talking about? I left your house ages ago. I rented it out to a Nigerian pimp for one year and that will be until I get all my money back. And if you ever threaten me again, I can assure you, until the end of our time, I will be hunting your ass, like a fly on your rotten stinking shit. I know where all your three baby mamas live, so don't fuck with me, you bonehead looser."
He immediately wrote back, "What! Are you crazy, don't you dare do that? I didn't mean what I said, I was just trying to scare you." She concluded he had a big mouth but his heart was jelly. "People like that are scary and unpredictable to stick around," she thought to herself. She had to move on than to live in uncertainty.
She took the money that was hidden in the house. It was almost 12,000 euros. Her body was tired, her mind was not functioning well. She took a long shower, scrubbed herself for two hours. It was one of the longest baths she had ever taken. She polished her nails, gave herself a pedicure and updated her profiles. She took some selfies and at exactly 2 pm on the 2nd of September she took the last sip of Hennessy and walked out of the apartment a winner.

Chapter Twenty seven

It was a full-blown summer and she never looked back again. Her first stop was at a kiosk, night store. She wanted to get herself an ice tea to cool her nerves and slake her thirst. There was an old Indian man behind the counter. She grabbed a bottle of ice tea from the fridge, opened it, and took a long sip before she had paid for it. She pulled out 20 euros from her newly acquired wealth, took another long sip, as she waited for her change. The old man held up the 20 euros and looked at it suspiciously through the light. He glanced at her and chuckled shaking his head.

"You can go to jail because of this you know that?"
"Why would I go to jail?" She choked, worried and afraid. He smirked, turned his head to the side and spat out whatever was in his mouth.
She stammered. "What, what do you mean?"
"This is fake," he yelled, "as fake as Chinese rice, are you trying to fool me?"
She was nervous, "No way," she argued.
"Do you want me to call the police," the man angrily threatened her.
"Wait, there must be a mistake, just hold on." She took out a 50 euro note and gave it to him.
He sort of scratched on it with his thumbnail. "It's also fake," he erupted laughing.

She stared at him in bewilderment. "You mean it?"

"Lady I know money. I hold money every day, I know when something is fake and when something is real, are you gonna pay me with the real money or you want to pay with something else," he chuckled.
"Something else, like what? That's the only money I have."
He licked his lips and pouted..., "otherwise I will call police," he threatened again and added. "You are going to go to jail for this and for a long time."
He started playing with his phone, as if dialing a number.

She froze and decided, "Ok listen, someone else fooled me too, I just changed 100 bucks a few minutes ago from a taxi driver, so it's not my fault," she tried to explain.
He starred at his mobile phone and asked. "Do you know the taxi number? All taxis are centralized, Where did the driver pick you up from? And where did he drop you off? It's very easy to find out, who it was. Either that or you can make life easier for yourself. Just put your soft smooth hands on me, give me a happy ending. Make me cum and I will forget about it."
She was alarmed and horrified, but she remained composed.
"Ok before anything goes down, just do me one big favor, can you please check the rest of my money and see if it's real or fake."
"If you promise me a happy ending I will, I have the best money control machine, direct from India," he laughed and added. "You know MX?"
"No I don't," she replied innocently.
"Best money counter machine from India, MX is my brother he said," and giggled. "I need to close the doors, this is very dangerous, but don't worry MX has all the answers, where are you from?"
"Nigeria?" She answered.
"Nigeria, oh Nigeria MX doesn't work in Nigeria, he

said," and giggled again. He almost ran from the counter to close the door and pulled the shatter down and warned her, "yeah, this is very dangerous mafia. It's worse than drugs. You have to be careful if you want to get involved in this kind of business."

"Where are you from?" She asked him. "Me? I was born in South Africa, I know Africa very well, Kenya, Namibia, Botswana, Zimbabwe, Zambia, I know everywhere but not Nigeria too many scammers not good for business. I am Patel, Patel is common Indian name, but you can call me Pat. Look outside, do you see the big sign, that's my name. But I have other businesses too. Money making businesses. If you need help I can help you. But not with this kind of business, I am warning you. Be very careful, with this kind of thing."
"I am not dealing in any business," she chided him. "Yeah, tell that to the police, I am not a fool, they all say that come, come." As he grabbed her hand and pulled her to the back office. He ran the money through the machine and for sure all the money was fake.
"I thought you said you only changed 100 euros, you have here 12,000 of worthless paper. That's a year in jail for every thousand euros, that'll make it twelve years in jail." She whimpered almost wailed. She was frightened and terrified, but she knew she had to be strong. She started complaining, "It was not my fault, these guys really fooled me," she cried out, "you see I did a job for them and they paid me with this kind of money."
"Not my fault either," he laughed, "that's your problem. Are we in agreement or should I call the police he said," as he took out a bottle of rubbing oil and added, "jail or no jail? Are you illegal here?" He intimidated her. "They'll send you back immediately, with nothing but only the clothes you are wearing." Chipo let out a heavy sigh. She gathered herself

and nodded her head. "Ok fine, give me a shot of whiskey, or vodka, at least something."
"I have something better," he squeaked and took out a pouch filled with small knots of white powder. He spread a line of cocaine on the desk.
"This wicked dirty old man knows his game," she thought. Chipo wondered how many times he had done this to other desperate women, she snorted the cocaine and chugged a half-pint bottle of che-ap whiskey. It didn't turn out as shoddy as she had expected. It was so much fun for her. She rubbed the oil on her hands, "Nein nein the oil is for big dad," he shouted, as he pointed to his little John, with his eyes closed. She took a glance at it and burst out laughing, it reminded her of her two year old cousin. "Just do the job," he insisted shaking, his hands were pressing between a cupboard and a wall. She tried her best to be professional, but she couldn't find his nuts. Before she could figure out the next move, he started humping, so fast like a little rabbit, his eyes suddenly bulging out, like he had been pricked. He was twisting and swaying, like a kid pressed with wee. He let out a baby cry sound. Chipo constricted her laughter as she assumed he had climaxed, though nothing had been discharged. He hurriedly pulled his pants up, feeling ashamed, but he was over the moon, with excitement.

"You can wash your hands in the sink. I told you don't mess around with big daddy," as he rushed out. Chipo looked into the mirror above the basin. She grinned and suppressed her laughter. He came in with a bottle of Jack Daniels in a plastic bag.
"Here take this. If you need anything, come back anytime, I am always here. Take this too he said," grabbing a packet of peanuts from the shelf.

The drugs were starting to get to her, she was just fidgeting around. "And here is some real money."

He squeezed 50 bucks into her hand. "Now you must go hurry up. I have customers coming soon, go hurry." In her head she busy was calculating, "50 bucks for a minute's work, which could be very profitable," she thought.

Chapter Twenty eight

Her situation had become worse. She was stuck with a bag full of useless money. She speculated that Marko had no idea that the money was fake. She wondered how he had become in possession of it, maybe he had been duped too. Unless of course if he was dealing in that kind of business. Her mind pondered and raced through a lot of theories. She was annoyed and disturbed by her own ignorance and naivety. She had been so much in love, that she had let her guard down and had allowed herself to be manipulated. Being desperate and lonely can make you gullible in a foreign place. It can be traumatizing and that can lead to changing your perceptions about humans.

She still had 500 euros of real money she had gotten from Susie, but that was emergency money, never to be touched. It was wrapped and hidden in Chamu's cellar without his knowledge.

"A weed smoker is never to be trusted especially if he is unemployed. The moment they run out of money they are capable of pawing anything," she reminded herself.

She met up with Chamu at the Mauerpark and updated him on the current situation. They agreed that she could come to his place anytime after 6:30 am. Because that's when his wife went to work, and she

had to leave around 5 pm before she got back.
"You have a friend for life, Chamu. I'll not forget you buddy," she said as she pulled out some packets of cigarettes she had nicked from Patel's shop.
"You might not believe it, but you'll know it soon."
"A Wey Yuh Naah Seh, Queen ah Queens, Zion, A Baaaaay, Wey di monie deh," Chamu shouted.

Mauerpark is an open-air entertainment zone in the heart of Berlin. It was packed with a lot of different types of acts. There were musicians, people performing acrobatics, karaoke, drum beaters, flea market.., It was a paradise for chilling and interacting. After a long chat with Chamu they joined his weed smoking partners who were sitting under a tree. She presented them with a bottle of Jack Daniels and their gloomy cloudy faces enlightened.

Ronni took the bottle and flipped it around smiling.
"Guys, you remember what happened last time we smoked and drank Jack Daniels." They all grinned.
"What happened?" Chipo asked curiously and they chuckled.
"Nothing good came out of it," Leo replied. "We ended up spending three years in jail," he snapped.
"Really? Oh hell, Chamu you never told me you were once in the slammer." Chipo said surprised.
"That was a holiday man. We had to detox, get rid of unhealthy substances in our bodies you know, clean up our system," Chamu declared.
"And thanks to who, it was all your fault Daniel," Leo yelled pointing at him. "You are the one who bought that Gora ganja, I had never smoked such weed. I mean think about it, Chimpanzees chew it before they mate," Leo elaborated.
"This seems interesting, so tell me more what happened?" Chipo insisted.
"It's quite an interesting story, if you take time to think about it," Daniel jumped in.

"Oh yeah very interesting indeed," Chamu said and laughed. "We were smoking at Leo's house," continued Daniel.
"No that's incorrect we had been smoking for two days," Chamu added.
"Oh yes, nonstop, at Leo's house Daniel admitted. "And guess who comes out with a master plan, Chamu." They all laughed.
"Chamu decided we needed more money for more weed and there was a bank across the road."

"Oh shit! Exclaimed Chipo. "No way."
"Hold on, yes he thought it was a good idea to rob a bank, that was directly opposite the apartment. So we hatched out a plan, which was to walk into the bank and take some cash." Daniel explained.
"Oh shit," Chipo jumped up excitedly, "And did you believe you were going to succeed." She asked.
"Well" Leo hijacked the story, "we walked outside the house, strolled like the Beatles crossing the zebra lines, towards the bank. Chamu was in front, followed by me, then Dani and Ronni were at the back. But the bank was closed because it was lunchtime, we didn't know that, yet we stayed right across the road."

Chipo burst out laughing. "Oh man, you guys are crazy"
"So we left and walked back to Leo's place," Ronni snatched the story.
"Which was again, across the road. We continued smoking and drinking Jack Daniels. After about an hour, we went back and robbed the bank."
"Well basically I demanded the cash with my buddies behind me, wearing no masks, just sunglasses" Chamu added giggling.
And they willingly gave us the money and we walked back across the road in the same format to Leo's apartment and continued smoking."

Chipo was laughing her ass off. "Within ten mins the whole building was surrounded by an army of swat squad." Chamu chuckled and they laughed. When the judge sentenced us he was laughing and he said you guys need to sober up. Leo concluded.
"Hey, guys do you remember Zeus?" Ronni asked,
"oh man that was some scary looking guy," Daniel said clapping his hands. "This guy was the bomb," he added.
"When we were locked up some Russians tried to bully us, as you can see we are all skinny and handsome huh."
Chipo roared her eyes. "None of us had been to jail before so we had no idea what to expect. The only experience we had was what we watched and saw on television," he elaborated.
"So naturally we were scared, thank God we didn't get raped, nope." He divulged.
"Oh damn shit," Chipo shouted.
"But these mean looking Russian guys," Leo continued, "wanted us to provide them with cigarettes all the time. And if we didn't offer them any they would threaten us. But we didn't have access to a lot of cigarettes only what our families brought us.
So as usual Chamu befriended this tall skinny guy, full of muscles."
"He was from Somalia," Dani yelled. "They called him Zeus in jail. He was believed to have killed nine people with his bare hands in his home country. And you know in jail word spreads very fast."
"Bloody hell nine people," she was alarmed.
"This guy never talked man," Ronni stated. If he liked you, he would just listen nod his head and grin."
"And agree to everything," Chamu chipped in.
"He never said no to anything, if you tell him, hey Zeus those guys are messing with me, they need to be taken care of. We have no idea what he did or say to them, but the guys never bothered us again."

"Oh man, Zeus... Zeus is the king. We send him 100 bucks every month. He is due to come out in about two years," Leo said as he pulled a joint.
" Phew, you guys have lived life, I don't think I would have survived in those circumstances," Chipo said choking from smoke. A group of other people joined them, among them was Lasti, from Zambia but had lived in Zimbabwe since childhood. He was quite a character, he was somersaulting, cartwheeling, and doing flips. He used to be a dancer in a music band and once worked in a circus. He didn't shy away from showing his skills and talents. He had a back-pack loaded with four bottles of Hennessy and diffe-rent types of juices.
"Whoa looks like its Christmas today," Chipo shou-ted.
"We celebrate Christmas every day my sister. I take Zimbabwe with me, wherever I go." He shouted ex-citedly.

Chipo was intimidated by the amount of alcohol and weed lying around. Smoking joints in public seemed so normal, no one cared about it. The mixture of the multicultural crowd was intense and very interes-ting. Almost every second person was from another country and people where grooving. There was no evidence of noticeable worries displayed by anyone. It was an open party. The atmosphere was awesome and the weather played along. It was a great place for networking and interacting.

"What's the occasion though?" She asked him.
But he just laughed.
"He got kicked out of the house by his lady." Chamu shouted.
"I am as free as a bird," Lasti declared. "Now I can do what I was born to do."
"And what is it that?" she asked.
He gave her this sheepish grin and chuckled.

"Let me show you, Chamu, Chamu Macheso encore," he shouted. Chamu obliged, and played his favorite song. Lasti started dancing, he had a strange way of moving. He could lock his knees and only move the lower parts of his legs simultaneously. Then he would twist his legs and kris cross them while creating a rhythm.
"Borrowdale dance babe, the horse dance," he screamed. A group of intrigued viewers stood by watching as he danced. Chipo enjoyed the moment, the mood reminded her of back home with her clique. Her worries were shielded away for a sec, but she kept an eagle eye on her backpack. Lasti and Chamu were well acquainted, a lot of people had gathered around and the group kept getting bigger and bigger.

She knew she was laughing, without actually being happy, she was smiling but wryly. It was all a show. Everything she did was for a reason, she was chatting and mingling as much as possible trying to find a suitable gap.

She came across Eduardo from Colombia. He was using a bong to inhale weed mixed with cocaine. Each time he inhaled, he would shake his head violently and let out a loud wolf cry.
Eduardo was a professional acrobatic. He told her he used to work in a circus training animals back home in Colombia. He ran away after he fell out with the mafia. He was using his Circus company to move drugs from one city to the other and across the border to other surrounding countries. One of his employees discovered their illegal, unlawful business and informed the police. But the police were part of the gang. So she was handcuffed and brought back to the circus. Eduardo was forced to shoot her and dissolve her in acid, not knowing she was five months pregnant. He only found out about

it when the husband came looking for her. He felt so much guilt and overnight he disappeared. The mafia went on to kill his family and relatives. He had only himself left in the world.

"The bong helps me sleep better at night." He told her. He didn't choke as he narrated his story, "I have seen far worse, things in my life. We all die at the end of the day," he reassured himself.
Chipo was hesitant to get involved in the bong business. After a few nudges, she tried it out. She had this rush of euphoria, intense excitement, she found herself dancing to bongo drums among a group of other revelers. She tried to do karaoke but her voice faded, but still the crowd cheered her on. The party was in high gear, as the masses were having a great time. In the middle of all that fun, Marko and Dino passed by.

Chamu gestured to her and she just nodded and shook her head, she had moved on for now. But somehow, Lasti had gotten wind of her situation and he took advantage of the long standing grudge he held against these guys. Being high on Hennessy and weed, he pulled Chipo from the crowd and stuttered "hey Chipo our puppies are here, yah these are the guys who messed you up hey," nah its okay, Chamu told me everything yah, now I have an excuse to do some damage, I won't allow anyone to mess around with my Zim sisters," he shouted as he approached them. She was confused.

There was no warning, nothing. He punched Dino, Dino flew to the ground. Marko tried to reason with him and he was body slammed. By the time people intervened, Marko and Dino were languishing on the ground and Lasti was already enjoying his drink. "That's why they call him Jokoniya, Awoooaaah" shouted Chamu laughing. Chipo had no idea what

that meant, but the message had been received. "Don't let anyone belittle you or fool you. If that happens just call me," he boasted
"There are all small boys. I can whip them with my belt like kids he said" as he guzzled his cognac. Chamu was rolling uncontrollably on the grass laughing, as Marko and Dino limped away like hyenas. She felt untouchable.

"Now I have a real bodyguard, a protector."
She thought to herself. The mood was so cool, so amazing. She sat down on a rock to chill a bit, and soon she hit it off with one chick, her name was Sia. They had so many things in common.

They talked about visiting different places and wanting to run a weed farm. The more they smoked and drank, the higher they got, and the more they became attracted to each other. They went to look for a toilet but being an open space, they had to walk further out to some trees. Without any hint, they started kissing. This was Chipo's first time to feel attracted to a woman, and Sia gave her the confidence and allowance to carry on. As they walked back from the bush Sia being the naughty one, would rub guys hair and she randomly gave one short man a wedge. That is she pulled his underwear out and tried to put it over his head. Before running away laughing. Sia made her become full of life, she was beautiful yet so simple, relaxed, and seemed very principled.

Chipo could not stop admiring her dark long hair with a body supported by African ass. She was easy to get along with. The more they talked, the more she fell for her. She was intelligent, logical, and very spiritual. Her big wide smile would cheer up anybody. Most guys that were around had their eyes on her, but she never took notice of it. Chipo was head over heels in love with her. Their chemistry was so strong you would think they had known each other for years. As they drank and smoked, Chipo realized she was a friend she could never have, maybe in the next life, she thought to herself.

The sooner she learned to let go of some things, the better. She didn't have time to experiment. She was a woman on a mission longing to find herself.
She needed to put her life together, without affording anyone the opportunity to know of her status or situation. She was afraid of being taken advantage of and her aim was to achieve her IT degree. That was her main focus. She was aware she might get lost along the way. She might be forced to do things she usually wouldn't do, but her objective was in the clear.

"Hey are you daydreaming," Sia nudged her. Chipo just smiled, "I wish I was like you," she mumbled, "How am I like?" She asked her.
"Well you are like you," and they both laughed.
"I have a feeling, I am almost certain, that guy there likes you. He has been looking at you the whole time." Chipo told her.
"Really, which guy?" That one she said as she pointed with her finger.
"Uh" she cracked up, "that's my little brother Alves," and they giggled like little girls.
"I think he is observing you, but he is very shy, watch, hey Alves come over here, I think she likes you," Sia shouted, but Alves just grinned and tucked himself into the crowd.

That night she slept at Michael's place. He was such a gentle soul. She had no idea how she met him or how she got hooked up with him. She had too many drugs in her system. She woke up and found herself in this beautiful huge apartment.

There was a note on the dressing table that read. "Please forgive me for this we had a very interesting conversation yesterday, there is something that you said to me that touched me and helped me in a way you'll never know. I know you might not remember what it was but it meant a lot to me.
Please don't be offended, the money is just that you paid for all the drinks last night, just a small token of appreciation, don't forget to close the door when you leave, hopefully, we'll see us again," cheers, Michael.

He had left 200 euros on the table. She thought of eating oxtail stew. She panicked, when she suddenly realized she had unknowingly used some of the fake money. She was pissed off with herself, she needed to get rid of it as soon as possible. She called Chamu up.

"Hey, Chamu should I bring some oxtail?"
"Him Naah Behave," he screamed.
"You have maize meal right,"
"Jah rises,"
"Cool see you in a bit,"
When she arrived at Chamu's place he was in a deep argumentative discussion with one of his friends Max.
"How would you feel? Every time your woman sprints to bed like a cockroach. Running to strip naked, katakatakata removing her clothes. As a man sometimes you have your own principals, your own plans. You jump in bed, you feel her thighs, uhh she is already naked, so now it becomes a routine, in out in out. No way man I can't live like that, me I want
to enjoy myself in my own house. No one wants things the easy way oh. It upsets me. And when I complain she says, I just wanted to make it easy for you now, hahaha," he mimics her voice.
"Easy for me my foot, is it so hard to remove a pant,

do I need a degree for that. I can just slice it with my nail if I want. I am a rude boy oh, I have warned her before, be discreet, cover yourself, and don't mess with my job oh. Don't just lay bare and expose yourself like that, it's not appealing. Let me be the man I want to be and take charge. Let me run wild with my own fantasies, I have different ways of how I want to discover that mysterious hidden gem, that has dethroned kings and Queens.

But if you just bare it like a bat suntanning, the mystery is lost. I want to fight and struggle for what is mine. For I believe if I suffer because of pleasure and I conquer. Let me feast with pride now, I have tamed the elusive mermaid." And he smoked his blunt, his eyes as red as peri peri.

"Don't let her bully you oh, it's your house now"

Chamu roared, "one solution to that" as he proudly sat up. "You need to punish her, punish her badly and hard, If she ever does it again, condone it sarcastically, but in your mind you must operate like a killer, be focused and nay her, give her a marathon nay, I swear, if you do it well well she will never throw away that pant again, she will always think twice. You can't afford to be taken for granted in your own house, man, be dominant."

"But oh boy admit that thing is sweet oh," Max yelled as they both laughed.

"Did I tell you about Pascal?"

"No what happened?" Chamu asked curiously.

"Remember that rich guy, with a blonde woman who is always at his gigs."

"The giraffe, the one that walks like an ostrich."

"Yeah that one, the guy invited him to his Villa for a drink and guess what happened, he begged him to sleep with his wife."

"Oh, oh, oh!"

"Yah man, he told him he has an agreement with his wife since he can't function anymore."

"But he is not that old now." Chamu replied.
"Some of these guys abused drugs at a very young age. He told him he can only use his tongue hey, he begged him. He told him he knows that the wife wants the real thing. So he is afraid if he doesn't come up with a plan she might start having an affair."
"Damn that's bitter."
"The only problem is the husband wants to be in the room, he wants to watch now."
"Eheh that boy must watch out oh, that guy will jump on him and do him too.
That reminds me, you know Abi is in jail, I feel sorry for that boy oh, he was just unlucky to meet such a cruel woman."
"You mean his wife"
Eh that Mandy woman, they have three kids together but she never gives him peace.
"What happened again?"
"You didn't hear, he is in jail now." As Chamu takes a pull of the joint.
"Abi is in jail, what did he do again, that guy can't even kill a fly."
"You are aware that they had separated."
"Sure I know that he was dating that Kenyan woman Natasha with big matakos."

"Exactly, he impregnated her and when Mandy found out that their relationship was getting too serious, she became bitter. Because she always thought Abi would one day come back to her. When that did not happen, what did she do? She banned
him from seeing the kids. That's when they started fighting, taking each other to court. The court granted them the same rights. That made her even more bitter, so she decided to set a trap for Abi, she invited him to her place pretending that she wanted to discuss something about the older son's behavior, you know that boy is naughty, he beats up

other kids. When Abi got to the house against the advice of his fiancee, Natasha didn't want him to go there alone. She told him that, the woman is wicked and he should be very careful. But you know Abi, he is naive and the ex-wife knew it. I heard when he got there, she was wearing only a pant and a small T-shirt, pretending like she was asleep, the kids were not home, yet 5mins before he arrived she had begged him to come early so that he could read a book for the youngest daughter. Women can be evil if they want to. The guy fell for it, she made him an offer he couldn't refuse, basically she coerced him into having sex with her. As soon as he left that apartment she called LARA the Rape Crisis and Counseling Centre, and you know how quick those guys are, there are rumors that they might have been waiting somewhere close by, because they were so quick. By the time Abi got home, police were already waiting for him. He was given four years in jail bro."
"Hey that's murder man, I pray for the kids," as Max rolled another joint.

"Chamu the water is boiling," Chipo shouted from the kitchen. In tough situations one meal of sadza will carry you throughout the day.

Sadza also is known as Ugali or Fufu in other countries is made of grounded maize meals and served with stew and vegetables.
Chamu was a master at preparing this special traditional dish. Chipo decided to take another long bath even though she had showered at Michael's place. She thought she had to take advantage of every opportunity available.

"Yaaa people saaample it," Chamu called out, as he walked in carrying plates of food.
"Oh man you do me good oh," shouted Max.

"After this I can doze off well well." Chipo added. Chipo dipped her finger in the sauce and sucked it. Sweat ran down her face as she devoured the food. "This is very delicious oh, Chamu, lekker thank you." She took a bite of the oxtail and followed it up with a fist of Sadza. Her mind raced back to the villages of Chirimanzi, at the Muchena homestead.

Every school holiday as kids, her parents used to send them to the villages. To herd cattle and help out with housework or work in the fields. Chipo loved herding cattle with her cousin brother Makiwa. One day they went out, as usual with their herd of cattle. The weather was partly sunny and partly cloudy. They walked for almost eight kilometers until they found greener pastures for their animals to graze. A lot used to go on during these pasturing periods. Some kids from other villages would challenge you to a fight or a race. If you lose or win at the end your bull had to fight their bull.

The Muchenas owned one of the best bullfighters in the village, so they were constantly provoked by gangs from other villages. Makiwa was a natural born fighter and very few people dared mess around with him. On this particular day it was quite. They were busy playing Nhodo, which is Shona traditional children's game, where you have lots of stones in a shallow hole and you try to pull each stone out one by one while tossing another stone in the air and catching it before it drops to the ground. As they played the game they didn't pay much attention to the animals or their surroundings. Out of nowhere came this roar of thunder. Lightning struck one of the trees next to them. They escaped death by whiskers and they were scared and terrified. They just started running in the direction of the village. There were a sudden heavy down pour.

Within minutes the whole sky had changed. There was thunder and lightning and the clouds be-

came aggressively dark. It was such an evil sight. Chipo was running as fast as she could but Makiwa was way ahead. The cattle were scared too, they were all galloping towards the village. It was chaos they were mooing and rustling, running so fast that some of the cattle overtook them. When they got to the river, it was almost flooding. Makiwa was in no mood for joking and Chipo sensed it. He told her to get hold of the tail of one of the beasts. But warned her to be careful. That once she got to the edge of the river to let the tail go otherwise the cow would kick her back into the water. She didn't think twice about it.
The urge to be heroic kicked in. Her fantasies suddenly became alive. It was a dangerous mission, one slip and she could be swept away. She grabbed the tail of one of the cattle and followed Makiwa who was already halfway through. She did not want to wait for three days for the water to subside. Once she got to the river bank she didn't let go, and the beast didn't kick her back into the water. She gave her a pat and they ran along with each other until they got home. Makiwa never waited for her. She found him in the kitchen eating sadza with oxtail. No one said anything. She just threw herself to the ground with her wet clothes and joined the race. It was a mountain of sadza and a dish full of oxtails. She had a fist of sadza in one hand and a chunk of oxtail on the other hand. They cleaned everything out. It was so embarrassing for them because the food was meant for six people. After the job was done, out of shame they began rounding up the dogs pretending to feed them. Chipo was proud of her adventure, she was running around telling everyone. Makiwa warned her not to brag about it to anyone otherwise he would be beaten up for exposing her to danger. That night Makiwa slept on top of the roof, her uncle was hunting him down. The next day he was mad at her. He took her to a nearby

river tricking her that he wanted to teach her how to whistle.
He told her that she had a thick tongue. And she needed to get bitten by a little black bug, that looked like a beetle and lived in water. After every bite he would advise her to fold her tongue and blow the air out, trying to whistle. By the end of the day her tongue was swollen, she could not talk. Miraculously the next day she discovered she was able to whistle. She only found out it was a ruse after she caught him laughing about it with her older cousins.

Ever since that day Chipo developed a love for ox-tail. She lamented the day Masivanda had to be put down. She still has the end of the tail as a souvenir.

Chapter Twenty nine

Chamu shook her violently, "hey wake up it's almost 5 pm."
"What?" She jumped up.
"That's the problem with eating sadza in the afternoon, it fills you up. When you are done eating, you have to catch a nap." Chamu said grinning.
"Oh, man! That was a long sleep," she complained as she yawned. She hurriedly walked to the bathroom, wiped her face, and cleaned up. She removed any noticeable traces of a woman being in the house.

She strolled aimlessly enjoying the warm weather. The good thing about summer is, that so many people loiter around, so it's very easy to blend in. She needed to find a job or any other way of making money. But without a work permit it was almost impossible. Someone told her about doing a black job. Working without papers. She found one job, cleaning dishes in a Chinese restaurant. She was getting paid below minimum wage but she was just happy to be doing something. During the day she would sleep at Chamu's place and in the evening she would work until late.
She made sure she provided Chamu with cigarettes and alcohol as a token of appreciation. The little money she got helped to maintain her girl's standards. It was a lot of work and communication was a disaster. On one particular day, her boss called her, asking her if she could come to work early because they

had a lot of reservations. The place was full of people and the Chef was getting pissed off by everything. He was hurling insults and throwing dishes recklessly. After six hours of none stop working, Chipo took a cigarette break.

She sat across the restaurant by a street bench. Her feet were painful from standing for long periods. As she rolled her right angle, she caught sight of a border control minivan parked in an alley. She thought nothing of it, when she stood up to walk back to the restaurant the whole place was surrounded by police. Searching for people working without papers. She made a smooth u-turn and removed her apron. She casually took out a cigarette and walked slowly away, expecting someone to call her back. She was worried and afraid that one of the officers might have seen her. She stood by the train station, observing the restaurant with a group of other passengers. From a distance, she could see clearly what was happening in the restaurant. Some of the customers were customs officers. They had guns and dogs. One young lady she had asked for a lighter earlier on was among the agents. She came outside the restaurant and was frantically looking for something.
Chipo stepped back and hid among the crowd. The train came and she disappeared smelling of duck.

Since that day she never looked for a black job again. She couldn't afford to get caught, without having sorted her papers out. Chipo became too familiar with the streets, she could walk from Warschauerstr to Nollendorf Platz. Catching the train was too risky and she was never in a hurry. At the back of Nollendorf was a popular street known as Kurfürstenstraße. There you would find all the cheapest prostitutes from Eastern Europe. The girls were charging any amount from 10 euros to do different types of sexual

acts. They were scattered all over the street. That's where she met Nigel. He was working the streets, hustling. He had his own small business going on and he welcomed her with open hands. Nigel took her to a place where his boys were peddling weed, that was his specialty. Chipo saw groups of African guys, in street corners, behind dura walls, and at train stations. It was as if they were selling sweets in the streets. The hustling was aggressive. They would approach anyone. The boys had no proper system of running their business. They would play loud music scarring the people away. It looked
as if they were higher than the customers.

"Once in a while, we get raided by the police, but it's of no use, they know we have no other way of surviving. Most of all these guys are asylum seekers or people who do not exist at all," Nigel told her.
"Meaning they are not in the German database, like yourself. Some need three hours to commute to come over here and some are based on the outskirts of Berlin."
After a week of moving around with Nigel, Chipo came up with a plan. Nigel had developed some form of trust for her, he was happy to tell her about his dealings. She showed a lot of enthusiasm and respect for him. He was paying for her food and drinks and she could chill at his apartment.

"Listen let's be a little bit smart, things can be done in a more organized fashion. I mean you have it worked out, money is coming in. But you could double your sales without attracting too much attention."
"I am listening go on, I am a good listener now" Nigel said. If you see ten African guys standing in a corner, with hoods covering their heads. I mean come on, you know how that is portrayed by most people. What are you gonna think?
Definitely everyone can tell they are selling drugs,

right? Not everyone smokes weed and this might upset some of the residents and business owners. So why don't we organize it more professionally? Bring all the guys together, talk to them, and come to an agreement. Put two guys selling at every station. They don't keep the weed with them, as two other guys can act as lookouts. And they have the weed stashed somewhere close by," Chipo suggested. "At least that way it's clean and organized." She added.

Nigel liked her way of thinking, so he kept her close, she was like a little sister to him. He protected her and he never made any sexual advances towards her. She wouldn't have minded though. Hey the guy was a street boss, he was taking care of her. The new system worked for a couple of hours, but after some of the deadbeats had smoked and drank alcohol, no one cared anymore. She was making thirty bucks for looking after the weed, and sometimes she would crush at Nigel's crowded apartment. But it was never safe there and she warned him a couple of times not to entertain his runners after peddling. But most of the guys were from out of town and needed a place to stay.

After selling the weed the guys would drink themselves to stupor, and then they would fight and argue against each other. They had no respect for the neighbors. Sometimes they would play loud music and be very disruptive. The guys were just hard to handle, they had lost all sense of reasoning. It's not that they were arrogant, they just didn't know any other way of expressing their anger. She thought it was caused by the stress of having no direction, not knowing what the future holds.
They felt they were being treated as social pariahs. It was not out of their choice. They sensed they were being marginalized and suppressed. One had to be in their situation to understand why they were

doing, what they had to do. Some of the guys were just too young and had been through a lot already in life. They had lost respect for any form of humanity. She was hanging out with Nigel a lot and she got to witness a lot of stuff first hand.

Nigel went into an emotional downward spiral and he started taking cocaine and gambling. With the money he made from weed, he would use it to support his other habits. He became depressed, he would spend the whole day in betting shops. And in the evenings, he was drinking and snorting cocaine.

"This is the trend right now, he tried to justify his behavior. Everybody is doing it, you need to try it too," he said, wanting to convince her. She had heard the same words before and she was quite familiar with the outcome.
"You are going to crash and burn Nigel, you'll end up six feet under if you don't change your ways soon man," Chipo warned him.
"Once you go overboard it's a slippery road to get back bro, man up," she would tell him. But all this was falling on deaf ears. He would make money from his peddlers, sometimes 10,000 euros a month, but within two weeks he would have squandered it all. He had fallen deep into an abyss, a bottomless dark hole.

It was not fun hanging out with him anymore. Chipo noticed upsetting and heartbreaking changes manifest themselves in him. She later learned that he was in the process of bringing his wife and children and the boat they were in had capsized.
"I think I ,m going mad, am I hallucinating? I'm going to kill you all!" He would shout. Sometimes, he could just stare at nothing for long periods.
He developed panic attacks and was suspicious of anyone who looked at him. The guy was losing his

mind. It was becoming scary and dangerous to be around him. One night as they were driving around, he braked so hard by the traffic lights and he just passed out.
Chipo being scared, the police might get called, got out, and ran leaving him slumped to the steering wheel. He was helped by some strangers who re-suscitated him. He became reckless he would carry drugs in his pockets, something he never did before. His peddlers began to take advantage of his state. He could not remember how much weed he had distributed. He was not paying his suppliers anymore and they were chasing after him. He was losing control of what was once a decent form of income.
She warned him several times but the more she did the more he accused her of being a snitch and working for the police.

Chipo reduced her dependence on Nigel. She revived her business relationship with Patel.
One evening she got very lucky. Patel saved her. Whenever she needed something she would visit him. He would give her money, alcohol, packets of cigarettes and he would allow her to just hang around. He would make her dust-up the goods and clean up the shelves. They had a mutual agreement. She had told him she was a Muslem so no sex before marriage. As long as he had his happy ending episodes. They had an understanding and he was very happy with it.
This particular day, she found Patel with his son Esmail. He asked her for a special favor and gave her five hundred bucks up front. He told her his 26 year old son was a virgin and in his words, "he wanted to experience the jungle fever." For five hundred bucks Chipo did not hesitate. The job was expeditiously executed. She had just killed two birds with one stone, "easy money," she cheered herself up. She walked out with a thousand bucks that night.

As she was a few feet away from the kiosk it started raining so hard, that she had to run back and seek shelter in their shop. Esmail was getting all whacked up and his father begged him not to fall in love. She sat with them smoking and drinking some free alcohol.

Chapter Thirty

When it had stopped raining, she left Patel's shop. It was cold and wet. She began to feel unwell. The closest place was Nigel's apartment and she didn't have anywhere else to go. She left Patel's kiosk shop around midnight. It took her longer than usual because the trains had been delayed. Usually a journey of about an hour, took her almost two hours more.

As she was about to turn left into the parking area of Nigel's place, she noticed police vans. She saw Nigel's street boys pressed against the wall, some were pinned to the ground. She kept on walking like she didn't belong there. She looked straight ahead, did not blink or breath, she was so stiff and afraid. She walked for almost a mile, without turning back or knowing where she was going. If she had been there thirty minutes earlier she would have been taken too. She thought to herself. Her body and clothing were wet and full of sweat yet it was cold. She drank a shot of Jaegermeister she had in her jacket. She started feeling dizzy, her legs were giving in. She didn't know what to do or where to go as it was 3 am.

From a distance she noticed a telephone booth. She barricaded herself inside and sat on the floor. She took a sip of the whiskey she had stolen from Patel. It was doing her no good. She started vomiting and felt very weak. With fatigue and this sharp pain at

the back of her head, she thought she was going to die. She passed out for at least an hour, only to be awoken by a loud thunderstorm which caused the cold wind to forcefully flush the door open. She was surrounded by vomit and a broken whiskey bottle. Feeling dizzy and trying to figure out what had happened, she was completely helpless.
It was easy to mistake her for a junkie or a homeless person, for which she was but in denial. She wiped her mouth with a piece of newspaper and staggered towards the train station. It had started to rain heavily. The time was dragging and the subway would only begin to operate after 4 am.
She bought a day ticket and went right at the back of the train, where she coiled herself up on the seat. She had no idea where the train was heading, but she knew it was a local train, so it would go back and forth. The train went up and down at least 4 times until It was 7 am and working people began filling up the stations. One old lady regarded her with a contemplative eye. She got up and put five euros next to her. Chipo felt useless, but she was too weak to act it out. She was smelling of alcohol and vomit and looked like a zombie.

When Chamu saw her, he was in shock. He backed off when he came close to her. She had this horrible foul smell. She was stinking and looked sick.

"Oh, man! Did you sleep next to a skunk, where you scavenging the whole night? You look like Zuze man, (*a well known sleepless naked madman from Kadoma*) and you smell like Zuze.
What a mess! Bless Jah you are alive," he ran a hot tub for her and she sat there for almost an hour. He made her hot chocolate.
"Chocolate for another chocolate," he tried to cheer her up. Chipo slept like a dead log. Chamu tried his best to make her feel better. He prepared soup and

tea for her. He went out and bought a lot of fruits and vegetables. "You gonna need a lot of vitamins, something is not right with you, oh?" he said shaking his head. "It's better if you have to sleep here today, in this house. You look, terrible man, you are not in good shape to be out in the streets," he insisted, but Chipo was hesitant. "How about your wife?" She said.
"Don't worry about that, I know how to handle her. It's only for a day, you need to rest," he assured her. "I'll tell her that you missed your flight and you are a long lost sister. Just don't worry about it."
"Thank you Chamu, I don't know how to pay you back man," she whispered.

"I know a doctor, he is a back door doctor we should go and see him," he told her.
He knew she didn't have a medical insurance card, so she could not go to the hospital or see a private doctor. She ate her soup, drank her tea, ate some of the fruits and felt much better. She was still feeling weak and tired. They went to see this back door doctor. When they arrived they found about thirty people in the waiting room, and it was almost 6 pm. No one talked to anyone.
The atmosphere felt weird, it was too silent. Most of the patients were beautiful women and heavily built guys.
"Chipo isn't the only one without a medical card." She thought. They were all in the same boat. It's always a good feeling when you see someone in the same situation as yourself. When her turn came, Chamu told her to wait for him until he had talked separately with the doctor. He went in by himself and she could partially observe them through the gap of the door. They chatted, bump fisting each other.

After their small talk, he called her inside. Chipo expected to see someone in jeans and a white coat.

The doctor was massive, a giant of a man. He was dressed up in an expensive blue navy suit with a scuff around his neck. It was strange though that he worked alone, with no assistance. He was very welcoming and over friendly too.

"Hello there," he said as he stretched out his hand, "They call me Dr. Neutrons, you wanna know why, because after I am done with you, you'll feel like you have been split into two, just like in matrix," he said giggling.
"Open your eyes wide, let me see what you hiding underneath those angel beauties. You look isolated, unstable, and I also understand you don't have a medical card or any money either, not even a bond note," he chuckled, "You are the 5th person I know from Zimbabwe, beautiful country I hear, how do you intend to pay me then, my darling?"

"I am sure I can find some money to pay you, sir," her manners kicked in. "You look young, very strong, great genes, beautiful to the wandering eyes. What could be wrong with you? Have you been up to no good?"

"Can you give me a cough please, breathe in, breathe out, your breathing is fine, heart rate is a bit amiss but good. You have so much to offer," he said as he touched her stomach, "can you please undress for me, for big Doctor Nu," as he grinned.
"Really do I have to?" She asked.
"If you want me to help your ass, yes," and he giggled again, "Don't be shy, Big Daddy has seen it all. I am sure it's not the first time to undress in the presence of a man," he scoffed. She did as she was told. He observed her body from top to bottom and shook his head.
"You are something else," he said as he rubbed his hands and placed them on her tummy. "Can you pee

for me?" His benevolent eyes shot up and when he saw the look on her face, he clarified. I mean in that small cup." He squeaked and let out a sheepish grin.

Chipo found it hard to make anything out of him. It was difficult to take him seriously. "Do I really have to pee?" She asked feeling insecure.
"Don't worry just a little test, for illicit drug use," he grinned. "Welcome to my world, I chose the best profession. Yes you must pee, pee in that plastic tumbler," he sternly stared at her.
"I'll look away, no worries," he said as he turned his back. "I can hear you," he called out and laughed. Chipo didn't know how to react. She just ended up laughing too. She had no choice, otherwise, he would demand his money upfront. He sniffed her urine and pretended to drink it.

"Nice and warm golden color," he said as he looked at her suspiciously, "looks like you have been naughty. Was it flaccid, did your lips swell?"
Chipo was confused, his condescending attitude made feel inferior. "You are pregnant," he blurted.
"I can see the babies swimming in there, but let me be absolutely sure here."
Chipo gave a big sigh, and wondered,, "How could I be pregnant?" The doctor just laughed. She started thinking, definitely not from Patel. She had not slept with anyone without protection since she left Marko. Oh shit! It couldn't be that asshole, her mind wrest-led with her thoughts.
"Yep, you are pregnant for almost three months."
"But I had my periods all this time."
"Me too," he answered and laughed, "you can go home, think about what you want to do with this mess. If I were you, I would abort it and make so-mething out of my life. I mean you have no man, no money, you are alone, it's going to be tough."
"There is no way I am keeping this fetus," she

murmured. "Any memory of this guy must be erased from my brain, I can't afford to be fucking pregnant. My parents would kill me," she was lost in her thoughts. "Don't worry," he whispered as he put his hands on her shoulder, "why don't you dress up and come and see me tomorrow. You are an amazingly beautiful woman," he said and smiled. "A young lady, mature beyond her years. Take this card and be on time 9 pm sharp. I'll deal with all your problems. Go on, there are a lot of other patients waiting outside." She grabbed the card and turned to go.

"Chipo," he called after her, "tomorrow 21 pm," as he wrote in his diary. "Good, see you then in some hours and consider it gone," he chuckled, and cracked up, "I am a doctor of doctors."
"By the way, did I tell you that one of my finest best friends is from Zim, Yep, we studied at the same university. He lives in Canada now. Aka Sigh, a very energetic, intelligent charming fellow, with dreadlocks bigger than Bob Marley's. He chose the wrong profession though, he should have been a lawyer or a politician, hard to win an argument with him.
He once told me, a farmer is like a doctor he can never die from eating his own crops. He knows the ins and outs of every fruit.
Are you a fruit Chipo?
Do you think you should be eaten?" He burst out laughing. She just scoffed, shook her head, and walked out.

She found Chamu outside smoking a blunt. He was looking at her, waiting for her to say something.
"Ignorance is bliss," She yelled out. He looked confused. "Huh you ok?"
"You are better off without knowing."
"As long as you are healthy, did he charge you?"
"Oh no, he was cool, not yet though, I have another life-changing appointment tomorrow." "He is a good

doctor, my sister, he helps all my friends, for a few favors, sometimes for free. Maybe you should smoke some weed," he suggested.
"That sounds like a million-dollar idea and drink some alcohol too," she proclaimed.

"Babylon Jah love, Big Man ting," he shouted.

Chapter Thirty one

Chamu's wife was short, stout, and kind of pompous. She was nonetheless kind and funny.
"It's a pity we meet for the first time and you are not feeling well," she said as she sorted out the seeds of her marijuana. "Let me help to put a smile on your pretty face. You know that a dog is a man's best friend. If you don't believe it, lock your dog and your wife in the boot of the car for about thirty minutes, when you open the boot, which one is really happy to see you?" She chuckled and giggled loudly whilst cutting the butt of her heavily loaded joint.
"You must come to visit more often Chipo," she said in between laughing before she could answer, Ch-amu stepped on her shoe with his foot under the table.
"I'll, that's a promise," she replied. "Next time I'll stay a bit longer, and by the way, I think you have the wrong profession. You should try to do stand up comedy."
The Dolby surround system was clean and clear. Only reggae music played in the background. They had Jamaican color lights flickering in the background. The room was dimly lit and Chamu and his wife were a perfect match. They got along so well, It was as if they lived in their own world. Maybe it was because of the common love of smoking weed.
After a few joints, and with the place turning into a chimney, Chipo seized to exist as they were chatting and flirting with themselves. The thing about weed

is once it's in you, it tends to control your mood, your attitude and it gives you that extra boost, that you become limitless. Chipo felt it that night. They were so loud she didn't know what kind of games they were playing, but it was quite serious. It sounded more like Monica Seles was playing tennis against Hulk Hogan, high squeak pitch vs a deep husky thud.
"You guys need soundproof walls," Chipo told him the next day. He just smiled and walked away.

"This guy your doctor friend, how well do you know him?" She asked anxiously.
"Well, he helps a lot of people like I said yesterday. I find him personally to be quite a reasonable person. He is cool, down to earth, you have nothing to fear. He is a man of his word. If he says he'll do something, he'll do it," he replied. "How are you feeling anyway?" he asked.
"Could be better," she said as she sipped her wine. She had to be mentally prepared. She had made up her mind, so she wasn't worried. She just didn't care. She had so much hatred for Marko, that anything associated with him, she was willing to terminate, execution style. She had become so mean and so intent. "Nah I'll take it out, do away with it," she grunted.

She went into the bathroom and looked into the mirror. She wanted to see herself repeat, the same words. "I am on my own, I am going to do what it takes, to save myself. I'll not regret anything and I'll not feel any remorse. No fatherless kids, she shouted and continued. Everything I am facing is a challenge, and I am going to come out a winner. Everything that is happening to me is only going to make me stronger. I am in this life to live it and not to be lived by it. There is no more looking back."
She looked aggressive as she stood there for a while staring at herself.

Chapter Thirty two

When she got to the doctor's other office, it was more like an apartment that looked like a pharmacy. There was a lot of medicine lying around, papers thrown everywhere, and so much literature packed in cabinets. He opened the door with a smile of a successful man. He was wearing tights as pants and a tank top with ever-active logo embroidered in front. He was comfortable enough to parade and horse talk while his manhood suffocated and searched for loose soil.

"My house is my oasis, full of endless exotic flowers that blossoms in darkness. I welcome you for a ride only the blessed get to experience. A man who respects another man and treats all women like hidden treasure, deserves to be called a king. And every king needs an exotic flower that blossoms without air or sunlight," he declared as he rubbed her cheeks, laying bare his intentions, leaving her blushing and speechless.
She was quite impressed at the package on display. It brought back memories she had long forgotten. Teds flushed in her head, the man who had instilled life in her at a very young age. She hid a smile as she remembered him modeling around the lounge in the same type of tights. And that used to scare the living daylights out of her.
"You are right on time," he erupted, "I was just getting ready for the biggest night of my life.

"Well 9 pm is 9 pm," she answered. "I am glad you know that, please feel free, make yourself comfortable. Uh, wine or whiskey?" He asked
"You have cognac?" She requested. He gave her a naughty look.
"I got the best," he replied and asked. "Ice or no ice."
"Two ice cubes, thank you."
"Let's talk a bit about you," he said as he offered her a half-full glass. "Talk about me, about what?" She proclaimed innocently.
"Well, there are certain precautions that have to be taken into consideration. And you should also know that there are always consequences to these kinds of procedures."
"I am not interested in counseling, I am fully aware of the consequences and believe me, I have meditated about it," she said and drank the cognac in one go.
"We could become very good friends, I admire your attitude but you have to understand, I am not taking advantage of you in any way. You don't have to do anything you feel uncomfortable with. Who knows one day I might need your help. Allow me to ease your pain, save your future. In the jungle, there are no rules. If a lion limps, the hyenas will attack, are we in agreement?"
She filled her glass and downed the drink like water.
"Some music then," he suggested as he did a two-step walking towards the stereo.
"Picture this I want you to relax and excite your mind, at the same time. No one starves in my house, satisfaction beyond guaranteed. Think of a place so beautiful, that your imagination will run wild. And then this place becomes filthy and inhabitable. All pipes and valves get clogged, destroyed. Everything has to be reconstructed. New blood infusion until all is squeaky clean again, wouldn't that put a smile on your face." Chipo was lost in her own world, the cognac was working its magic.

"You still have your jacket on, you don't feel safe?" He asked her.
"That's it, no wonder why I am feeling so hot. I didn't realize it," She replied. "I do have some stuff in here, that need to be maintained under a certain temperature. You shall become reborn again my god given flower," he continued, and went on "everything shall become alive again. Your dream of a wealthy life, owning your own house by the beach, far away from anything else. Where you'll feel secure and loved. Where you'll be at peace with your surroundings, with no one around, but just you and the birds, dressed in nothing but a straw hat, completely butt naked, and me observing your every movement a few feet away." He whispered as he removed her jacket.
Chipo was getting high from the weed she had smoked before and drunk from the alcohol.

Dr. Neutrons knew his job well. It was like a bear falling on top of a rabbit and he foretold her of the pain to come. She wondered what made elephants run so fast at short distances. She pictured the number of sperm whales stored in their belly.
She debated on whether she should have pleasure out of it or play dumb. Dr. Neutrons was not in the mood for fooling around. His face had transformed into a scary creature. If she was to survive this encounter, then she needed to be in a different world.

Her mind switched to the first day, Teds had plowed her plain thonged field. She remembered him smelling the grass, telling her its gonna rain, she felt him feeling the texture of the leaking walls. He uprooted the bushes and pulled the weeds out, whilst massaging the soil as the ground swelled up, bulging out, adjusting for a proper landing.
She observed him plant his seeds and sprinkled the plants. She felt the roots sprouting, spreading into

every vein. It was glorious and satisfying. Her damp body became slippery and flooded. The spirited captured soldiers were quickly flushed into oblivion.
She smiled slyly at the seemingly inevitable victory but only to be flipped over violently. Her vision switched to Graeme. That dude could make it rain like a Waterfall.
She remembered Ted threatening her, "if you ever touch that Waterfall guy again, I am going to snap your neck out." She was becoming a bit hazy and more like in a vegetative state. She needed reinforcement. The spirit of MaMoyo, her totem was dying to be unleashed, to seek vengeance. Her eyes popped out as if her nipples had been electrocuted. Masibanda was scuffling with MaMoyo, squeezing each other's breath out. They had woken up the beast of Mutare , and provoked the ghost of Mutoko. They were now free to roam and were on a roll, she had summoned and commanded, the souls of her ancestors, gran of her grannies. As he desperately tried to fathom the ocean and tear her into pieces, his eyes suddenly bolted out, choked and frozen.
His back stiffened as the shadows of the unknown warriors hovered above him. Lifting the heavy burden, off her cursed back. She watched her soul stare awkwardly at the old fighting bear, losing what it thought was an easy meal. As he struggled to run uphill, almost snapping the foot of a mountain goat, he winced and stumbled, fell on his back, rolled over, hunger and thirst in his eyes, as its meal invitingly lay in wait. Out of breath, out of strength, eyes glazing, snarling like a dog refusing defeat, he clutched her ankle with his paws. Not willing to give up, she mewed like a cat and smiled.
"You think you can come to my house, brutalize me, pummel and abuse me.
Well, I am gifted and a step ahead of you. I know each and every corner of my oasis, my weapons are invisible, hidden in every sac and are very effective.

When I start fighting back, you better be at your best," she bragged about herself.
She felt a new energy and power flow in her body. She poked him cautiously like a dead lion, waiting for a sign of life.
"You got no idea, old man," she downed the rest of her cognac and poured some on the floor, celebrating victory with her ancestors. She pulled a cigarette and made smoke rings while lying on her back with her knees up.

"Yeah I have faced similar foes before, ask Ted and Graeme, tied them ass up, beat that one," she silently propped herself, seeking assurance.
For some reason, her surroundings had become battlegrounds.
"You wanna listen to my heartbeat," she chuckled.
He grinned and wormed himself towards her.

After what seemed like an eternity, he got up and blended some juice.

Chapter Thirty three

"This is papaya juice and pineapple juice, some natural remedies to soothe you out. After this, I want you to take a hot shower."
"No more cognac?" She asked eagerly.
"No that's a hormone booster," he said and laughed. "We don't follow any protocols, usually any form of alcohol is prohibited, so is grapefruit juice."
"So why are you giving me all these things then?"
"Because I am a doctor and I know how to treat my patients. Here put these pills under your tongue and put this in baby Chipo, when you are done with showering. Be prepared for some heavy bleeding, hemorrhage. There will be abdominal pain, yes, but it's part of the procedure, you will feel weak, dizzy, nauseated. You will not die. Don't worry. This is where you require my services."

That day she was beaten, stabbed, suffocated, and executed. She spilled blood. It was like a chicken slaughterhouse. When it was finally done, she had mixed feelings. He gave her some more medicine. She didn't want to look at the products of her conception. "You can stay until you are fully fit, my home is your home," he told her. She just curled herself and slept.
Dr. Neutrons did his best to make her feel comfortable. He gave her presents daily, basis, perfumes, handbags, and money.
He was very calculated, charming, and more active

when he was under the influence, which was his greatest weakness and strength. He had weed for breakfast, cocaine for lunch and both for dinner. He was high all the time but he had his business under control. He allowed her to stay for a couple of days and dressed her the way he fantasized. She loved it. "At least he buys me new clothes," she would joke. During that period she witnessed some strange movements.

He would pop in and out with different elegant, well-dressed women, and disappeared for hours behind closed doors. At one point, there were three of them living in the apartment. After four days Chipo was strong enough to go back to the streets. She found Chamu playing his guitar and singing:

"Out of the light, the rays shine
Out of the trees, the birds sing
If you look deep down your soul,
there is a ray of light,
that will sing the song of the water,
As the waves swell the wind shall blow
If you look deep down your soul."

"Wow, you come up with a new song every day," Chipo said clapping her hands. "Soon you will be the next Oliver Mtukudzi," she added.

Chamu was as high as a kite, his eyes were so small. He looked drowsy, blinded by the light.

"My sistren one love," he muttered, "oh is this for me?" he asked when he noticed her holding a whole pack of cigarettes. She put her new clothes into the cellar and slept as she needed the energy for the long night.

Chapter Thirty four

With Nigel gone, Chipo didn`t have anyone to chill with. She would go on long aimless walks trying to figure out how she could improve her situation. She came across an African bar -restaurant called Africa one.
She sat inside the bar. Most of the people were speaking Swahili and she figured out they were from Kenya or Tanzania. As the night dragged on, more customers filled the place.
There was one particular regular woman, who was abusing alcohol. She would absorb a shot of tequila and guzzle her glass of beer in one go. Most of the guests seemed to be familiar with her antics, as they scoffed at her and minded their own business. She was an earthquake of a woman loud and aggressive. When she talked the whole bar would turn their heads and protest silently.
They knew her well enough to respect her abusive temper.
And then the inevitable happened, she provoked and disrespected a well known local musician.
A Tanzanian guy called Mani, she accused him of having smoked all her weed and of wetting her bed. They were quarreling and she put him in a headlock before swinging him like a rag against the wall. She was short but as tough as a bull rhino. When Mani got up, he wanted to walk away but she took a needle out of her bra and poked him a couple of times on his chest, leaving him with dots of blood on

his shirt. The owner of the bar ran and tackled her to the ground. A few other customers joined in and chased her out, but after a couple of minutes she came back and threw a big stone hitting an innocent customer on the shoulder and ran away.
The bar was full of drama and entertainment as two women battled it out dancing on top of tables.

In one corner was a group of well dressed, curved beautiful Kenyan women. They were celebrating the return of their friend Sontia who had been incarcerated in Brazil, South America. They invited Chipo to join them for a wash down. Chipo cringed at the thought of being jailed in Brazil. "Jesus Christ!"
She said in disbelief and continued "You have some of the world`s most dangerous criminals in those jails," Sontia just smiled.
"Every one of us here has been in jail for one reason or the other," Sontia baffled her. She talked about her experiences and agony, and her journey from Germany to Brazil. They listened with glee and levity. Sontia had befriended a Nigerian man, she had met in a club. The guy who she called Texus, had swept her off her feet and lavished her with love and gifts. They spent almost every day together. They would meet for dinner and they would go dancing together. Most of the time they would drive around, meeting some of his friends and business partners. He told her he was into import and export of cars. He flew with her to Spain for three days on a holiday, and stayed in a five star hotel. They drank the most expensive liquor, ate lobsters and caviar.
He introduced her to some of his female companions, she felt like she was part of the family. She had met his brothers, sisters and his uncle. He had trusted her with a delivery of 15,000 euros to a business partner.

In three months they had planned to move into a

new apartment together. They were making future plans and for Sontia, she was so excited, as she had never been in such a relationship before. She was head over heels. She rarely had time for her friends. It was because he was spending so much time with her. When he suggested he wanted to propose, he came up with a brilliant plan. He was going to do it in a romantic way. He would take her somewhere on an Island, surrounded by water and sand beaches. So they decided to fly to Brazil to an Island called Ilha de Tinhare. It was the first time for her to fly outside of Europe ever and she was ecstatic, over the moon. She was blissed out. The place was paradise, the weather, the beach, the hotels, the people, it was as if you were on another planet.
They spent the first days chilling, relaxing at the beach.

On the fourth day, he went on his knee in full view of all the guests at the bar. The euphoria of marriage and having kids made her drunk and blind in love. They were supposed to stay in Brazil for two weeks but Texus received an urgent telephone call the next day and he had to attend an important business meeting in Argentina. When she went swimming that morning, Texus had gone to buy some souvenirs and when she came back, she found him waiting in the room with their bags already packed and ready to go.
"This business deal is what I have been waiting for, for a very longtime. This is what is going to finance our wedding," he had told her. Sontia thought it must have been very important and she quickly put on her clothes and they left for the airport. To her surprise when they got to the airport, she discovered they were not going to fly together to Argentina.
He had bought her a ticket to fly back to Germany by herself and he was going to fly to Argentina alone. He was in such a hurry, hence there was no time for

too many questions. He gave her a long kiss and told her he would join her in a couple of days and would make up for it. "My babe please forgive me, but I need to do this, I love you," and he was gone. That was the last time she ever saw him.
Disappointed and without further ado she galloped to the check in point.
The awaiting dogs greeted her with enthusiasm. They ran towards her waging their tails and barking viciously, showing her tough love. The hounds almost hugged her as they circulated their prey dangerously and playfully.
"They were so excited to see me," she joked. Chipo and the women laughed. Sontia explained, she was so confused, in shock, and because of the language barrier it made the situation catastrophic.
One overzealous policeman tripped her to the ground and choked her with a button stick. She was soon surrounded by about twenty other policemen dressed in riot gear. They tore open her bags and before long she was exposed. They discovered cocaine hidden on the artificial floor of the bag.
She just fainted.
The policemen were laughing and mocking her. They gave each other high fives and congratulated their dogs.

She had to spend the next five years in jail, living and sharing the same cell with twenty hardcore murderers and gang members. When she finished talking everyone was quiet. Some had tears in their eyes. Petra, one of the bubbly women broke the ice. "The most important thing is that you are well and alive and thank God that Texus bastard was caught and sentenced to fifteen years in jail. More tequilas, yeah!"
They all shouted. Chipo could not believe it was real. She thought no one could be that cruel to the point of setting up their own girlfriend in such a way,

let alone someone they had just proposed to. But then again she thought of her own situation and she drank the tequila quietly. Sontia didn't seem bothered.

She had passed that phase. Whatever she went through during her incarceration had made her a stronger and mentally impenetrable person. She looked fearless, cold and yet friendly and humorous. Chipo gathered she had not encountered any positive scenarios since her arrival. She wondered if that was the norm before you could integrate into the system.

What astounded her was the fact that most of these women had been in Germany for so many years and seemed not to have achieved much.

They had been hustling the same things over and over again. There was never any mention of education or trying to learn any form of skill. It was depressing and the future looked bleak for her.

The party continued until it was time for her to go. It was almost 6 am and the other women were still drinking and dancing.

Africa One bar and restaurant became her favorite place to hang out. Most of the gossip was just about how to make money, by unscrupulous, promiscuous or any immoral means. Chipo struck a conversation with a smartly dressed German guy. He knew a lot about Africa, especially Kenya. He talked a lot about himself, about what he had achieved and how many houses he had built.

He told her that he wanted to build a hotel in Kenya, because his ex wife had moved there with their two kids. He complained about how she nearly made him broke and that she had cheated on him.

He lamented how he had paid for her cousin to come to Germany and had looked after him in his house.

"Since I had a big place with many rooms in the cellar, I decided to accommodate him. I gave him the basement to use as his bedroom and suddenly, my

wife became very religious. For two years she would often go in the basement for hours of prayers.
It was only after she became pregnant and gave birth to a black child that I realized the so called cousin was her Kenyan boyfriend."
He burst out laughing, but you could tell the guy was hurt. Nonetheless, he had accepted the situation because he loved his wife and they continued living together. "She had two men in the house, one husband and a boyfriend," he chuckled. "In the end, she divorced me and kicked out the boyfriend, Mani you know him, the one who got poked with a needle the other day," he giggled, "I saw you sitting right here, we are buddies now. By the way I am Peter," he sighed as he sipped his beer.

Chipo listened with interest and disbelief. "She then sold my house," he continued and elaborated,.. " took my money and went back to Kenya. Someone told me she is now living with some Massai guy, straight from the bush," he said forcing out a dry laugh. "I hope she is enjoying drinking goat blood and dressing in sheepskin, now my kids have to sleep on a floor made of cow dung."

Chapter Thirty five

Peter picked her up from Chamu's place the next day and took her for dinner. He was very uncomfortable with himself. He laughed at his own jokes, that weren't funny.

"A friend of mine used to wear the same red shirt for dinner, and he wondered why he never got any chicks, Ha!Ha!Ha!" He laughed. Chipo thought maybe it was because of the age difference; She couldn't get the vibe, but she just laughed along, too.
"You see when I was growing up, my family went to the same place for holiday every year, Ibiza! How stupid is that, my father took us to the same spot, and we would meet the same people every year for twenty years."
"Wow! When was the last time you were there?" Chipo asked.
"About two months ago," he chuckled and continued "yes I know it's a bit weird but, I get to meet people I have known, all these years and some of them are married and have kids, its fun."
"Is that a German thing?" Chipo interrupted.
"Yes maybe," he said bopping his head, as if in denial.
"In a way it is, Germans like to know their surroundings. For instance, in Ibiza, we know Ben is running a superb cocktail bar, there is Miguel with a long white beard, who makes excellent delicious fish. He knows me and he knows my friends. I

also get to see familiar faces, and its nice. It's once a year reunion," he said roaring with laughter.
"We Germans, we believe in working very hard for our money. So when we go for holiday, we also party hard, in peace of course," he chuckled and continued, "not like the British, they don't know how to drink beer, they are always violent. If we are comfortable, we'll spend money in peace, huh, no strange faces are loitering around.

Why do you think the Germany economy is so strong? Our mentality, our patriotism is rooted deep in our bones, we die hard and we are very loyal if we feel appreciated," he gloated.
"Made in Germany huh," Chipo says sarcastically.
"Yes, yes he confirmed. We are perfectionists. We give more than 100% in our work, that's why in some companies you'll find that, three generations are working in the same firm. And it's a tradition that can go on forever." Chipo was astounded.
"That's some deep loyalty right there!" She said as she nodded her head.

Chipo had a quick analysis of him. She thought, he was normal among Germans, but he was also in denial of with his own feelings. He was proud to be German, but he was still not sastisfied with himself. He lacked balance and as long as he had not come to peace with himself, he would always be miserable, regardless of his good deeds. She soon discovered how contradicting and insecure he was with himself. He had a way of talking that made someone feel inferior.
He would use words like you people, us Germans. He was so shallow minded and insensitive, Chipo was disturbed by it, and she made it known. He was full of dry humor, "Please don't tell me tomorrow that your cousin is dead and you need money for the funeral and then the following week it's your nephew

again, or that your mother lives in a hut and you want money to build her a house. Ha!Ha!Ha! Yeah, yeah I am not stupid, I know you, people," he said and continued to chatter like a parrot.
"Why would I tell you that?" Chipo smirked, definitely not impressed.
"Well you Africans always need money for one thing or the other and when you see a white guy you think he is rich. You believe Europe is a land of milk and honey. You are all brainwashed," he crackled. "I can imagine the shock, when you get smacked in the face, after discovering it was a malicious deception. As soon as you land on your banana boat, you become disappointed and some of you became mentally disturbed," he sneered almost getting a seizure from laughing.

Chipo was getting pissed off.
"Yo, yo, yo, you keep on saying you Africans, do you know that Africa is a continent, not a country.
I am from Zimbabwe and we are totally different from West Africa or North Africa, we have different cultures, different traditions. In Nigeria alone, there are more than 170 million people with over a hundred languages."
"Really?" He exclaimed. Chipo added "There are more than a billion people that live on that continent. If you are so much offended by the Africans, why are you spending time with me? You can't just put everyone in one box. If I tell you Europe is all one, are the Germans the same as the Albanians?"
He chuckled, almost choked as he gulped his beer.
"Huh that's a joke, Albanians never, we Germans are the pillar of Europe, Albania should be in Africa or Asia," he scoffed.
"You see how judgmental you are, anything that is not good enough is associated with Africa. Now I understand why she left you, I am sure you never appreciated her. Taking her to the same place every

year, my ass, you must be messed up in your head. You got it all twisted up buddy, you thought you were better than her, huh, condescending, more superior, that kind of shit, shame on you and shame on your holiday buddies too. You know what that tells me, you are afraid of change, what you learned from your papa, is what you want to keep on doing, because you can't come up with anything better."

"But why change something that is working," he challenged her.

"I feel sorry for you. Your mentality is the same as sleeping with a woman using the same position for eternity, just because she cried once. I pity you," she concluded, whilst clicking her tongue.

"Don't get me wrong, I am talking facts here, Africa is the richest continent in reality, but also the poorest in reality," he snorted. "There are so many factors why it is the way it is, and you know that. You guys wiped out the whole tribe in Namibia, more people than the Jews that were killed during the 2nd world war."

"What do you mean?"

"You should know your history, you started it."

"No, no I did not mean to provoke you," he almost yelled.

"But I am talking from what I read, what I see on television and from what I hear. I mean look at Africa, its a joke, 3rd world or 4th world, whatever, corruption is rampant, widespread everyone is corrupt. Nigeria a perfect example, wealthy, should be the Saudi Arabia of Africa, but they are one of the poorest countries in the world, yet they have got so much oil, and all those reserves. Huh!

They produce oil, sends it somewhere else to get refined, and then buy it back at double the price and sell it to the consumers 5 times more than the original price. Isn't that a shame, to your leaders. You have one ex-president living in a house with 500 rooms, yet people are living on 50 cents a day,

uhh, what a joke." He was shaking his head. Chipo was uncompromising, but she knew the guy was right in some ways. "There is corruption, yes but who brought it to Africa, who is financing Europe, is it not African resources, why is France siphoning almost 200 billion from its former colonies? Is it not to run the French economy?
Do you think the Eiffel tower was built by the Gods? Why is Gerhard Schröder, an ex kanzler of Germany, the Chairman of Gazprom? Wasn't he in charge of the negotiations to built a gas pipeline from Russia to Germany, isn't that corruption?" he burst out laughing and responded.
"Ha!Ha!Ha! Schröder, I never voted for him, he is African or Arabian anyway, five wives! That's unheard of here," he gloated. "He is big-headed, he will die a lonely man," he stated.

By the time the bill came, the atmosphere was tense. It was made more unpleasant when he chose to pay only for his food and drinks and Chipo had to count her pennies to pay for her own share.
"You must be a stupid selfish man" she erupted and added, "I am sure even as a kid you were selfish. You invite me for dinner, you choose my food and recommend expensive cocktails. You think I like to drink all this milk and then you make me pay.
You asshole, it's you who will die lonely." She said as she got up.
"But in Germany, it is like that," he giggled.
"Go to hell," she banged the table and walked out. She was so angry, for she had not budgeted for that so she went to Africa One to cool off.

There she met Wicknel also known as the Angolan Giant. He was huge, tall, and as dark as ash. He didn't waste time in boasting about his superiority in bed. "You know what they say in Angola, if a man cannot satisfy his wife? He loses all credibility in his household," and he laughed. "So far in Angola, every man is respected," he said as he drank his beer. "My music is popular around here, I'm a successful music producer. You can ask anyone here. I speak French, Portuguese, English, and German. If you need any help, let me know." He was well known in the nightlife scene. A few ladies in the bar drank on his tab. "Some of them are my back ground dancers and they help me out, when I am organizing my events," he told her. Chipo thought since he was a music producer, he knew a lot of famous people, so she paid attention to him. Peter walked in, like a king, smiling broadly with two heavy African women and acted as if they had never met.

Wicknel invited Chipo to his studio, "there is a tune in my head and I really wanna play it before I forget the words. I only work during the night you know, I am like an owl. When you guys go to sleep, that's when I start my day. Sometimes I can go for two days without sleeping," he overstated.
"There is a band recording tomorrow and I want to finish up some beats for them. Maybe you can put your voice on one of my songs," he charmed her. She was over the moon. She could not wait to hear her own voice, singing in a professional studio.

The music studio was some miles out of town in a secluded industrial area. Once at the makeshift studio she realized he actually lived in the studio. He told her he wanted to take a nap before working and asked her to hang around. The bedroom was a tiny room filled with a squeak double bed. There was no couch, no chair to sit on. She had no choice but to sit on the bed.
Chipo was suspicious but wanted to while away time until it was time to go to Chamu's house. They started kissing and in the process, he removed his shoes with his feet. Within a second, the whole place was

consumed with a horrible stench. She backed off holding her mouth.
"What's wrong?" Wicknel asked innocently.
"Your feet man, do you mind if you put your shoes outside." Immediately and promptly, he became upset, "are you saying I smell?" he shouted, "how can you disrespect me like that in my own house?
I bought you drinks the whole night, now you are saying I smell. When you were chopping my monie, why didn't you tell me that my monie stinks, were you not chopping it? Get out of my house," he was in no mood for compromising.

Chipo thought to herself it's 2 am.
She had no idea where she was and trains had stopped moving. She tried to apologize. "No, I didn't mean it like that but, I am sure you were wearing your shoes the whole day, and it's normal that they become sweaty or you stepped on some poo poo, dog shit, and you didn't notice it," she frantically tried to explain to him.
"Huh, so now I smell like dog shit, you have no respect young lady get out of my studio, I want to sleep, you chop my monie and you disrespect me, do you know who I am," he yelled.
"But how am I going to get home, I don't even know where I am," she stammered.
"That's not my problem, I didn't drag you here," he threw her out and banged the door.

Chipo had to walk for almost 3 km, not knowing where she was going. She was so scared she might get stopped by the police or come across more weird characters. She was grateful when she saw a moving yellow light, she knew it was a Taxi.
She waved it down, the driver gave her a mean look and sped off.
She was nervous, her blood ran cold. As she walked alone, the night became mysterious, shadows blown

by the windy melted into the darkness. The cold breeze stalked her with cryptic mutterings, hardly disturbed by the clattering of the dark souls waiting in wings. After walking what seemed like a death sentence another Taxi driver roared past scrutinizing her before swiftly gliding to a halt. As he rolled the window down he gave her comforting advice. "This area is not good for prostitutes, better go to the city center more money there, money, money." And he shook his head whilst rolling his eyes. She just nodded like a swan and jumped in.

Chapter Thirty six

It was a young Turkish driver with a bald head and a clean-,shaven moustache. "I thought you were a ghost," he laughed "no one walks around here in the dead of the night, its pretty dangerous, especially for people like us. This place is a Nazis area. Where do you want to go?" he asked.

Chipo sighed, "Wedding," she answered. "You want to go to Africa one, I have been there. I met a very lovely lady from Kenya, Nancy. She was
very nice. She would call me and I would pick her up and drive her everywhere. She didn't always have money, but she was very clever," he laughed.
"I had a fight with my boyfriend and he kicked me out, yeah and now I am on my way to my Aunt's place. How much do you think it will cost me to get there?" Chipo lied.
"For you, I can switch off the meter and you can pay with a blow job," he snorted like a kid. She was stunned.
"Well, that's what Nancy always did. Are you from Kenya, I know and I understand everyone is looking for money, it's not easy to make money, but I am always willing to help," he defended himself.
"I'm from Kenya," she, said "and you, where are you from?"
"What do you think? Some people say I am Italian, some say I'm Iranian but I'm Turkish, from Turkey."
"How old were you when you came here?"

"Me," he said, "I was born here," and he chuckled.
"So why do say you are Turkish, you are not, you are German," she deliberately provoked him.
"No, no, I'm not German, I am Turkish, I'm building myself a nice Villa in Antalya. When I retire, I'm going back home," he smiled.
"It's strange though, I've met people from England, of Indian, Asian or African origin, born in the UK. When you ask them where they are from, they never say they are Indian or Ghanaian they always say they are British."
"They are stupid they have lost their identity, he yelled. "I mean I don't know about that, maybe the laws of integration in Uk are different than in Germany, well, we are always referred to as the Turkish, I'm proud to be Turkish," he said and he laughed.

Chipo saw that she was in a recognizable place.
"Can you please just stop anywhere around here, I want to get some money from the machine," she asked him politely.
He scoffed, wasn't impressed. He had thought he was going to get a blow job. The moment he halted, she exited and walked towards the cash point.
Unexpectedly she started running the opposite direction, leaving the Taxi driver shouting after her.
"Schlampe, Ich mach dich alle. Verpiss dich nach Afrika!" (*Bitch, I will kill you. Piss off to Africa!*)
She continued running and turned into a oneway street where she knew it would be hard for the driver to follow. A few yards from Africa One, she met Chamu.
He was shaking, filled with panic. He had been running too. They both stared at each other breathing heavily. Finally, he said, "Hello sista, oh man, shit gonna blow today oh."
"What happened?"
"This boy BJ he got carried away, he asked me to accompany him somewhere, we have been on the

road the whole day. We get to Macdonald's, we wanna chop. Guess what happens? Two unmarked police cars had been following us. We were lucky because we sat by the window and we saw everything they were doing, I didn't know what was happening. BJ just got up and told me oh boy, shit gonna happen now, you better run, the car is hot."
"But what was inside?" She asked, adjusting herself.
"What else, drugs now. I told this boy to chill. He was flashing too much money, buying bottles of champagne in the clubs, moving around in 100,000 dollar cars, stupid man. Dressing up in gold chains like Mr. T and he knows he is not clean, a very dumb guy, no brain Umugu.
Money makes people go crazy. He was a calm guy back in the days. That's the problem with being born poor. Once you have this monie, you don't know how to deal with it. It's true oh, these guys are not stupid oh, they see everything, everything my sister and when they think they have enough evidence on you, you better run before its too late.
Don't mess with the Germany police oh, these guys know their job. No matter what you do, you only succeed because they want you to succeed. If they decide enough is enough, they wont hesitate. The mafia, all these gangs might think they have everything under control, that's a lie oh, those riot guys, if you see them marching towards your home, lord have mercy. They are trained to split bones in a nice way. You'll feel pain but you don't know where the pain is coming from Gestapo style. Just one hit with that baton stick will make you stiff like a rabbit on fire. What's your own, why were you running?"
"Some stupid dick head was bothering me, that's all, we go for a beer."
"I can do with a joint."
"How were you able to run, your chest is packed with smoke," she laughed. "My sister when it comes to saving your life, you'll surprise yourself.

You should have seen the way I took off, I said wind carry me oh, Rasta man is fire." He said and chuckled. There was an ambulance siren from a distance, Chamu crouched and spread himself on the ground, Chipo burst out laughing.

"I am always ready for war my sister, just practicing, testing my flexibility. You know hiding from these people is the same as hiding in water," he said and chuckled.
"They can see you nice and clear and they'll wait for you to come up for some air."
"Well, then you need to be smart and do better than that."
"Escobar was caught on top of a roof," Chamu mumbled as he walked. "I want to show you my hide out area." He took her to a place with a cluster of old buildings. Among the maze of high rise ghost apartments, on the 13th floor was Karen's Sheeben.

The entrance was guaranteed with a code word, "Shekare." The place was packed with all different kinds of people. Mainly mature Germany, Italian and Turkish men, surrounded by Kenyan and Brazilian slay queens. The lounge was filled with couches and small tables, in the middle was a conjoined long wooden standing tables with bar stools. The Shekare, Karen the party host was expensively dressed to her last jewelry. She glittered with pride as she strolled through her successful venture.
She knew everyone by name, when she caught a glance of Chamu she nodded her head with a big smile on her face and cast a wry look at Chipo.
Chamu gave her thumbs up and Chipo responded with a half smile. Her domineering persona stood out, she was hyperactive, very talkative and quick witted. As she moved around chatting up people, two beautiful scantily dressed ladies patrolled the floor serving drinks, paying little attention to their

mini-skirts. Chipo had never been to a Shebeen before. She embraced the idea of grouping friends and their friends together and selling them Alcohol. After gulping a few beers Chamu left. She stayed behind and engaged in a conversation with a group of male patrons.

At exactly 3 am the Sheeben queen switched on the bright lights, spewing shining torturing rays sending people scampering out. Chipo got into a vehicle with two men and they ended up smoking weed and drinking alcohol in a secluded area of a park. When she woke up the next morning she was naked, the two men were lying naked next to her, Jason and Heinrich, she remembered their names. Without fear she raised her head cautiously partially covering her breasts. From a distance, she could see people and cars roaming by.

When she looked behind her, to her surprise they were more than fifty naked people. Chatting and moving around with no care in the world. She thought she was dead and living in paradise. Where everyone moved freely without fear, or shame since there were no snakes offering anyone any apples.

"You want a banana bag," asked Heinrich. "Banana bag," she replied and roared her eyes feeling offended.

"Vitamins, some liquids to rally you up, it's a perfect way to start a day," he added.

"Where are we?"

"We are in a park, Tiergarten," as he got up and stood in front of her stark naked. "How did we end up here?"

"How do you feel?"

"I feel naked."

"This was your wish last night to sunbathe naked, Berlin style, remember. Try this juice, it's quite good."

"Yeah yeah, of course, I remember." She pretended

to scour around. "Whoa how can someone feel so free to move up, and down skin deep, naked in full view of strangers," she uttered. "It's an art that can only be accomplished by the brave," rattled Jason. She found it funny in a way and very weird in a big way. She protested silently shaking her head. She gave a wry smile at the thought of naked women lying around in parks in South Africa.

"This is a new world unheard of," she thought to herself. "How can your manhood catch a borne if women's private parts are so cheaply exposed?" She asked Jason.

"Uh you get used it, and in the end nothing happens anymore."

"I mean if your dick has a continuous erection," Chipo continued, "there will come a point in time, where the engine will stop functioning, because of false alarms, and everything becomes kind of immune and the spark disappears. The blood is diluted and loses it's purpose," she elaborated.

"I grew up like this, I can go to a sauna or sunbath naked with my family, mother and sisters and it's perfectly ok," Jason confirmed.

"Whoa!" She was surprised. "In Zimbabwe there are no nude parks," asked Heinrich.

"Have you ever been bitten by a mosquito," Chipo replied, and they all laughed.

Chapter Thirty seven

After two weeks she returned to Dr. Neutrons for a check up, as planned. Unexpectedly he offered her a job as his runner, because BJ had absconded and he needed a new innocent face, someone to help him liaison with his associates.
Chipo was staggered by the offer, she was not prepared for it. She became wide eyed and grinned totally perplexed by the sudden turn of events. Although hesitant she was very grateful. Having a job and a roof over her head is what she had prayed and wished for all along. But she was cautious and feeling insecure. For some reason, he thought Chamu had told her about his other unofficial side. When he realized she was ambivalent about his proposal.

He pulled out a stack of cash and said, "because of my confidence in you, I am willing to pay you upfront half of the money you'll get. This is a good start for you. You'll raise enough cash to finish your studies, without having to work in McDonald's, and you can stop whenever you want. I'll personally help you get a small apartment for yourself and maybe we can find a way to make you legal, huh you like that don't you."
She just nodded her head and he continued, "I can help you get a German citizenship, but you have to be very loyal and stay focused. One slight slip can create massive problems for us.

We'll not communicate by phone, you'll get a new plan route every week and all you have to do is follow the instructions. There isn't much talking in this business, it's take and give. Your radius will be 5 km from the city. So its easily doable with public transport.
In some cases, you'll have someone escorting you."
She agreed to everything without fully understanding what it was all about. He had some form of arrangements with brothels, pimps, prostitutes and clubs. He was treating most of them and supplying them with class A drugs and anabolic steroids. As novice as she was, the money was too good to ignore.

She ran figures in her head. "In five months, I can earn enough to buy myself a nice condo back home." She thought silently and smiled. Being homeless for a while had given her a new fighting spirit, she quickly settled in her new environment, a nice small, apartment of her own. She could cook, take a shower, and do whatever she wanted. She felt she had accomplished something major in her life. Little did she know, she was going to be stuck in it for one unforgettable year. She learnt to be discreet and anonymous.
She assumed membership of a religious cult devoted only to Dr. Neutrons. In a way she was isolated and brainwashed.

Being a runner had a lot of side effects, for each day she wondered what would happen if she got caught. Basically, she was suffering from anxiety and depression. She become a serious user and immune to the fatalities it had caused. Dr. Neutrons was pulling in big time cash. All the back door patients were regular users. They had a data base of their clients, they knew when someone needed to top up, medical history of the clients, profession and

so on. Customer satisfaction and supplying a quality product was the main goal. It was a membership club. No new clients were accepted without recommendation or some rigorous vetting.
Chipo was moving with the flow. She used to post pictures of herself on the grounds of any university or surrounded by groups of students just to keep her parents and family at bay and entertained. After all, she was working and sending money home.

The worst part of her job was dealing with unpredictable behaviors, of tribes from another planet.
They had plenty of money and the craving to party.
Most of these nerds had little regard for others.
She had complained to the Doctor about it, but he had brushed it aside as part of the business.
They were so self-centered, arrogant, and had not a spark of decency.
Chipo had created a list according to their inhuman behaviors, on number one was Carl-Pitt, he was one of the worst culprits. He had been adopted by a wealthy gay couple and had inherited most of their wealth when they passed away. He was a spoilt little brat. He once spent a week in a brothel, showering hookers with money and champagne. He could stay for a month in a hotel yet his villa was a few kilometers away. He was a party animal always looking for action and she had to follow his trail, providing him with his basic needs. At one point he slapped Chipo accusing her of stealing, after he couldn't find his roll of cash, only to realize he had it in his jacket. She would always get rewarded handsomely to keep her mouth shut. He was unpredictable and short-tempered, on two occasions he almost raped her thinking she was one of his call girls. The worst part was when he let her in, while he was getting his private parts shaved. He was reckless and out of his mind. But he always avoided trouble with the authorities. The only good thing about him, that she

liked, was his music. When he was sober, he was a completely different creature. He was humble, quiet and down to earth. He would sit by his piano and rap a few songs for her. He would play the guitar and write lyrics.
Listening to his music made her understand him better. He was angry inside, lost, and seeking revenge, blaming the world for his existence.

On number two were the twins, Lya and Ella, they were a menace to the society.
Chipo predicted one day they would kill each other or murder someone. Fighting was an everyday thing. One would accuse the other of using her makeup, misplacing her hairbrush, or for snorting all the cocaine. They fought about almost anything. One time as she was making her rounds, she found them trying to drown each other in a pool. Ella was accusing Lya of sleeping with her boyfriend. Chipo had to jump into the pool to separate them. As she got out of the pool, twin guys came out of the house bragging and laughing at them.
"You just got pranked," the guys shouted.
Then there was Carsten and Lisa. They lived the Hollywood life. Chipo had turned down a few holiday invitations not because she didn't want to, but she couldn't leave or fly anywhere. Lisa was pretty, outgoing, and a fitness freak. One evening, she requested that she needed an urgent delivery around midnight. Chipo was about to go to bed when she saw two missed calls and UB initials popped on her screen. She knew what that meant. UB was for Usain Bolt, which meant urgent speed delivery.
She went to the pickup spot, fuming with anger, but Lisa had specifically requested for her and it was a 10,000 euro order. It was unusual since she had already delivered their weekly consumption.
When she arrived, there was a party in full swing. Lisa practically dragged her inside.

She was bombarded with a series of drinks within a short period. Soon she was hitting tequilas, margaritas, getting high on cocaine.
Everybody was in a party mood. Groups of couples kissed, danced, and made love in the open. She found herself chatting and kissing with some long- haired guy. Lisa called them upstairs, as she entered the room, Lisa fondled her boobs and they started kissing, as Carsten and the long haired guy watched.
She felt Carsten grinding her from behind and Lisa went down on her. It was a strange setup. She tried to push Castern's head away, only to be left holding a toupee. He started making out with the long-haired guy.
She had no recollection of the rest of the evening but whatever happened in there, she knew they were all going to hell. She found 2,000 euros in her clutch and assumed it was her gift for the night.

When she entered her apartment it was 2 pm and she was late with her deliveries.

Chapter Thirty eight

Dr. Neutrons was waiting for her in the dark, without her knowledge. He was furious. He had a pistol on the table. Without raising his voice, he told her he had lost 2,000 euros because of her incompetence and she had to reimburse it.
She was in a state of shock. She couldn't believe he was capable of getting that much angry.
"If we don't deliver on time, our customers will move somewhere else. I've worked hard to get where I'm right now and I am not going to let anyone jeopardize that. I have people to answer to.
Your job is not to entertain my clients, this is why its called take and give. If this ever happens again, you will find yourself on the streets, with nothing", he asserted his authority.
"You have one more chance, you hear me?" he repeated himself. "If it happens again, you are out. Now go and take care of my clients and make money for me," he ordered and walked out.

She had a terrible hangover and could not recall anything. Her memory was completely blank. In her head she began to question herself, how Dr. Neutrons had managed to get into her apartment. She blamed herself for being careless. Her lack of responsibility had betrayed her. Lisa started bombarding her with calls and messages. She began to stalk her and pursue her relentlessly. Her effort paid off, and she was too rich to ignore.

Their moonlight tryst flourished behind closed doors. Her income increased rapidly, but she remained cautious, afraid Dr. Neutrons might find out. Lisa was not someone to hang around with for too long. Her cocaine habits were excessive and Chipo feared for her life. She was beginning to get too comfortable and slackening. She was aware the moment she let her guard down, was the moment she would fall into a deep pit. She reminded herself of rule number one, "don't get high on your own dope, don't fuck the customer, and always keep an eye on the ball. No slackening, stay vigorous," she yelled and pumped herself like a madwoman.
When she got back home that evening, she dulled her psychic pain with vodka.
Out of paranoia she turned her apartment upside down, worried Dr. Neutrons might have installed hidden cameras. She changed her front door lock. She felt unsafe and haunted.

It was a quiet week and she remembered there was always this Ghanaian guy called Nana trying to invite her to one of his parties.

She had not been to a normal party for a while and she thought it would be a cool way to relax, freshen up, mingle, and maybe get acquainted. She called him up and he added her name on the guest list. The event was in a club called Felix and was filled with very posh, well-dressed people.
She walked in like an ostrich on heels and ordered a table and a bottle of Ciroc Vodka by herself. The music was amazing.
She was having a blast and had money to spend. Her aim was to let go, to fly solo like an eagle.

Nana would pop by once in a while for a small chat, The waiter brought another bottle of Ciroc and a bottle of Ace of spades, "Damn that's some real

shit," she said to herself. The waiter told her, "drinks on Ginibs!"
"Who the hell is Ginibs," she screamed.
"Me," some tall skinny short dark looking guy with a wide smile, dressed in a very expensive navy blue suit was staring at her. "If he can afford an Ace of spade, definitely he can afford me", she thought and blushed.
"Do you mind if I join you," he asked politely.
"Show me your hands," she shouted.
"What?" he asked confused,
"What size shoe do you wear sir? I beg to know," she teased him. And he cracked up, "just kidding, but its important size matters," she said smiling, as she pulled him in the VIP cubicle. "Feel free to join," she said. "Thank you, I was beginning to feel lonely, what's a pretty thing like you doing drinking all by yourself?"
"No I am not drinking alone," she replied.
"Who else are you drinking with then, I don't see nobody here,"
"Ha!Ha!Ha! You have no idea, look again," she challenged him.
"How much vodka did you drink?" He questioned her.
"I'm drinking with my ancestors," she shouted and he burst out laughing. He was startled, panicked, and started searching around.
"I don't see anybody here."
She put her hand on his shoulder and whispered in his ear, "don't disappoint me, they'll be angry, look again, be spiritual." He was perplexed.
She laughed and said, "let me introduce you," she smiled and added, "this is aunt Pefe," as she pointed to an empty seat, "and right there
is Mbuya Chura, next to you is aunt Eliza and that's aunt Mary my protectors."
"I'm happy to meet you all, hello everyone," he said with a bow. He then went on to pop the bottle

and poured six more glasses of Ace of Spades. Chipo loved the sound of the pop of the bottle, so sexy, so fulfilling, It was like a spiritual awakening in her. She was filled with effervescence, bubbles, and fizz, just like the sparkling wine. That's when she realized she was born to make money.

Ginibs was very confident with himself, money seemed to flow easily, and he had a habit of pinching his nose. She wondered if he was a snorter, but she didn't want to scare him.
"How come you are alone?" She asked him curiously.
"No, I am not." He answered as he grabbed a glass of Champagne and poured it on the floor, "my ancestors want to drink too," she giggled uncontrollably like Madam boss. They had a good laugh. The guy was full of himself, very humorous.

He ordered the most expensive cigars, They were balling, but all the time she was scheming, how she could get that thick watch off him. She recognized it because her boss had one exactly the same.

"He has a suite at the Adibas hotel and he has an Omega watch, flew in on a private jet, wearing a Zoot suit, oh man that's some serious big dog right there, presented to me on a silver platter, this kind of chance comes once in a lifetime," she pondered about it.

She knew one way or the other she had to take him out. But her options were limited, she excused herself to go to the bathroom. On her way, she met two beautiful cock nosed chicks. They snorted some good shit in the bathroom, and after that, they were the best of friends.
When she got back to the table, he had ordered another bottle of tequila, "who is gonna drink all this shit man, two shots would have been enough," she

protested. "Hahaha," he laughed, "whatever I do, I do by the bottle hun, come on look at a lady like you, smart, cool, calm, just chilling by yourself and you are successful on your own." He boasted.
"Uh, uh," she pointed to the empty seats.
"My apologizes aunties," he responded as he nodded his head to the empty seats. "You know what Chipo, today is your lucky day, I'll make your wishes come true, whatever you like is on me."
"Hey girls how are you doing, its been a while," she said as she pretended to welcome her two new best friends. She saw his eyes lit. He looked like a little boy opening a present. He snapped his fingers.
The waiter almost fell as he ran to their table, "two more Aces of Spades," he demanded. The bottles came burning on fire. They had sparklers attached, and all eyes were on them, Ginibs felt like the Godfather. He gave the manager another 200 euros to have a security guard stationed at their table. There were DJs on rotation and DJ Aisher The Turntable goddess, the Afrobeat queen came on and the club exploded.

Ginibs sent another 200 euros to the DJ to make him play Chipo's favorite song, Disappear by Winky D. She was so excited. She sang along, jumping up and down. He had just made her the happiest person that night and she was ready to return the favor in kind. Nana was beaming, knowing he would get a percentage of the drinks, "No photos please," Ginibs complained, Chipo thought oh thank God, no evidence. She kept a permanent smile on her face, like a call girl.
He suggested they continue the party at his hotel, chauffeur-driven, five-star treatment he had bragged. They followed him like little ducks. When they got out of the car, he had passed out.

They had to literally drag him into his hotel suite. It

was such a luxurious place, and Chipo wished she could stay there forever. They pumped the music up, and suddenly Ginibs was awake. The bar was fully stocked. While she was snorting some lines with Kyra, he was in the Jacuzzi downing shots of tequila with Natalie. They walked out of the hotel around eleven in the morning, 50,000 euros richer.

She had found another avenue for making money. On her way home she was angry with herself. She remembered uncle Magandi's words when you want to do something, do it, and do it to the fullest, go for gold. When you want to hit someone, hit first and hit him hard that he doesn't get up. If you want to steal, steal everything because if you are caught, the punishment will be the same.
Whether you steal 20 bucks or 100,000 bucks, you are still called a thief. She beat herself up for she had left behind a drawer full of valuables amounting to maybe up to 500,000 euros. "Why did I hesitate? Why didn't I just grab everything?" Her thoughts ran wild.

Chapter Thirty nine

She called Chamu up, Since madam was around, she met him downstairs, All her valuables were stored in his cellar. She gave him 200 euros and he started ululating, and singing, "A Mi Fi Tell Yuh, A We Seh, praise jah, big up sistren," he screamed.

Mhondoro inonwa muna Zambezi,ho
Mhondoro inonwa munambezi
mhondoro inonwa muna Zambezi,ho
Mhondoro inonwa munambezi

"I Hear You," she said and he ululated again.
"The chickens are coming home to roost," he shouted, "Jah bless," Chamu knew how to appreciate and praise someone. She loved it, It made her feel proud and useful but he was too loud, attracting too much attention and it made her uncomfortable. She kept looking up to make sure the wife wasn't observing them from upstairs.

When Chipo wasn't working on the weekend, she would call up Kyra and Natalie for shark fishing. Sometimes they would succeed, especially with old men, and they never got into any trouble because most of the people were too embarrassed to report it to the police.

There was a Beyonce concert, at the Mercedes-Benz Arena, and they had been planning for it for quite

sometime. Not in a million years were they going to miss it. They dressed up like Beyonce clones. The show was an incredible, exhilarating, thrilling, rousing, and electrifying performance.
They had never witnessed anything like that in their lives.
"This is how life is supposed to be lived, we love you Beyonce!" Chipo screamed into the crowd.

The after-show party was at the club Pearl. It was another level of entertainment. There were more people in the VIP area than on the dance floor. They went direct to work, "victim identified," Kyra chuckled, as she sipped her Champagne.
"To the left, to the left," she sang. "Should be an easy one," Natalie confirmed.
"Where?" Chipo asked.
"The blonde guy looks 40 I guess. The one on the table of four people," she emphasized.
"Something is strange," Natalie complained and questioned. "Why is he sitting alone?"
Chipo was curious. They observed him for some time. He was turning down self inviting groupies, "Maybe he is gay," Natalie said pissed off.
"Maybe he is just waiting for his wife," Chipo answered.
They turned their attention to other big fish, but that night, it was hard to sell. It seemed like all the Beyonce's of the world had come out to party. There were lots of beautiful attractive women. Each one was more beautiful than the other.

Chipo got a tap on her shoulder. "Are you going to let a gentleman celebrate his birthday alone. Today is my big day and I wanna celebrate it with someone special, do you mind if you join me on my table," He asked politely. Chipo looked at him like, who the hell are you, with one eye fixed at his table. "Your table looks empty," she teased him. She thought to herself

play hard to get, but not too hard otherwise he will be intimidated.
He saw the look on her face and he was a bit unsettled.
"I am Stefan by the way, I am a model agent looking for potential future Heidi Klums or should I say future Naomi Campbells," Chipo could see her girls suppressing their excitement.
"Hello I am me and these are my two friends, partners in crime, we do everything together."
"Oh yeah, of course please do join me, you and your beautiful friends, just go round that way and I'll let the bouncer know, you are part of my crew," he suggested.
They got their decorated bands and were now fully fletched members of the VIP. "Kyra and Natalie should have been go go dancers," Chipo yelled to Stefan and added, "look how they shake and whine, so sexy hey."
Kyra and Natalie did a lap dance on Stefan and he felt proud, as he noticed other men observing them cheerfully. Some of the ladies were irritated and offended by their acts though.
As usual, bottles flooded the table, but he was a smart drinker. He took his time but kept dosing them with shots of tequilas. He reminded Chipo of her homeboy Terry.
"I have a friend called Terry, he is exactly like him," she whispered to Natalie. "He would buy you alcohol and make you all drunk, and afterward he would do his stanky leg dance, and the funny thing is, he has only one leg," they both laughed.
Stefan was a ladies man, a charmer, very talkative, He could have been anyone's boyfriend.
He was a good dancer too, and he kept on encouraging them to drink and drown shots. They were mildly inebriated, at least that is what they thought, but they lied to each other.
Stefan suggested they go to another place.

He took them to some strip club, where they almost got chased away as they were creating competition for the strippers. They were too intoxicated to know what was happening. And then the white ashes were lined up on the table. Stefan became wild. That was home for him.
They each pulled a line and they felt reinvigorated, as they became alive again. By the time they got to the hotel, Stefan was so active, so wide awake you couldn`t steal anything from him.
He began making other appointments with one of his friends, Markus, who sounded crazier than him as he was on speakerphone when they talked.

They left his room around 5 pm and as Stefan staggered towards Berghain Nightclub, a well known, notorious Techno club.

Chapter Fourty

While Chipo was on her way home she got a disturbing call from Suzie. She could tell in her voice, that something terrible had happened. Suzie begged for her help, for she wanted to meet up with her immediately. Chipo was hesitant as she had not slept the whole night but nonetheless, she instructed the Taxi driver to turn around. She found Suzie in an empty alley, moving about nervously she was in distress. She had two big suitcases, no makeup, no adornments, but just a cigarette stud in her hand. Her eyes were tired and her skin scratched. She looked wasted. As soon as she spotted Chipo, she ran towards her and cried out, "oh my sister thank you, thank you for coming, I don't know what to do."
"What's going on?" Chipo asked as she sat her down next to some garbage containers.
"Oh man shit gonna happen oh," she yelled.
"What shit again?" Chipo asked politely, mimicking her heavy Nigerian accent.
"You know our sex games now?"
Chipo rubbed her forehead.
"This time all gonna blow oh, everything went south now, oh Mamawe what have I done," she cried out.
"What happened Chipo asked again?"
She gasped, "he wanted something different."
"Oh boy," Chipo chipped in, "that smells like trouble."
"Hey this white man," Suzie said as she clasped her hands.
"He begged me to place two small blue tablets like

that, into his eh rectum," Chipo's eyes bulged out. "Oh boy," she yelled out giggling.
"It's no joke oh, I asked him if it was safe and he told me not to worry and that it would make him feel like an Alien cruising around the globe. I didn't want oh, but the man begged. He cried, I said ok, only this one time I'll do it, but never again. So I did as instructed, tied his hands, tied legs."
"Uh uh uh hey," Chipo exclaimed.
"And when I started doing my thing, oh boy hell broke loose. The man started shaking violently. At first I thought it was part of the game then I realized something was not normal, something was amiss, he was convulsing oh, cardiac arrest."
"Whoa, whoa," Chipo shouted.
"I said oh this man is gonna die at my hands oh, hey I panicked. He had foam coming out of his mouth. I cut him loose and performed CRP."
"CPR," Chipo corrected her.

"I then called the ambulance, but I had to run before they catch me. You know ambulance people always come with the police now. And the first thing the police will say, before even finding out whether he is alive or not: is Ausweis bitte. And you know my papers are not in order. If I had stayed they would put me in jail, and deport me. I couldn't risk that oh, I still need to take care of my parents back home."
Chipo was shaking her head. "Is he dead?" She inquired.

"Me I am Nigerian I took off, I just took off, I don't know my sister, now I just need a place to crash for a few days, just to cool down. I think I'll head back to Italy, Od, God please have mercy on me," she sighed.
"What's up with the bags? Where did you find the time to pack all this stuff?" Chipo asked inquisitively.
Suzie shrugged her shoulders, "it's my life now ehe, I am always prepared. In desperate situations, you do

mad things oh." She took out a vial filled with white powder and snorted a line, and extended it to Chipo, but she declined.

They took a taxi to Chipo`s place, as they entered her apartment Kyra called her.

Chapter Fourty one

She was still high from last night and she could not stop complaining about what had transpired.
"What a wasted night? We thought we had hit a jackpot, he fooled us all. Stefan had three for the price of none. Lucky bastard!" She shouted.

Suzie nudged her and excused herself as she wanted to go and buy cigarettes from the kiosk she had seen around the corner. They talked for a while and Chipo heard loud disturbances of voices shouting from Kyra's apartment. She was screaming and her phone went dead.
"Kyra what's going on?" Chipo yelled, and at that moment her own door was kicked in. She got up in shock, as two guys dressed in black walked in. They just stared at her without making a move. She could neither scream nor run.

"Chipo can you please come with us. If you open your mouth you are dead," the guy said as he took out his gun.
"You remember him," he showed her a photo and enquired, "you know Ginibs?" She collapsed in panic. She tried to talk but couldn't. She stammered, "yes of course very nice guy I remember him."
Before she could say anything else, she was slapped so hard she flew against the wall.
"From now onwards, I do the talking, and you do the listening, ok?" Chipo nodded her head in fear.

"Let's make it look like you just took off in a hurry," he suggested as he started pulling out clothes, out of her wardrobe. "Uh, you packed already looks like you were about to abscond," he said as he knocked Suzie's suitcases to the floor.
"You kept all the loot to yourself hey, smart girl."
She was nervous. She trembled as she did what she was told.
They went outside her apartment, his arms wrapped around her, like lovers.
As she got down the stairs, she saw poor Nana's face had been reformed. His eyes were swollen, the lips tore apart. His forehead had been extended. He looked like some weird creature in a movie. The guy was in pain but managed to force a smile. He looked at her apologetically. They knew he had organized the party, so somehow he had information about her or the other girls. Nana's look instilled fear in her.

She was blindfolded and pushed into the car. Chipo began preparing for the inevitable. She wondered what would happen to her. "Would they kill me, put me in a wheelchair, cut off my tongue, or maybe rape me. She preferred the last option as long as they used condoms. The threatening aspect of death played in her mind. She was sitting between two heavily built guys and two others were sitting in front.

Suzie pretended to remove something from her shoe as she witnessed the drama unfolding from a distance. Chipo speculated whether any of her friends had been killed. She was powerless, and she needed to find strength. She wished for a miracle. She tried to be strong, to make light of the situation. It was all a big misunderstanding.

"If I have to die", she thought, "it would be cool if it happens while having sex with my idol, Jah Pray-

zah. That would be a soulful death", she exhaled, tears coming down her chicks. Chipo thought of her family, her mother, and her father. She had betrayed them. They had worked so hard to give her everything she wanted as a child. They had shown her and her brother's love. They had instilled discipline in them and taught them respect. She had failed them. She had thought somehow she would work it out on her own and win them over by being successful.
And would bury her past behind, her mother would have forgiven her, and slapped her on the wrist for her sins. Since they say mothers always know, she thought of her sisters and brothers, and the things she should have done for them, that she didn't do. The fights and memories they shared together. She felt so selfish for not getting in touch with them more often. If she could do it again, she would love just to spend as much time as she could with them. Her mind raced back to the day before. Just yesterday we were having a field day. Why didn't I hit the books like my sister? How come I got involved in all this?
Love of money and success had fooled her.
Nothing good was ever predicted, in doing wrong. She was out on a limb, alone, exposed, and vulnerable. Nothing had been forced upon her. Everything was of her own choice. No one dragged her into it, but it was too late, to pass the buck and pull the plug. She felt apprehensive about the whole situation. She wondered what crazy Pokello would do in a situation like that. Maybe jump out of the car, and do some karate moves, she laughed inwardly.
In the midst of thinking, the car came to a halt after what seemed like hours.

She was dragged out of the car violently and as her blindfold was pulled away, she came face to face with a short light skinned aggressive guy.
He does a three punch combo in her stomach and she drops to the ground.

"You fucken steal from the boss? Do you think you tough? You orchestrated this shit didn't you? You think you are smart? You are illegal here right? You can't go to nobody? We kill you, throw you in the sea nobody will ever find you and they won't even miss you either. Get up, Miss!" He commanded as he whacked her with the back of his hand.
She dropped to her knees bellowing. "You wanna be a fuckin gangster? If you want to become one, here is the deal. I want everything you took back.
The watch, the diamonds, everything!" She was aroused, and her face flushed. Now she knew she had a big problem.
"Who the fuck do you think you are, Get the fuck up, you piece of shit," he said as he pulled her up by her hair.
"What diamonds?" Natalie anxiously asked. Kevin giggled and punched Chipo in the stomach and pushed her to the ground.
Kevin swiped his hands and clicked his tongue, swayed as he moved towards Natalie. She was pleading for help.
"Please, please, they forced me to do it."
One of the bearded guys removed the piece of cloth around her eyes. "What did you just say?" Kevin demanded as he walked towards her.
"What did you say? You flat assed slut," he yelled and slapped her.
"My ass is not flat," she screamed back at him with an angry face.
Everyone laughed. She stammered again.
"They, they forced me to do it, I'm telling you, I told them I didn't want any part of it and they said...," She got whacked again before she could finish.
"We not in school here and I hate snitches." She fell to the floor, "get up booby trap female dog, bitch, you steal from my boss, huh. He entertains you, shows you love, buys you drinks, you snort his cocaine, and then what do you do, steal his shit.

How ungrateful, nevertheless there is a lesson to be learnt here." He pulled her up by her hair. She was sobbing, "I could have made you my girlfriend if you were not so stupid," he shouted and drilled a fist into her stomach.

She wailed, "I don't wanna die please, I am sorry I just want to go home."

"Too late for that tonite you'll die," he yelled and dragged her up again and gives another blow to the stomach. She winced and fainted. He spat at her and moved on to Kyra.

"What have we got here? What a waste of beauty," he screamed as he stares at her with an evil grin. He slapped her so hard, that he had to shake off the pain from his hand. Kyra stood there stone-faced like a stooge. She didn't move, wince or blink. She just kept looking forward.

"What the hell, you got a metal plate in there or what you tough bitch," looking at her suspiciously and in an aggressive way as he rubbed his fist. His hand was numb and painful.

"Wait till my boys deal with you. Ever seen one of those anacondas before?"

"Let's rape these whores boss," shouted one of the bald men. There was a loud cheer from his crew. A tall huge guy wearing a Brazilian bandana threw away his trench coat and stood in front of them, full monty, mocking and teasing them. He looked like he had done this more than a hundred times.

"Yeah all of you are done, which one I should start with," he whispered as he licked his lips starring at Natalie.

"Not you Morris," Kevin objected. The big buffed guy was confused. He murmured, and protested, "Cut the mumbo jumbo out," shouted Kevin. "Sam you take the tough one out, follow it up with the cry baby. Don't let me down dawg, mess up that vulva, ram that bitch yo,"

"Boss let me go first, man, you know I just came out

of jail," Kevin squeaked. "Okay let Ashraf have a go, nail that piece of shit." And then someone fires a gun into the air.
"What the hell is wrong with you Kevin? No rapes today!" a female voice barked, "I told you all already, didn't I say that before? Times are hard we need to improvise, by thinking business. Our task ahead is complicated, we don't need any distractions," she ranted. "Let me holla at you Kevin." He wasn't impressed by the intrusion. He was frustrated, annoyed and hesitantly followed her. "All you bitches die tonite, puta," he shouted and pulled out his gun, waving it clumsily, as he spat on the ground.

Kevin and the woman in dark glasses discussed for a few minutes. He was contemplating, openly agitated, and in dispute. Finally, he laughed and clapped his hands, grinning sheepishly.
He came back to them rubbing his hands and laughing horribly. "Change of plans, your lady luck has just smiled upon you. Thank queen Magda for her kind heart and her vision. That woman there is the reason you are still alive. I feel bad though. Your little ones will forever be tight. Sam give them something to drink, whiskey, you all drink right, yes you do, you'll drink what I want you to drink. David come on, welcome the ladies, show them some hospitality. Bring some chairs, sit, sit, all of you sit," they did as they were told.

"Okay here is the deal," Kevin continued with a devilish look. "I want you to relax, soon we'll go for a ride. No one will get killed for now, all is gonna be fine, as long as you do as you are told. If you defy me or my men and if you try to escape or do anything stupid, that'll be the last time you'll breathe on this earth. You do as I say, you live."
"Whatever you say, whatever you want," mumbled Natalie.

"Shut up you snitch, you squeal on anyone ever again, you'll be the first one to go. You understand! I know everything about y'all, drink, relax, it's a long safe journey." He was excited and was trying to be nice, but you could still tell the fury in him. The other guys kept looking at them in an intimidating way. Someone mentioned M13. They were beyond horror-struck. M13 was widely known as the most notorious South American gang living in the USA. The gang was known for violence and their trademark was cutting up their victims. The girls were even more terrified.
"Don't liquor them up," the bald guy shouted.

Chipo and her friends were bundled into the boot of one of the vans. After what seemed like ages, the van stopped. They were taken out of the boot and brought to the front, to sit amongst them. The group was made up of six guys wearing Mexican hats, reeking of booze and weed. Most had tattoos protruding around their necks and wrists. They were chillingly quiet and had mysterious aggressive gazes.
For some reason unknown to anyone, they had flutes and guitars packed in the car. One of them sitting at the back seat was playing with drumsticks, constantly licking his lips, whilst starring at Natalie, who was sitting next to him. Chipo heard Natalie say, "please don't hurt me whatever you want I'll do it." The second guy grinned showing his goldplated teeth. He kneeled and removed Natalie's underwear and threw it at Chipo. The driver pumped up the volume. He was yelling something in a different language as he watched Natalie's head pop up and down through the rearview mirror. Sounds of mourning and groaning filled the whole car. Kyra was stone-faced as she watched, one of the guys unbuttoning her trousers, waving a gun in the air.

Chipo immediately knew what to expect. When the guy sitting at the passenger seat jumped over and

joined them at the back. Her mind was running wild. She thought of how back in the days rapists were pilloried, whipped, and exposed to public abuse.
The guys didn't talk. Just their facial expressions and their silly whimpering said it all.

From her many experiences, she had discovered a way of separating her body from her mind.

Chapter Fourty two

She would let her mind wander away in the wildness and engulf her thoughts with a web of visions.
She remembered on several occasions when she nearly got bitten by snakes, and the many times she had cheated death.
One particular afternoon her dad decided no one would eat meat that day, because their chores were not up to satisfaction.
Chipo and her brother and some kids from the compound, decided to go hunting, accompanied by 20 dogs. They were carrying knobkerries, axes, and catapults. As they got to the paddocks, the pack went wild. They had caught the scent of a wild animal. As the group ran after them, suddenly, two springboks were visible. They took one look at the dogs and they sprung up so quickly, they were gone within a split of a second. One went to the left and the other went to the right.

The dogs also split into two following the animals, but the springboks were too fast. They were left biting the dust. Most of the guys in the group split and followed the directions of the dogs. Chipo and a few other younger guys ran after them but were too slow to catch up. The group was almost five kilometers into the forest, but the dogs and the older boys had disappeared. They could not hear a bark or a whistle that made them worried but the sky was clear and sunny. Out of nowhere, the unpredictable

happened. Dark clouds unexpectedly and rapidly enveloped the whole paddock area. Within minutes, the sun was gone and there was a bolt of massive lightning. A big storm was on its way. It became so evil dark and frightening. The dogs came back one after the other from nowhere and sped past them, barking and howling. The mood was scary. Chipo and her small troop of friends started sprinting towards home.
She knew the older boys would soon catch up and overhaul them. The dogs were running in a single file and it was now raining heavily. As Chipo led the group, more and more dogs were overtaking them.

Then something strange happened. As the dogs were running in a single file, they suddenly split into a V-shape, but Chipo continued to run straight ahead and in a mixture of thoughts, still wondering why the dogs had split. She was about ten meters away when she raised her head and saw a small yellowish tree in front of her. Her senses warned her, they were no yellowish trees in the paddock. That's when within a few meters left, she looked further up and realized it was a big long snake on its tail waiting to bite. She side stepped to the right side.
Hocky, her favorite dog from the blues jumped and met the snake in mid freight as it launched its strike. Chipo took one split glance and bolted like a bat out of hell. She never looked back until she was safe inside the house. Hocky limped home a few hours later and died the following morning.
When she narrated the ordeal to her father, he was so shocked and furious. He got his gun, called a few farmworkers to accompany him, and around midday, he brought home a 2.5 meter dead long yellowish snake with lots of bite marks, and three dead dogs.

Hocky and his crew had just killed the most dangerous and poisonous snake in Africa, "the Black Mamba" (Rovambira) her father described it.
"But it's not black why is it called a Black Mamba?" Chipo inquired.
"Because when it bites you, you turn black within a minute. Its venom is so poisonous that it can kill a dozen men. In a single attack, not only can it strike more than ten times, but its also capable of running up to twenty kilometers per hour. So consider yourself a very lucky young lady. Thank Hocky for that and you are banned from going to the paddocks on your own!" her father barked. He ordered the other men to pour rat poison in all the holes around the farm. He was afraid it might have had eggs close by, otherwise, it would have easily, escaped especially confronted by such vicious dogs. The Black Mamba was burnt and the ashes were buried together with Hocky and the three other dogs; Blacky, Cherry, and Cheetah.

Kyra poked Chipo and she gestured to her. They glanced at this short guy swaying and twisting on top of her, his plain tiny wriggled rump causing them to cackle out, laughing. The guys were so annoyed they felt embarrassed to continue abusing them.

As the van made its way, Chipo saw city names she had never heard of before: Hannover, Bielefeld, Rheine. The latter rang a bell, but she was confusing it with Rheinland. She remembered her history lessons, a terrible war had occurred there.
Then she saw the name Autobahn, and her mind immediately went back to one of her favorite teachers, Mr. Muponda. She wondered how someone could know so many interesting stories about European countries.
Germany in particular he knew the history like the back of his hand.

The method he used in teaching made them feel like children sitting around a fire listening to the many tantalizing, thrilling, and stimulating stories from their grandfathers. The whole class would pay attention with so much bewilderment and enthusiasm until the atrocities and the brutalities of the second world war sunk in and then unlike a dream, they realized, it had all come to pass. It was not just a cool story anymore.
That is when I learned the word Blitzkrieg.
Mr. Muponda would go, "here is a big word take note, it's very important, Hitler wanted a lightning war, he wanted a Blitzkrieg." He explained. "Hitler wanted his weapons to be transported at lightning speed because he wanted to end the war quickly. So he created the Autobahn (*motorway*)."
Chipo never forgot that word Blitzkrieg. She saw another road sign Arnheim- Rotterdam. She was puzzled but didn't think much about it until she saw a big illuminating billboard with a "Welcome to Amsterdam" sign. That's when it hit her that they had left Germany.

How was that possible? She marveled. "These guys must be real mafia, they had crossed borders without getting controlled or stopped by the police." She thought to herself.
They were taken to a hotel and booked into a room with four beds inside.
"This'll be your home for some hours, try to sleep, Natalie you are coming with me," shouted the gold platted guy. Kyra And Chipo stood there with blank faces, staring at each other. Natalie followed him joyfully. Three of the guys stayed behind with them.
Chipo's mind was intertwining with thoughts, Amsterdam was known as the drug capital city of Europe. So, instead of killing them, they had decided to use them as drug mules, to compensate for what they had stolen.

That night, she could not sleep. She had watched movies about, women swallowing drugs and getting caught and spending years in prison. She thought of Sontia's story. It was almost 5:30 am. If she did not turn up, Dr. Neutrons was going to be mentally ill, extremely mad and she knew automatically their relation would be over. Later that afternoon, Kevin brought an attractive looking girl, with lots of food and facial creams and toothpaste. He also bought different pairs and sizes of clothes and shoes. His attitude towards them had changed. He wanted to know how their journey was and whether they had slept well.
Then suddenly his face betrayed him. He became fearsome. He had registered that Natalie was unaccounted for. He looked around, burst into the bathroom, and fumed furiously.

"Uh, she is with Moses, I'll call them right away," stammered a nervous guy.
Kevin was visibly not amused, "I hope you guys didn't abuse these girls. I made it clear they were not supposed to be touched."
"No we did nothing like that," they all replied in a chorus.
He sighed, "Okay this is Lya. She is going to be your guide, and that means you do whatever she says."
Natalie and Moses staggered in. Kevin scooped him with his feet and choked him until Lya jumped in and pulled him away.
She took him outside and they exchanged harsh words. When she came back, it was as if nothing had happened.

Chipo and her friends remained silent and nervous. The aggression had made them numb. Lya took them to an exclusive five-star hotel. When they arrived, they noticed there was a group of familiar faces sitting by the foyer. That was done to instill fear and show them that they were surrounded. Lya showed them their suite. Inside the room were four different types of bags on the floor. "I thought we are supposed to be leaving today?" Chipo whispered to Kyra.

"Who said that?" Lya shouted and cautioned, "no discussing you want to leave today to go where?" she added.

"Nah nothing," Chipo conceded.

Kevin walked in later with a bunch of tickets.

"Tomorrow morning we are leaving at 5.00 am sharp. We are taking the ICE back to Berlin and each one of you'll carry one of these bags. There are very important documents in these bags. No one must ever open them, no matter what," he fumed.

"The documents in those bags are your life, that means your life depends on them. Your job is to do as you are told. If you lose one of them, you might as well kill yourself. So my advice is don't lose any one of them. Wherever you are, there will be about twenty people watching all of you all the time. Once you are in Berlin, do as you are told and follow the instructions. After that, you don't owe me anything and I don't owe you anything. You'll be free to go, but let me explain very carefully. If anyone of you tries anything stupid, I can promise you, for the rest of your life, you'll be working in a brothel in Mexico for free."

They didn't know whether they should be happy, or relieved, because he'll let them go, or should be scared about what was in the bags.

"I choose to be alive," whispered Chipo to Natalie.

"Me too," she replied.

These guys had everything mapped out. No fingerprints were to be detected. They had people waiting at every train station in case of an emergency.

Chipo and her girls were dressed up as businesswomen. Their seats had been reserved, and each one of them was given a brand new tablet and earphones. For them not to get bored and to blend in with everyone else. It was a morning train, and most of the passengers were working people. Their gadgets had Facebook, Emails, and many forms of communication blocked out. Four people were placed on both sides of the carriage to observe them.
Their bags were placed in different compartments as instructed, and further away from them.

Chapter Fourty three

The journey was going to take approximately thirteen hours. It was hell for them and Natalie was noticeably nervous. She kept on trying to make a conversation. She was cracking up at anything she was saying. "I am thirsty, you too? Hahaha, I feel like drinking some beer, hahaha, maybe tea, yah hahaha." One stare from Kyra made her zip her mouth. Lya brought them some drinks and encouraged them to read or just listen to music. Kyra was leaning against the window, covering her face with part of her jacket. It was hard to tell what she was thinking. Her face was plain, and she looked as if she wasn't bothered at all. The other passengers seemed to mind their own business. Some were on the phone, others were just staring ahead, while others watched films.
ICE is a very fast train. "What a luxury," she thought. There was internet, a bar, and a restaurant. The seats felt like you were sitting on a plane.
On the screen in the middle of the carriage, they displayed how fast the train was going, transitioning into the name of the next stop and time they would reach Berlin. After about half an hour into the journey, two conductors approached them from both sides and checked their tickets. Everything went smoothly, "a piece of cake," thought Chipo.

She wished she had looted everything from Ginibs. Her main worry was if anything horrific happened to her and she disappeared, no one knew who she was. She didn't have any form of identification on her. It was gut-wrenching to be in her situation and she was overly aware of her heartbeat. Since the time she got onto the train, a simple jerk startled her. She felt every thump, at times it skipped a beat or it added an extra throb. If she had to be spooked, she was sure she would collapse and die.

She needed to keep reminding herself that things could be far worse, she thought of what Susie had endured coming to Europe. Her mind was agonizing with different concerns.

"What if Kevin breaks his promise and decides to kill us all since we know so much already," she murmured to Kyra.

She was so nervous, her stomach was rumbling, she asked to go to the bathroom. She stood there observing herself in the mirror and commenced talking to her reflection.

"Chipo you are a woman now, be mature, take responsibility, and be accountable. Get your shit in check and your priorities right, otherwise you'll live to regret this life."

She thought of Haima, one of her friends back home.

When Chipo told her she was leaving for Germany, she was so depressed. She began a campaign to raise money for her own ticket.

"If you go without me, if you leave me behind, by the time you are back, I'll be dead. How do you think I'll ever find work in this kind of situation. You have graduates who are begging in the streets, digging for gold and me with nothing, where do I fit in? Even prostitutes are out of business. The only way is to become a small house. If the guy is rich, I won't mind being the second or third wife. At least I know my life is comfortable. But eh this HIV disease is not a joke, it's spreading like a flooded dam.

How can I die because of sex? It's even worse if

you are faithful and your partner is not. Look at what happened to Ellen's sister. She was such a nice woman, now she is gone, the husband is gone, kids orphaned. Why should I get married to another man's wife.
Either you go and prepare the way for us, get a house, a car, and a good job. When I come over, everything should be pico Bello. We'll rock Germany oh," she would say and laugh. It made her smile.

She was made to jump by a hard knock on the door. They were five hours into the journey.
Everything was going as planned. Lya was magnificent, she fed them and the girls in a strange way admired her character. She was vigilant determent and strong-minded.
Unannounced, the train slowed down and came to a halt.
"Oh shit border control," Chipo spoke softly to Natalie. They became worried, alert, and nervous. There was a message relayed, it said that the train had an engine failure, and they had to wait for another train to tow them.
Chipo wondered how the hell that was going to work, "I smell a rat, this is a trick so that the police can arrest us," she nervously muttered to Kyra.
They were not allowed to disembark since there was no station. After a long period, kids were becoming restless, and smokers agitated.
The girls were sweating and getting paranoid. Chipo heaved a sigh of relief when the other train finally arrived and conjoined them. Lya was consistently on the phone.
Chipo guessed Kevin wanted an update all the time. He must have been concerned and fearful considering her bag alone weighed almost four kilograms.
Once the journey resumed, they calmed down and went back to their thoughts. Chipo fell asleep and dreamt when she was back at her father's farm.

There was a snake hidden behind one of the closets. They ran out in panic and terrified. Her cousin Lovemore who was the brave one, took out a long fork tiled stick, went back inside the house alone and choked the snake by it's head before killing it. He then sat next to the fireplace as if nothing had happened, then they heard the maid screaming from the chicken coop. They ran over to her and found a large python had swallowed one of the rabbits.
Lovemore came to the rescue again, he took out a net and threw it over the python, the big snake could not escape, he dragged it out and set it on fire. He then went on to pick up the other smaller snake and threw it on top of the python. As they observed them burn, the python looked directly into her eyes and let out a cry like a grown baby.
She was horrified and woke up with a jump, her clothes were full of sweat. Kyra was staring at her with a smirk on her face.

"Nightmare hey the ghosts of the sharks," she chuckled and wore her earphones.
The dream was so surreal, she tried to remember it in detail. Dreaming about a snake was not the best omen in her situation.

"Everyone proceeding to Berlin must get off at Hannover Train station and change to platform 16," a voice came out on the loudspeakers. She saw Lya's eyes roll and gesturing to another person behind her to move. She signaled to Chipo to follow her. She looked troubled and distressed.
"Okay, this is what I want you to do, listen to me very carefully, we are going to get off at the next station in a couple of minutes. I want y'all to walk in a beeline, about five meters apart.
Try to look casual, there will be two guys in front of you wearing bomber jackets, one white, one red. I will be behind you with two other guys.

The place is full of cops, stay clam, no panicking, or hesitation. They are just doing their job. They won't stop you if you behave normally. They are just manning the station," she repeated.
"If you see any K9 police dogs, you should change direction and leave the station, someone will get in touch with you and pick you up, you understand."
Chipo exhaled, rubbed her forehead, and wiped her mouth.
"Any fun tricks will get you nabbed, take it seriously," Lya threatened them.
She told the others about the new instructions and her stomach cramped. Kyra offered to walk in front, Chipo in the middle and Natalie at the back.

They sat silently with their heads leaning backward. As the train halted Kyra got up, wore her jacket and went to pick her bag up.
Chipo was next, she yawned as she got up and went the other direction. She basically dragged her bag out, and stood in a small queue that had formed, waiting to disembark. Natalie was a few meters behind when Chipo jumped out and placed her bag on the floor pretending to tuck in her blouse, whilst checking out the situation, and at the same time waiting for Kyra to get ahead of her.
Natalie did as Chipo was doing, a bit too obvious though. The cops were milling around and there were cameras all over the place. The ladies were stiff scared and brittle.
They took the elevator down into the main passage hall, with a lot of shops. The place was crowded, as people were in a rush to get to their destinations. Kyra was leading the way at full throttle. She looked tense and in no mood for nonsense. She acted as if she was talking to someone on the phone.
Chipo could see the two guys with red and white jackets turn into platform 16. She had a fixed smile as she walked, pretending to greet one or two

people with a nod. She did her best to blend in and make herself comfortable. She moved with confidence and an extra catwalk step to prove she knew the area and that she was accustomed to it.
A few meters away there were three policemen watching people as they went by. Chipo began to laugh and seem engaged in a long conversation. She was rumbling in her mother's language.
"Please Lord, whatever my sins are, don't let me get caught, just let me through, I promise you I will make it up to you," she blurted and prayed in Shona.
She was startled when Natalie jolted her aside as she stormed past her. Chipo was lost for words and in confusion. Just as she turned right into platform 16 climbing up the stairway, her hair stood up as two policemen were coming down towards her. She melted. It was as if a current of high voltage had zapped above her.
Natalie ran past them without a blink and almost bumped into one of them. She was in such a rush that anyone would think she was about to miss her train.
Chipo went into panic mode. She started speaking in tongues in an American accent.
"Hannover is such a great place, the people are really nice, I just had a bugle with ham and cheese and a cup of cappuccino, I am in love with this place." She smiled as she went past them, her heart double beating. They didn't even take notice of her.
When she got up to the platform, Kyra was smoking a cigarette and having a conversation with a guy in a suit.
"Uh clever idea," Chipo thought to herself as she looked around for a single passenger. When Natalie took heed, she too started fidgeting and sneaked up to an old woman with heavy bags.
As the train approached, they were now vexed.
They had lost their reserved seats and it was packed

with a number of tourist groups. If anyone of them wanted to make a go for it, they could have succeeded, but they were too scared.

Chapter Fourty four

The train's last stop was Berlin Ostbahnhof. Plans were constantly changing, but their instructions were always to follow the red white bomber jackets. When they got out of the station, they jumped onto a bus.

Chipo was ordered to get off on the next stop. As soon as she got off the bus, a stranger put a jacket over her bag, and stared at her, "You did a good job," he blurted, kissed her on the chick and disappeared into the parking lot.
She stood there scratching her head, asking herself whether that was the end of her adventure. Lost in thoughts, a short pony-tailed lady on a bike approached her. "Hi you look lost," she said.
"Oh yeah! "Where am I?" Chipo inquired.
"Eastside wall, Warschauer Straße,"
"Oh yeah, right, thanks."
"You dropped a yellow envelope in the trash bin behind you," she shouted and winked at her.
"Me?"
"Kevin said thanks," she shouted and rode away. Chipo checked the trash bin, there was an envelope with 5,000 euros inside. She wasn't impressed, but it was a good start.
She was very much unsettled and looking over her shoulder in fear because she believed the guys were very dangerous and were well connected.
She nervously waved down a taxi and made the

cab driver drive around in circles until she hastily demanded him to stop in front of a hotel.
She gathered that she needed to be alone and have time to think and assess her situation. The thought of what had just transpired made her afraid and was skeptical of going to her own apartment.

She stayed for almost two days in this hotel before moving to the next hotel a few blocks away.

During that period, she found it hard to eat or think. Her body rejected any form of food, she tried to digest. Chipo was nervous and thoughtless, nothing made sense to her anymore, she just wanted to be alone and to calm her nerves down.
She was smoking at least two packets of cigarettes a day.
At times, she thought she was envisioning circumstances that didn't exist. She was experiencing nightmares and the thought of her parents freaked her out.
Since growing up, her aim was always to please her family. She wanted them to be proud of her and to lead by example.
As she lay on the bed facing the ceiling, she remembered the time she once got lost in a forest.
Someone had hired a truck that belonged to her father to carry crude gold and she had insisted on going along with the driver and some of the workers. The client was a spiritual man and he had explained that his spirit had led him to discover the gold mine.

At 9 am, while the workers were loading the truck, Chipo an avid bird hunter armed with a catapult and a small ax that she took underneath the truck's seat decided to explore her new surroundings.
She wandered aimlessly for a few meters without notifying anyone. From a distance, she saw a troop

of monkeys or baboons gathered around a tree.
She ran towards them and when she got to the tree, the animals had disappeared. This infuriated her and she swore and cursed, "fuck that, shit man, crazy creatures." She turned around with her head down and walked back to the truck, daydreaming about what had just occurred.
"How did the monkeys disappear so fast? Maybe I got distracted by a bird or I just didn't pay attention."

Startled by the dark shadow that appeared, caused by the clouds covering the sun. She lifted her head and realized she had walked much further than she had run.
Baffled and confused, she looked around, but neither the truck nor the workers were in sight. As she scanned further, she found herself in the middle of nowhere.
In her head she knew she was very close by, so she stood there trying to catch any sound of voices from the workers, but she was disoriented, numb and dizzy. Her memory was vague. She knew they had branched into the forest from the main road and had not driven so far away, but she had no idea where they had come from. She had lost all sense of direction.

She remained motionless for a while hoping to pick up any form of echo or movement. From a distance, she thought she heard cars passing by and decided to follow that direction. Her thoughts were running wild.
Her lips were beginning to crack, she had no water, no food and she was only wearing a pair of shorts and a T-shirt.
She walked for almost an hour but the forest kept getting thicker, bushy and mysterious.
There were a lot of unexplained, spooky noises

manifesting. The wind would suddenly change direction, she would get the feeling that she was being watched.
Everything was just suspiciously evasive and unnatural. Then she came across a freshly walked path, she followed and after a while, the path came to dead end.
There was a broken fence with a sign ripped out of the ground written. "Keep out beware of lions."
Now she was frightened out of her wits. Paralyzed with fear, she headed for the hills until she could not run anymore.
She sat on a big stone trying to catch her breath and that's when she saw a tree of wild Nhengeni fruits (*sour plums*).

A lot of fresh eaten skins lay scattered on the ground. She did not think much of it at that moment, but then it just clicked in her mind that most wild animals ate the same fruits. She cautiously observed her surroundings but did not see anything strange. She continued eating the plums, then dazedly, she caught sight of a tree stump.

As she carried on plucking the plums away, after sometime, the stump became visible, and her heart stopped. All along, what she thought was a tree stump, was actually a big fat python mesmerizing her with its colour blending. It got closer and closer without her being consciously aware of it.
Fortunately, pythons are very slow. She took to her heels and showed the python a clean pair of feet. Now she was vigilant and alert that there was danger in the forest, but that was the least of worries. The sun was scorching hot, hence she was getting tired and dehydrated.
A lot of animals were seeking shelter under the thick bushes.
Once in a while ,she would get startled by clumps

of shrubs shaking due to sudden quick movements caused by animals hastily running away when they felt her presence. That day she walked for miles, changing directions whenever the path came to an end.

In other words, she was going in circles. Around 6 pm, when the sun was about to set in, she came across a motorway. She could not hide her joy. She was beaming with delight. Although she wasn't aware of which direction led her to the city, she just kept on walking and was happy to see cars go by.

Her weapons were scaring away the motorist, so she dumped them, knowing no one would ever stop for her in that part of the area.

From a distance, she heard her name being called out, "Chipo Chipo Chipo!" She turned around and saw a group of men with dogs running after her. Her first thought was they wanted to kill her. She took off running back into the forest. If it wasn't for the dogs that brought her down, she had no idea what would have happened to her.

When the men finally brought her back to the truck, the spiritual man asked her if she had sworn or said something disrespectful. He went on to say that the area was a sacred ground. He told her how they had tracked her footsteps to the border of the game reserve. They were afraid she might have been eaten by lions until they picked up her footsteps where she had stopped to eat sour plums and they had seen big thick sinuous lines of a python trailing her.

When her father heard of the nightmare, she remembered him saying, that he would have hired a helicopter to search the whole forest had she not been found. The hotel room was stuffy and smelt of old wet carpet. She sat up sweating and went outside by the balcony to smoke.

Chapter Fourty five

She vowed that she would never go back to her apartment. Her ordeal had served as a wake-up call. She needed to be legit and live a normal life. Too many unpleasant savage dingus had occurred simultaneously and she knew there was only one way it was going to end and that was by death.
She was worried a spell had been cast upon her, without her being fully aware of the implications.
Her love for money and the benefits it created, left her fearing for her well being.

Her mind, body, and soul were too far separated and in conflict. Most of the things she had done were either because of naivety, desperation, or depression. Her obsession with glamour had lured her blindly, and now she found herself in a bind.
She felt so wretched and low spirited. Her life had no meaning, no direction. It was a hopeless case. Chipo grappled with herself, agony and despair had crept into her unnoticed. Her situation had become worse and she blamed it on impetuous, lack of wisdom, and the greediness of a comfortable easy life. Looking back she wondered what she could have changed, there was no one to comfort her and she was not sure about anything anymore.

Her adventures had left her dry and burnt out. But once something has been broken, it can never be perfectly fixed without noticing the scars. She was full of maybes and ifs.

"Maybe I should have gone back home?
Maybe it's all part of surviving in Europe?
Maybe I should seek asylum?
Maybe I should have kept the baby?

What if I cannot conceive any more?.
What if Schneider had not lied?
What if Marko had not stolen my money?
What if I go to jail?"

She spent a lot of time thinking about getting into the asylum program. She wanted to know how long it would take to be accepted so she could start studying. She had achieved her B2 certificate and wanted to work on acquiring her C1. The idea of becoming a political prisoner ran through her mind. But she needed guidance and Chamu would have all the answers.

She turned up unannounced at his door. He stared at her and shook his head in disbelief as he scrutinized her.

"Uri mombe yemashanga iwe," (*a person that leaves his/her house without a word and comes back after a long time.*)

"Dr. Neutrons is breathing fire, he has been searching for you everywhere, I thought you got killed, murdered or kidnapped," he snapped.

Chipo remained cool and calculated and then she said, "I went on a wild ride, but it's over now. Tell Neutrons I am now a junky, a drug addict, a street kid, a mad person, whatever suits."

He sneered at her, "you just killed something good yo, I hope you got something better," He said and appeared disturbed by her decision.

"Come on sister, street life is for dogs and rats, you have had a good start, not everyone will have it easy as you did. Why are you looking too clean and smelling so good anyway? You got something going on I don't know about?"

Chipo pulled some money from her jacket and offered him, "here are 500 bucks. I want you to have my back," Chamu saw the money and his eyes popped out. She continued, "I just came back from the dead, I need a new start, I can't do this anymore, I was this close to getting killed. Don't ask me by who? What I need right now is a good clean start. What can you suggest for me?"
"You know I am always there for you, you are my sister, is this money real," he asked as he sniffed it.
"I need to get into the system, I need to exist," she demanded.
He took a long deep breath, "well uh if you want, but I wouldn't recommend it, seeking asylum will be one option. Hold on let me print some stuff out just so you can educate yourself about it. You know I have helped a lot of people and um it depends on how plausible your case is, whether it is believable or not. It's a process so it takes time, and they might agree, or they might not. If I were you, I would find a boyfriend. So many guys would marry you at a drop of a dime very fast."
"No marriage of convenience, not my thing, I wouldn't want to be with someone I don't feel."
"If I was single, I would marry you without hesitation," he chuckled.
"Nah I am good," she responded.
"Sister don't ever underestimate yourself, forget about any conventional means, customary or traditions, it's a different world out here. You have to do what you have to do." He stared at her and pulled some papers out of the printer.

"Okay here we go try to go through these and see if it works you, just the top one is more important."
"In Berlin, you must register yourself as an asylum

seeker at the Landesamt für Flüchtlingsangelegenheiten (*State office for Refugee affairs*).
Registration will last two days. On the first day, your Ankunftsnachweis (*Arrival certificate*) will be produced, which acts as your temporary identification document and is the requirement for your right to support services. The arrival certificate features your name, birthday, citizenship, and a photo of you. You must also provide your fingerprints before it is issued. On the second day, a medical examination takes place and you reserve your first support services. Make sure you bring all of your identification documents and papers (*passport, birth certificate, personal ID, or driver's license*).
Following registration, you'll be placed in an acceptance center, which serves as your accommodation and provides you with everything you need. The duration of your accommodation in the acceptance center normally lasts up to six weeks or six months. It's a process like I said," he assured her.

"Let's go and have a chat with one of my old sisters, she has been around and she knows a lot about it."
"Is that safe?" she asked and continued, "I don't want people to know about my situation, I cannot trust anyone," she hesitated. "Don't worry she is tight, she is like a big sister to me, I know her for a long time and she'll teach you all. It's good for you to have as much information as possible."
To sweeten the deal, she gave him another 200 euros, "just a little token of appreciation and I don't want any trouble from Neutrons."
"Nah as long as you don't owe him money, he doesn't own you." Chipo wanted to always make it clear with Chamu, that for his help, she was willing to compensate him. It was more like paying a consultation fee. He would never ask her for money, but she knew he needed it.
"Whoa, you are good to me my sister. Before we

leave, I gotta dedicate this to you, you gonna love this new track, just hold on." He grabbed his guitar and adjusted the string. "I wrote this especially for you. He put on his Jamaican hat, cleared his throat, and he began to play.

"This is a dedication to my sistren Chipo, one and only, stay strong and blessed, sista, enjoy this one,"

"You have a home, in my home
You have a place in my house
The fire that I lit, is to keep you warm
The food that I cook is to feed you
I traveled a thousand miles I'm far away -
from you
I have been up and down, high and low -
my love."

"That's so sweet of you," she felt like crying.

Chapter Fourty six

They went to aunt Lucy's house, and the song was still ringing in her head. Aunt Lucy was very welcoming, a typical well built African woman. She was wearing African attire from head to toe.
The lounge was decorated with African artifacts. She had black and white photos of her family back in Kenya plastered all over the wall. It was easy to tell how much she cherished her roots and how she kept in touch with her culture and tradition.

Parts of the apartment was divided with pieces of clothing, partitioned into rooms and concealing hidden secrets. The place was quite big for someone struggling and seemed to have multiple entrances. Regardless of her situation, she was a jovial person, ready to let out a big laugh. It was 11 am and they found her drinking a glass of brandy Chantre.
Chipo presented her with another bottle because Chamu had hinted to her in advance. Koffi Olomide was blasting in the background. There was delicious African food on the table which included, samosas, chapatti bread, roasted chicken. They ate and chatted.

Finally, she said, "yah Chamu told me you are interested in stories," Chipo just smiled. Well, I'll tell you about my personal experience, direct from the horse's mouth," she giggled.
"I was in an Asylum camp for 12 years, so I know

how everything functions. People came and left me there. I witnessed a lot of sad moments, cruelty, both from the officials and the asylum seekers themselves. Once you get caged, you are labeled as an animal in a Zoo, you can't do anything on your own. You're fed, given water, food, you are made to believe and think that you have no future.
Your country failed you, so why should we be tolerant to you, you're here at our mercy, nothing belongs to you, we can come into your house when we want, we can take you out when we want, you're stuck in the camp. You can't work, you can't study, you are not even motivated to do anything.

I felt sorry for the young professional social workers," she lamented and continued, "they're really out there to help you out and to make you feel human, but they're forced to hear stories that only exist in movies. In the end, I'm sure they all need some sort of counseling themselves. Because I stayed there for too long, I knew all of them by name,. Some became my friends, Senait, Jana, Jonah, Sagal, Eike, a lot of them, eh Fatima, Annie, Monica. A few of them fell in love with the Asylum boys and even got married. Jana was a workaholic. She would come into the camp around 7 am and leave well after 8 pm. She had so much sympathy and empathy for the refugees, that sometimes she wished she had 100 hands. To be a social worker you need to be really dedicated. It has to be in you.
It's not something you can do naturally, because you learned it.
Jana would complain about how terrible she felt every time, when one of the asylum seekers she was looking after would get deported. When you spend a good amount of time nurturing your hostages, you become bonded with them.
You try to help them in each and every way, from the basic requirements. And when that person is

suddenly taken away, without having completed your mission, it can be very depressing and disheartening.
There were gangs formed according to their ethnicity, Moslems, Christians, Arabs, Africans - it's the same as putting a pride of tigers and lions together with a pack of bears in one place, you all become scavengers.
Discrimination takes place, racism is born, you're separated, divided, and judged. Naturally, you move around with people you can associate with.
The majority of the refugees were coming directly from extremely poor areas, where basic sanitary and hygienic measures were unknown. They had never used a toilet before, they would shit in plastic bags or in a newspapers and just dump the shit anywhere. You would find people washing their feet in sinks meant for washing dishes, shitting in urinals. Someone would just slaughter a chicken and throw its intestines on the floor.
One woman made money from witchcraft, she would charge people, promising them a lucky charm for early release or falling in love. I heard she got stabbed and died, after promising and giving false hope to some kid. She told this kid that his papers were going to be processed and he would be transferred somewhere better. That didn't happen, because he got a letter, that said he was going to be deported. That's when he lost it. He killed her. It's all because of frustration.
The place was worse than a slum. What do people start doing if they have nothing to do the whole day. They turn to alcohol, they turn to whatever makes them high and forget their problems. It's psychological torment, you've no idea what tomorrow holds for you. Occasionally, the cops would come in the middle of the night, kick open the doors and drag one or two people out. They were straight away taken to a waiting plane, back to their countries. That's how

you get deported, no warning, no time to pack. You are sent back with what you've on you. If they find you with no shoes, no shirt, that's not their problem. Ask that Ghanaian banker Adoboli, he had no time to say goodbye.
A lot of people have been injured, maimed, or killed, while jumping out of buildings. They would jump from 2nd or 3rd floors, trying to avoid capture.
I met graduates, skilled workers, but here they are not recognized. Their skills are useless, they all have to start from Zero, like anyone else. Look at the taxi drivers, especially the Persians, those guys are academics, professors who ran away because they were being persecuted. They are political refugees, what are they doing here, driving a taxi, wouldn't that kill your soul, your morals, your personal being. You are given 40 euros a week enough for diapers and fed with food meant for prisoners. Your options are very limited.
Some women turn to prostitution. I have seen women leave their husbands and kids and engage in promiscuous, immoral behaviors, making money by selling themselves to other refugees, or the security agencies," she laughed and sipped her drink.

"Even some of these young boys, they are sexually exploited, abused, molested, and offered money for their silence. They have no hope, and they are extremely vulnerable. The worst medieval means of torture, the greatest punishment you can ever apply to an individual alive, is psychological torture. You're lied to, by relatives and friends, you're made to believe that the grass is greener in Europe, that there is something so good it's worth dying for, only to discover it's all a hoax. That thought alone of building castles in the air and coming over here with high expectations, thinking you are going to a place where everyone is successful, where there is a democracy, then you discover the inhumane,

ill-treatments that is inflicted on refugees, can get you crazy, mad. Refugees in many countries are considered to be trash among trash.
A lot of people suffer from mental health. Some individuals sell all their possessions just to come here and when they arrive they discover they are better off having stayed back home. It's a big struggle and definitely not for the fainthearted.
You can feel that you are alive, but you are not. It's like a lion biting a chunk off, of a Zebra, and letting it get away, only to follow it later and finish it off. Dying a slow painful death, your destiny is determined by someone else. Another force is in charge of your whole being. Any pain that is thrust upon you, you will feel it to the bone, and you can't do anything about it. After all these horrific experiences, you will need life long professional help, my sister, you'll become a psychiatrist yourself by the amount of time, you will require to heal. Not only will the situation traumatize you.
The kind of stories you will hear, what people went through to come here, it's like jumping from a frying pan into a big fire. For 12 years I stayed in a camp, right now there are people stuck in there for the past twenty years, what else are you going to do, your life is over. But I guess why worry about birds shitting on your scalp, you should be happy that dogs don't fly. Maybe things could be worse, but one thing for sure is, it's better to die here in Europe than in Africa.
As soon as you are out of the camp, the sky is the limit. Six people, you hear me, six people, usually occupy one room, filled with bunk beds, cramped like maggots. If you don't get rejected and you stay there for a long time and you are lucky, you can get your own room. The waiting time alone will drive you nuts. Most of the time you will hear, that someone has been rejected after waiting for a year. It is that waiting period where human beings start

to improvise. People will try to make the best out of the worst situation. Some will tell you business is thriving. I know a woman, who opened her own makeshift restaurant, cooking from her bedroom, she is still there right now, selling ugali, for two euros. She is not the only one.
There were these guys who removed furniture in one of the rooms, so you had 12 people living in one room, and turned the other room into a bar. Every night, we would drink and dance there. What else can you do? Nothing my sister, it’s a small slum world on it‘s own. The system is not very encouraging, I guess its the German way of doing things, of pushing you without being pushed. It‘s the same as welcoming you into my house but not feeding you. You‘ll always feel like you are an outsider, there is no togetherness, no support for that. And these things have to be implemented from the moment a child is born. You can‘t teach an old dog new tricks.

When I first arrived here, I came through Frankfurt airport. I saw a lot of African people working there, and that was hope for me, but when you look deep into it, it‘s more like a marketing tool, face-value thing. When tourists or business people land at the airport, they all get the feeling that Germany is open for business, multicultural, cosmopolitan city. It‘s just my thinking, everyone needs a role model, someone who inspires them.
When I talk to my sisters and brothers in England and Canada it‘s a different world. They all have big houses because the system allows you to earn according to your brain and your strength. Do you know that some of the best-paid workers in Germany carry trash? The guys you see running around with your rubbish bins, they get more money than a first year lawyer. There is one thing about the Germany system though, regardless of which way it goes, it works.

It`s the goal, the objective is always achieved. Good or bad. The Germany law was designed for the Germans, but that was a long time ago. The events have changed, it`s now a multicultural society so the laws need to be adjusted, to accommodate the masses. I have always wished, that one-day African countries could adopt the Germany mentality and way of doing things. They could learn a thing or two about how countries are governed. Our presidents are incapable of governing.
I personally believe Germany should sell their expertise and knowledge to developing countries. No one dies of hunger here.
Food is the cheapest commodity in Europe. We just have to go to Aldi and with 10 euros I can feed myself for a month. Africa is the richest continent, yet the poorest, huh we are cursed" she laughed and added, "They need a big gathering, brew lots of beer, invite a mecca of people and dancie non stop for a year until the spirits are appeased. It's a sin to be poor my sister. They should replace the name refugee with, The Lost Explorers, TLE." They all laughed.

"No one deserves to be a refugee or to be separated from their loved ones. Look at Canada, France or Austria for instance, their president is a 27 years old, a young man, what a wonder. When I was born, he was still itching in his father's balls," she said and chuckled, "Yeah, it's like a grandchild telling his grandfather how to behave, otherwise, he would get spanked.
That`s why we need more Malemas in Africa, to monitor and persecute the abusers of powers. I don`t blame the Europeans or Chinese for taking our resources, If you walk into a blind man's house and you see he has gold stones which he is using as stools, are you not going to offer him a leather couch in exchange of those stones.

Our leaders are blind, selfish, short-sighted, and there are followers, period.
So you see, we are following, followers who cannot follow," she said and cracked up.

"You know that in my country there is a whole city with people with brown teeth, why, too much fluoride," she answered herself.
"They cannot even afford to provide clean water, yet they have helicopters, private jets."
"I am a grandmother, I haven't seen my own grandkids in 10 years. When my dad passed away, I couldn't attend his burial, I was not allowed to travel. As soon as I leave the country, it's a one-way ticket, I am not allowed back in. But again it's all about luck, maybe I was unlucky, my ancestors were not strong enough. But you, you, I can feel, positive energy in you, and it's dying to come out.
You are going to be successful in life, you just need the right guidance. You look pretty, and you have a lot of lucky charms swirling around you." She concluded.

It was a scary analysis, a very discouraging narrative. Whether she was being hyperbolic or not, Chipo found herself in quandary. She didn't see any other way out. She was going to go back to Zimbabwe and face her demons, at least she knew she would be surrounded by her family. It had to be a smooth exit.
She was going to seek asylum and ask immediately to be deported. That meant she would never again set foot in Europe for the rest of her life.
Aunt Lucy invited her to stay over for the night.

Chapter Fourty seven

As she lay on the carpet that night, she thought she had seen a child ghost. She had a series of dreams and this child ghost kept appearing. She wondered if it was the child she had aborted. She awoke with a jump, covered in sweat. To her astonishment, she was completely naked and two women stood over her, sprinkling some form of liquid on her body. Out of breath and overpowered she could not talk. She wasn't sure whether she was dreaming or it was real. Strange enough she could hear voices. The place was covered in smoke, through the dim lit room she saw two other women in one corner, half naked performing a cleansing ritual. Her clothes were being washed in a dish full of blood.

The women were muttering in an ancient spiritual language. She thought she was wide awake but she was not aware of her surroundings. Everything panned out in front of her. She was violently choked and pressed to the ground, as someone tried to force down her throat, a small round hairy creature with teeth.

Her mind became blurred, she thought, she was about to be sacrificed. It was a terrifying experience for her. The whole place was scary and eerie frightening. She could not talk or scream.

Death flashed before her eyes, she summoned herself to calm down. It's only a dream and if it's not then you better start kicking and throwing punches, at least you would go down fighting, fighting

like it's your last breath, she told herself. With all her strength she raised her arms in defense, protecting her mouth and then half asleep she gathered all her strength and threw a devastating right and left hooks that shook and banished the evil spirit into scampering to the unknown world. She lay there for a while, afraid to open her eyes. When she finally did, she had a breath of fresh air and smiled at what she had conquered. If she can clobber an enemy in spirit, she can annihilate anything in reality.
When she sat up, Aunty Lucy was a bit jittery. She had a table full of food, decorated with candles and Holy Crosses. She anxiously looked at Chipo and there was fraught silence.
"Breakfast is ready," she said hastily. "I feel so sorry for your demons, the way you were punching and kicking in your dream, my God, that was a massacre." Chipo just grimaced. Her expression immeadiately vanished when she got up. When she realized she was stark naked, she pulled the blanket up around her.
"Where are my clothes? Who took them off me?" Aunty Lucy smirked.
They were all over the place, full of sweat and dirt. I put them in the washing machine and I ironed them for you."
"That's impossible, how did that happen?" Chipo was becoming disturbed, resentful, and irritated.
"I want my clothes now," she said as she wriggled towards her. Aunty Lucy recoiled and flinched.
"Your clothes are behind you on the chair," she stammered.
As Chipo put on her clothes, she was spooked and startled. Her pubic hair had been shaved. She had a look of horror on her face and her anger rushed out in palpable waves through her arms. She tossed an iron at Aunty Lucy, hitting her on the forehead, sending her crashing to the floor in agony.
An unknown big heavy woman with two swollen

black eyes, rushed out of the bedroom holding a broomstick.
"Don't mind her, she is mentally challenged," Aunty Lucy screamed. Chipo threw plates of food and candles, whatever she could get hold of at her.
As the woman ducked one of the candles hit the curtain causing it to catch fire. Aunty Lucy struggled to get up screaming hysterically!
"My house is burning, my house is burning, Mama Titi pulled down the curtains, hey girls come out and help her," she yelled.
Chipo turned to see who she was calling. Through the open door, she saw a naked girl stretching out from what appeared to be a big cooking pot. Amid the confusion, she took the opportunity and dashed out of the apartment, almost half-clothed, bumping into a group men who had queued outside the door, leaving them gasping.

She went filled with fury to Chamu's apartment, kicking the door in without warning. She slapped him hard and dragged him down by his dreadlocks. She grabbed a knife from the table and sat on him cutting off his locks one by one.
"You piece of shit, you set me up." Chamu was in shock. He covered his face to protect himself, "hey sista what's going on man? Stop that? Are you high? What has gotten into you?"
"You sold me to a witch, you evil person, how can you do that, I trusted you so much. I gave you money to protect me."
"But sista I've no idea what you are saying, what happened? I didn't force you to stay with her, you agreed to spend the night yourself. I've no ill intentions towards you. How many times have I helped you, now stop cutting my dreadlocks and tell me what happened."
Upon noticing his innocence, she goes off him and sat on the couch, Chamu still stunned, looked

disheveled, as he picked up some of his locks which lay scattered on the floor, expressing disapproval at her.
He struggled to gather his breath, "my sista, you cannot just jump me and smash me like that. What if I had fought back?" He wiped the blood from his mouth and added, "I would have hurt you. Look what you did to the door, my wife will be very upset."
"Chamu I'm confused here, I want you to tell me, what you know about your Tete Lucy," Chipo demanded.
"If I knew she was a woman not to be trusted, I would not
have asked her to help you. I know that she has helped a lot of women and no one has ever said anything bad about her. Why are you so angry with her?"
"She did a ritual without my consent," Chipo yelled.
"Uh, a ritual, that's a bit weird." He started
laughing. "Wait a minute maybe it's true, all I know is there was once a rumor, that she was involved in trafficking girls and forcing them into prostitution, but these were just unsubstantiated accusations."
"Well, those accusations have just been proven to be true. That woman is a witch. If she did something evil to me, by the grace of God, it's better for her to disappear from this earth, because I'll bring thunder and lightning into her house." Chipo shouted.

Chamu's phone rang, a woman can be heard wailing on the other side. Chamu was aghast as he listened. An imprecise micro expression visibly stuck on his face. He felt a little uneasy as he put the phone down, perturbed. "Did you burn the place down?" He asked calmly. Chipo just stared at him.
"This is an arson man you can go to jail."
"They were doing some illicit activities there, I doubt they'll report it to the police."

Suddenly Chamu pulled out a big grin on his face and let out a long horse laugh.
"You beat the shit out of that big woman, damn, you heard the way she was whining, it's as if she had wee in her mouth. Chipo I cleanse my hands in front of you. I had no idea about anything. I respected her as my sister. What she did behind closed doors, was none of my business and out of my control."
"You need to give me back 300 euros," Chipo said boldly.
Chamu's smile disappeared, "uhh," he gasped.
"You know something is bothering me a bit. Do you really believe she is capable of doing what you say you witnessed? If it's true, a lot of mysteries have been solved. A couple of years ago a body of a naked African girl was found murdered floating in one of the channels, back then it was pinned on Nazi groups but no one was ever prosecuted. But back then people said the last person this lady went to see was Aunt Lucy. It's beginning to make sense now.
Cy, her ex-boyfriend went from being normal to insane. They quarrelled with her because she kept disappearing in the middle of the night and he accused her of spending hours crouching in a large white metal pot."
"A cauldron," Chipo added.
"Yes that big bhodho," (*cauldron*) he replied and continued, she got so mad at the accusations, the next morning Cy was found sleeping on top of a tree, no one knows how he got there, Chamu narrated and laughed. "And since that day he has never been himself, his head is always jerking and once in a month his mouth gets misplaced."
"He has a hemifacial spasm," Chipo elaborated,
"That's correct, scary thing hey!" Chamu shouted.
She looked concerned and worried as she listened to him. "You have the money on you," she insisted, to his surprise.

Chapter Fourty eight

Chipo left Chamu's place disoriented and went to buy herself a used phone. As soon as she logged on her account, she was bombarded with messages from Dj Lionel. She called him up and they decide to meet.

Their appointment for dinner was at 8 pm, but she decided to go there 2 hours earlier since she didn't have much to do. She was surprised to find him already waiting, with a big white teddy bear. They had interesting conversations and talked a lot about themselves. He was very direct in his approach and he made it clear, that he wanted to catch up on the lost time. He expressed his feelings and laid out his plans.

Chipo was hesitant to tell him about her shenanigans. However, she did not deny him either. He insisted on her to meet his mother since she had been diagnosed with cancer. He was worried her fate would come sooner than later.

"I don't want to overburden you," he said, "it's just that my feelings are genuinely and indisputably strong. I know you might say we don't know each other that well. We could wait for another six months, but we'll only be torturing ourselves. Why wait for six months for something we can do today. What if after six months we discover we have nothing in common. We might as well go all in now, than drag on and only realize it's neither, what, one of us wanted." He tried to convince her.

She felt good to be courted, but she decided to play hard to get.
"I'm sure and positive we can get along," he assured her. Chipo was lucid to the fact that she was illegal, and a person of no fixed abode, yet to her own surprise she remained adamant. She decided to play the string game. That is when you release a captured bird with a string tied around one of its legs. As it chirps and sings, lauding itself for escaping, you start pulling back the string randomly, reminding it you are still in control. She had developed this mental capacity for making a dire situation seem normal.
"Did I ever tell you my mother's wish has always been to go for a safari, somewhere in Africa?"
"Why don't we make that place Zimbabwe?"
Her eyes blossomed. She wondered if he could read her mind. Her plan had been distracted. When he mentioned Zimbabwe, she saw a way out.
"I Cannot just move in with you and your whole family just like that. I need to meet your mum the formal way," she said politely.
"That's all taken care of, I have told them we know each other for two years," he assured her. "You could come for dinner tomorrow."
"I think that's a good start," she replied.
"I could cook a roadrunner and some sadza with muriwo," Chipo snapped and laughed, "whoa very impressive, you have done your homework, haven't you."
"Uribho," he showed off with his shona skills. "When I make up my mind about something, I go in head first, I leave nothing for discussion or to doubt, either I am in or I am out. It'll be a blessing to adapt to your cultural beliefs and be able to greet your mother, or should I say my mother in law, in her own language Makadini Amai."
Chipo was head over heels. It gave her confidence that he had put in the effort to get to know her

tradition and culture. She felt consumed with the whole idea.
A twitch on her back warned her, "Don't miss out on a good thing, it's only a bird's droppings."
She smiled at herself. "What if you discover I am crazy? What are you gonna do?" She belted out.
"Then I'll be crazy with you."
"What if I am possessed by an evil spirit and I like to roll in the mud and snore like a pig?"
"Oh that's easy, I didn't tell you I've a small farm with a couple of pigs and chickens. I inherited it from my grandfather, I've seen pigs play in the mud, and I've heard them sleep and snore, I find it cute, can you imagine a fat pig letting out a squeak constricted sound," he joked and they both chuckled. The more Chipo tried to make life harder for him, the more she found herself falling for him. "I didn't know you are a farm boy" she responded mischievously.
"Own me and I'll own you," he whispered. "You know I was brought up very differently. I was the only child for ten years before the twins were born. My parents were 90% of the time traveling around the world for work. I was basically raised by Mama Buba. She was originally from Zambia. She made me who I am today. She taught me manners, how to respect your elders and behave in an appropriate way. She was with us since I was born and I had never known anyone else except her. She was always alone. Her family was still living in Zambia.
One day she brought a man home. She was so excited and shy, I remember. She told me not to tell my mum about it.
Each time my parents were away, this man would come and sometimes he would bring his friends, and they would make a party in my father's private bar. I used to call him uncle Mike. He was a cool guy. He would bring me stuff every time he came to visit. He loved our house so much, that he would sit by my father's bar and Mama Buba would serve him liquor

and play a lot of African beats. I actually got my D j skills from him. And then one day, I was telling my mum about what I had learned from uncle Mike. She didn't say much, as she was more interested in knowing what else was going on when they were not around and I was excited to tell her everything I thought she liked it.

The next morning Mama Buba was gone. I never saw her again. I was told her relative got terribly ill and she had to rush back to Zambia. It was hard for me because I didn't want to have another baby minder and I was hoping she would one day come back. And then after about two months, my dad went missing, he was kidnapped. The kidnappers were demanding money something like two million bucks. My mum refused to pay the money and my dad was never found. It was suspected that Uncle Mike and his friends were involved. Uncle Mike had used information Mama Bubba had provided him to plan the kidnapping.
Nothing was ever proved to be right but since then, I was always taught never to trust anyone, no matter what."
"I am really sorry about your dad. I had no idea you went through such an egregious situation at such a young age, must have been very terrible for you. I mean that's some crazy shit man. I wouldn't blame you for not trusting anyone. I would do the same thing too."
"Anyway it happened, I just hope wherever my dad is, he is doing ok. I've to go home and start marinating the chicken," he said as he got up and observed her, "I think you'll need some time to yourself too."
"Oh yes, I need to take care of some business," she lied. She remained in the restaurant for a while, trying to figure out what to do with her sore throat. There was something disturbing her and it bothered her a lot. It was a burning sensation she

experienced during urinating. She attributed it to nervousness or a mild fever. Her thoughts criss-crossed to Aunty Lucy's wickedness. The sharp pain in her lower abdomen brought back bad memories but she shunned everything aside and popped pain-killers.
All along she had been wondering what had happened to Susie and how the other girls, Kyra and Natalie were coping. She went to Chamu's place to remove her belongings.

Chamu was in a jovial mood as usual. He was preparing to shoot his first video for a summer song.
"You are blessed to find me here, I just got back yesterday from Stuttgart, where one of our fellow Zimbabweans was found dead after three days in his apartment," he recounted.
"I am sorry to hear that. Did you know him well?"
"I met him sometime back in the days at a reggae festival, a very intelligent man, he came here in the 70s. He was a university professor married to a Russian woman and they had three kids. But she destroyed his life. She met some young Ghanaian guy and kicked him out.
I think he was almost 60 years old when his wife divorced him. She took everything; the house, the money. She cut all communication with his kids, and that put him under tremendous stress which turned to depression.
The guy just woke up one day and lost his mind. He started drinking and smoking. His University fired him from his job, and he was left living, I should say squatting in a one roomed apartment.
To make things worse, since he came here, he never even once, went back to Zimbabwe and he had no contact with any of his family or relatives. The thing is when most of these guys came to Europe back then, they thought they were so special. They thought they were better than anyone else back

home. So they neglected their families and when things went haywire, he had no one to turn to. Most probably he was ashamed and embarrassed. Now he has died a pauper."

"That's a sad story and the kids never bothered to contact their father," Chipo asked quietly.

"I heard only the eldest daughter used to visit him once or twice a year."

"Whoa, that's brutal."

"Oh you got no idea, mixed children, if they don't grow up with both parents, or their fathers, they can easily stray away. In this case, the mother fed them with the wrong information. She told them that he was a loser and a bad influence on them, an alcoholic, a whole lot of other garbage stuff. And as kids you know, they are vulnerable, they believe anything.

"In the end, they are the ones who suffer, it's a pity," Chipo added.

"So you want to take the bags?"

"Yes thanks a lot, Chamu, its time to move on."

"I'll get the keys then."

She removed all her luggage from the cellar and called a taxi.

Chamu wished her well with a big hug and she was gone. She took some of the valuable jewelry and pawned them for cash. Her aim was to look as glamorous as she could for the dinner, with her future in-laws.

She booked a decent hotel for a week, hoping by then she would have moved in with Dj Lionel. For the first time in her life, she decided to go for a manicure and pedicure.

She was going all out on her looks. She had her feet and back massage. She had Dead Sea Mud Mask on Face and Body applied.

She felt like a brand new person and she looked good. As she exited the hotel, she looked the part of being a beauty queen. She was startled when she caught a glimpse of someone who looked like Kyra sitting in a car with two men. She waved at her but the car drove away at a high speed. She thought she must have mistaken her with someone else.

She stood by the side of the hotel, waiting for Lionel to pick her up. There was a group of street people, junkies gathered around sitting on the pavement. She cracked up with what she saw. One of the junkie guys brought flowers for his drunk junkie girlfriend. She grabbed the flowers and thew them to the ground, shouting at him.
"Why do you bring me flowers, what can I do with flowers, why didn't you bring me a beer," and she staggered away with two beers in her hands.
The guy was in shock as he rushed to gather the flowers rumbling and mumbling.

Dj Lionel came to pick her up exactly as expected, right on time, one minute to seven, 18:59.
To her surprise, he was wearing a Moss 1851 tailored fit Navy textured Tuxedo. She recognized it because that was Frank Bruno`s favorite brand. Frank Bruno was her father's favorite professional boxer until he got knocked out in brutal fashion by Mike Tyson.
Up until then, her father had big posters of him hanging in his office, and he had admired his style and sportsmanship, until he got beaten.
"I'm supposed to be looking good, not you," she jested. "Oh it's you, I didn't recognize you, mama Mia you look delicious, like a chocolate cake," he said as he led her to the door.

He had everything planned out, the music in the car was slow and romantic. He had memorized his lines to perfection.
"You look gorgeous, I am glad I met you. I hope you'll like my cooking."

"Is that all you gotta say?" Chipo teased him. He wasn't impressed about that, he cleared his throat and sighed. He was having trouble in reinventing his approach. She had distracted him finally he spoke so fast it was hard for her to digest it.
"There is a lot I haven't told you about myself, I would, however, prefer you to find out on your own. My plan is that we chill out, by the fireplace, and sip some wine, hopefully, somewhere in the midst of the flame, a sign will appear, and we'll have to figure out, what it is. If the flame blows left, I get to decide what we do for a month, if the flame blows right you get to choose your own bedroom."
"What if the flame stays upright?" Chipo smirked.

He changed the music and said, "I believe there is always that one woman in a lifetime, that every man wished they could've had and that one woman cannot be easily bent."
"What's up with flame?" She insisted.
His facial muscles tightened, "I'm not into this for sex, I'm not into this for pleasure, I'm into this because you live in me, as long as I'm alive, I want to be with you and not anyone else.
I want you to be the last person I'll give my love to," he said sternly looking at her.
"You talk big game how can you be so sure, come on, that's an old one, tell me something new," Chipo joked. Maybe you are a per vet or a stalker, a lot of questions need answers here.
"I guess talk is cheap," he uttered and never said another word again until he stopped the engine.

"We are here," he pouted. Chipo fumbled with the lock. She stammered as she turned her head towards the house.
"What the heck, you cooked in a hotel?"
She found herself facing a massive building with no neighbors in sight. She was still in awe when he

opened the door for her. "What kind of a DJ are you again, are you like DJ Black Coffee or something?" He chuckled."Nah this is not a DJ`s taste, "welcome to your new home."
"Hold on, no I'm not getting in there, looks scary, you have a black butler" she amused him, and he laughed hilariously.
"It's my mum`s house, she inherited it from my Grandfather. The food will get cold if we don`t enter soon, come on," he said as he extended his hand. Chipo hesitated. She was doubtful and ambivalent. This was a too big shoe to fill. With a house like this, it was easy to get any information about her if anyone dared to inquire. But DJ Lionel was persistent, "we could leave immediately after dinner if you don't feel comfortable," he assured her. She felt like she was in a movie. Big golden chandeliers covering the ceiling. Two meters long family hierarchy paintings filled the passage. The place was squeaky clean. It was built to last a few generations.
The mother was amazing. She was tall, silver-blonde, curvaceous, dressed in an elegant Alex Perry Crystal Decorated Long Sleeved Gown. She looked dazzling, majestic, she reminded her of Isha Sesay; very communicative and entertaining.

Chipo drowned in the accolades afforded her way. The two sisters were just darlings. They thought she was an actress.
Lionel played the perfect host. The food was prepared in small portions, Chipo ended up making the sadza after three failed attempts.
The roadrunner had been stripped to the bone and served as filet. The sadza was too heavy to eat for the sisters.
They started making dolls out of it and started playing the muppet show. "Girls that's unacceptable and disrespectful, show some manners," the mother rebuked them.

Chipo found it fun, not once did she ever imagine making a doll out of sadza. "But mama it's almost like clay," shouted Jessica. And it feels like clay, only smoother," added Sally. The mother concealed her embarrassment by pretending to cough, as Lionel buried his discomfort in laughing sardonically towards the sisters.

"Have you thought about what your uncle offered you, it's better than spinning and scratching and juggling," she mocked him. "Mum, we talked about that already," he complained.
"Chipo maybe this makes sense to you. His uncle is the minister of security, and he has offered him a traineeship in the police service. Of course, after he qualifies, he will rise very fast. Who knows, maybe he might be made chief of police or become a mayor. Having any sort of carrier in life should be a priority for all kids. I'm sure your parents would agree with me Chipo."

She was caught unaware, she forced a grin and swallowed her dessert before she could answer.
Lionel came to her rescue. "Mum I thought we said no discussion about nothing," he reminded her. "Well definitely education is the key to prosperity, and as a person, you feel fulfilled to achieving what has been set as the standard norm. I can't wait for the day I'll put on my graduation gown and toss my cap into the air celebrating four years of hard work," Chipo chipped in. Lionel just smirked. "There'll be a time and place for these kind of life changing discussions, today is just about exchanging presents, and displaying our excellent hospitality. While I am at it I would like to propose a toast," he said as he got up.
He grabbed his glass, and cleared his throat before continuing, "as we always do it all the time, I want to give a toast to my two beautiful darlings.

Whatever the future holds for you, let the heavenly angels always shine upon you and I will always be in the near when you need me," he continued, "to my wonderful mum, I got nothing but love for you and you are going to be proud of your son because I am going to make you proud. Last but not least to Chipo, welcome to the family, I can guarantee you once a Wolfgang gets hold of you, all the wolfs will fall in line and support. Sorry about the sadza, I still have a long way to go. Thank you again for being my guest, and I'm looking forward to seeing you in that chair every day.
Cheers everyone, and goodnight to you two, your time is up."
"So what do you think?" Lionel asked as he drove her to the hotel. "You got a great family," she answered. Her mind was occupied by the thought that his uncle was a minister of security and he was about to enroll to become a cop. "Is that all you have to say, you seem absent-minded, is it the chicken," he chuckled. "No thank you for everything, it was awesome, beautiful evening, I greatly enjoyed it. It's just that my life at the moment is not where I would want it to be. I am on a rollercoaster."
"Well don't let it worry you too much, where there is a will there is way! The offer is still open, you saw the place yourself, it's big enough for one more person."
"Oh you kidding me, that place is big enough for ten more families man, you got a lot of hidden secrets, you know that," she yelled at him and advised, "next time at least give me a hint of what to expect. What if I had walked in there and the whole table is full of cops?" "Well, we would have sat with them and have dinner. Are you afraid of cops?"
She swallowed her saliva, "It's always good to know what you are getting yourself into, that's all. You need to know your surroundings and mark your territory like a Wolf."

After he dropped her off, she sat by the hotel bar. She was mulling things over. Her relationship with Lionel was turning up to be dangerous. She remembered Schneider's words, "stay away from the police they can be brutal."
What Lionel's mother only had to do was ask her brother to screen her name and she would be exposed. Her mind raced back to the time she met Gunther, and how he had expressed himself and gave her vague summaries about Germans. She thought of all the stories she had heard, what she had gone through and observed.
There were a lot of contradictions. Some of the events were based on hearsay, as very few people could narrate information based on personal experiences. And if it was related, it was all to do with the system, and the system made people the way they are.

She reflected and speculated about all the different versions associated with the German culture. She concluded that several members of the minority groups had misguided personal issues regarding ways and mentality of certain German individuals and organizations. A lot might have lacked the skills and education to find a decent job or did not possess the necessary permits required. And that led to biased assumptions and disdain for the hosting nation. The inflexibility and the intolerance or slow to adjust coupled with a never bending bureaucratic system led to a habit of blame game while questioning their unfair treatment. Most of the victims had inherited negative tendencies and attitudes passed on, from their guardians, associates and cultural institutes. Germans are no different from any other nationalities, it's just that they don't know it any other way. Their beliefs, their patriotism and principals are based on the expression, a leopard cannot change its spots. They are deeply embedded and

permanent, unless certain adjustments or miracle spiritual cleansing are carried out before birth.
However, being adventurers and venturing into unfamiliar territories leads to experimental tests and weakened dilution. You could sprinkle ashes all over or spray paint on some parts, but when cornered, they can easily shake off these ashes and reveal themselves, or with time the paint will fade away and if not constantly recoated, it can unmask its true colors. But one thing for sure is that they remain resolute, mentally strong, focused, and unbearable.
Typical "Die Mannschaft mentality," as Dr. Matthias once said profoundly. This resentment came by not because of the hurt, but because of the history, that was created long before they were born. The sins of their great grandmothers who bore the unwanted kids that overwhelmed and asphyxiated the rest of the tadpoles, and be born a nightmare.
A lot managed to escape and overpower the zealots, but were born marked with regret, as they never wanted to be part of it. Up to now, they despise themselves and those that are like them, but they can never be anything else.
They find solace in being as far away as possible, eliminating any signs of remembrance and preventing any flashbacks.
Alcohol is addictive and it makes life easier. Certain parts dissect from your body and become what you have always wanted to be, while the other parts fall in anger into soft folds, as they observe in disgust their stubborn self migrate into forbidden lands. They wait impatiently and awkwardly for the loose souls to return and become whole again. By now, they're used to it, for they're aware it's only for short periods, that is if they don't mingle with the Bavarian brothers.

Her thoughts were destructed by a familiar voice.

When she turned around, she saw Kyra with dyed black hair rushing out of the hotel surrounded by three men. She assumed they were guests at the same hotel, but the receptionist told her the name didn`t exist in their computers.

When she got to her room, the whole place had been ransacked, her clothes thrown all over.
She was confused, in panic and could not report the incident, afraid the police would be called in.

She had placed a small bag with her fortune in a hot water dispenser and it was still intact, she sighed with relief and sat down trying to calm her nerves.

After a while, she got up, left the hotel and disappeared in the middle of midnight.

Quotes from the Author:

If all I had was you in this world, it would be enough.

Nothing wretches the heart more, than the occurrence of a mystifying dream.

Acknowledgments:

If you ever crossed my path and looked at me for one reason or the other and if you breathe the air that I breathe, you are part of this project.

Thanks to Robert Heyde (my graphic designer), Dr. Awes for her contribution and endless support. My silent prayer warriors, you know who you are, I will always uphold you and cherish you.

In Memory of:
In memory of The fallen heroes that once crossed my(our) path. You left fingerprints of grace on our lives. Innocent, John, Callisto, Kuda, Mary Svikiro, Chakanetsa, Julius, Svondo, Babamukuru and Mai-guru Muchena, Tete Elizabeth Svikiro, Mr./Mrs. Mombo Sr, Kelvin Muvirimi, Roy Turikai, Elvis Mavondo, Tom Nyandoro, Anopa Makaka, Fred Magwera, Derrick, Theodore Gonyora, Tony Trevor Chikonzo, Jacob Chivava, Cosmas Farirepi Mazun-gunye, Tichaona Joseph Pasi, Hajj Awes Al-hamdany, Fusire, Sibanda Sr, Vivian Gavi, Vivian Mkumbuzi, Ronald Kanoyangwa, Mwanaidi Juma mwaisaka, Mr. Tata Tembo, Paul Gram, Paul Adolfo, Mr./Mrs. Mfengi, Mr. Chigura, Mr. Andrea, Mrs. Kettle, Mr. Kershaw, Charles Gasura, Douglas Shamu, Luckson Moyo, Mr. Mavesere-Senyuwa, Mrs. Nhende, Ashley Nyagumbo, Heinrich Chimani, Mr. Sango, Vusu Sibindi, Alex Banda, Mr. Mudzingwa Sr, Shingi Farai Mvududu, Edna Magandi, Getrud Nairosi, Farai Kusemamuriwo, you shall not be forgotten.

Author's Note:

Commuting by public transport can turn out to be a blessing if you are looking for inspiration.
Offering a helping hand and showing empathy resulted in meeting Chipo.
Venturing into underground hair salons and drinking in illegal shebeens contributed immensely to the development of the project. I went out of my way to helping different individuals and through that Susie was discovered.
By nature out of interest and a bit of pleasure I showed compassion and love to diverse cultures, that expanded my horizon and gave me the flexibility to write freely and without bias.
After gathering the ammunition I needed for this particular kill, I hibernated for 4 weeks, only sticking out my nostrils for fresh air and some fresh feed once a week until the first draft was completed.

I gained 5 kg in the process and experienced a couple of cold shoulders and roaring eyes accompanied by long wild hurtful stares. Once in awhile the wolf cried reminding me that time for hibernation was almost over.
The name "I came in Blind" emerged after listening to too many hyperactive youngsters and hearing a lot of the same eager, naive, and vulnerable stories, during my research work. Initially, this project was proposed as a documentary, but after a lot of consultation and encouragement by some of the students who had experienced the same treatment, I decided to write it as a novel, with an adaptation into a film in mind. A lot has changed since my fieldwork and some of the structures and places might not exist anymore. The identities of most of the people have been concealed, for the sake of protecting their privacy. A majority part of the book is based on field notes and memory.

Other parts are based on one on one talk, and the rest is based on stories among peers. My devoted German friends have contributed profoundly to showing me the many different ways of understanding and integrating into the German multicultural society, in exchange for a trip to Vic Falls Carnival Celebrations.

This book serves as a memoir of the people I have come across during my expedition, and for those who feel marginalized in one way or the other.
One thing without doubt about Berlin is that it is an amazing historical city, full of dedicated patriotic people. After years of being surrounded by a wall, there are only a couple of things Berliners want; free public transportation, peace, music, and cheap rent. I just have to teach some of them how to smile. Mind you Germans are the most welcomed tourists in the world, just not in Germany.

No wonder why President John F. Kennedy said, "Ich bin ein Berliner."

A shining light tainted by a dark spot,
discovers its superiority amongst stars.

A sacrificed lamb

Chipo.

Printed in Great Britain
by Amazon

56129626R00192